Microsoft®
Access VBA
Programming

for the absolute beginner™

Microsoft® Access VBA
Programming

for the absolute beginner™

Premier
Press™
MICHAEL VINE

The Premier Press logo, For the Absolute Beginner, and related trade dress are trademarks of Premier Press and may not be used without written permission.

Microsoft, Microsoft Windows, Microsoft Visual Basic, Microsoft VBA – Visual Basic for Applications are registered trademarks of Microsoft Corporation in the United States and/or other countries.

All other trademarks are the property of their respective owners.

Important: Premier Press cannot provide software support. Please contact the appropriate software manufacturer's technical support line or Web site for assistance.

Premier Press and the author have attempted throughout this book to distinguish proprietary trademarks from descriptive terms by following the capitalization style used by the manufacturer.

ISBN: 1-59200-039-8

Library of Congress Catalog Card Number: 2002116160

Printed in the United States of America

03 04 05 06 07 BH 10 9 8 7 6 5 4 3 2 1

Premier Press, a division of Course Technology
25 Thomson Place
Boston, MA 02210

Publisher:
Stacy L. Hiquet

Marketing Manager:
Heather Hurley

Acquisitions Editor:
Todd Jensen

Technical Reviewer:
Keith Davenport

Copy Editor:
Kristin Landon

Interior Layout and Project Management:
Argosy

Cover Designer:
Mike Tanamachi

CD-ROM Producer:
Keith Davenport

Indexer:
Larry Sweazy

Proofreader:
Darla Bruno

This book is dedicated to my two children,
my son Spencer and my daughter Olivia
who was born during the writing
of this book on October 22, 2002.
I love you both so much.

Acknowledgments

Writing any book is not easy, especially a technical programming book. It takes many great, patient, and talented people to write, edit, design, market, finance, and produce a book and the accompanying CD-ROM. Without the great people of Premier Press, it would be impossible for me to share with you my knowledge of programming in such a professional and fun manner.

I would like to acknowledge Todd Jensen and Andy Harris for their continuing commitment to this series. Thanks, guys.

I would like to thank Keith Davenport with Davenport Enterprises for his excellent work on CD-ROM development and technical editing. Thanks, Keith!

When it comes to inspiration, I give credit to my father Alex, who in his own right is a great writer. Throughout my life my father showed me what could be accomplished with words and has instilled in me a desire to write that has never left me. He has always been a supporter of my endeavors regardless of where those endeavors took me. Thank you, Dad! I love you.

Beyond the technical and business workings of creating a book, the author must be fed, loved, and encouraged. Without the support of my lovely wife, Sheila, this would never have happened. Thanks, baby, I love you.

About the Author

Michael Vine has taught computer programming, Web design, and database classes at Indiana University/Purdue University in Indianapolis, Indiana, and at MTI College of Business and Technology in Sacramento, California. Michael is a Certified Microsoft Professional in Visual Basic development with more than ten years' experience in the Information Technology profession. He currently works full time in a Fortune 300 company as a software engineer developing enterprise Web applications with Java, J2EE, Oracle, and Web Logic.

Contents at a Glance

Contents

CHAPTER 3   Conditions   49

CHAPTER 4   Looping Structures   77

Functions Continued 99

Code Reuse, Modules, and Advanced Form Concepts 123

Advanced Data Types   149

Debug Windows, Input Validation, File Processing, and Error Handling   171

Introduction to Database Languages   203

Database Programming with ADO   229

Object-Oriented Programming with Access VBA 263

Microsoft Office Objects 287

Letter from the Series Editor

Microsoft Access and other low-priced database management systems have lowered the threshold for database development. It is now possible to build a functional database in an afternoon with no programming whatsoever. However, it doesn't take long to discover that databases are hard to build correctly. When you want your data to do something interesting, you'll probably need to learn some programming.

Computer programming is sometimes seen as a 'black art' that requires years of practice. A subset of the programming community is interested in data programming, which has its own aura of mystique. People who can program and create well-formed databases are in high demand.

Fortunately, programming is not nearly as difficult as many people think. Microsoft has included a powerful subset of the popular Visual Basic language directly in the Access software. All you need is a good teacher who can show you how to harness this power. Michael is that teacher.

In this book, you'll learn more about databases-how to create them in a flexible and powerful way, how to write programs that create and manage databases, and how to build programs that can take advantage of the full power of a database management system. You'll also learn how to program well. There's a lot to learn, but it will be fun. Every chapter includes a game or diversion you will be able to write. Michael is a database pro, but he's also a very experienced teacher and writer with a friendly, easy-going style.

Although the focus is on fun, this is a serious programming book as well. Throughout the book you'll see explanations of how the concepts are tied to more traditional programming projects.

Whether you're an experienced programmer looking for a quick guide to Access VBA, a serious Access hound making the jump to programming, or a beginner wondering what this whole programming thing is really about, I think you'll enjoy this book and learn a lot from it.

Best of luck to you as you begin your programming journey!

—Andy Harris
Series Editor, *Absolute Beginner* Series

Introduction

Microsoft *Access VBA Programming for the Absolute Beginner* is not a guide on how to use Access and its many wizards. There are already many books that do that! Instead, *Microsoft Access VBA Programming for the Absolute Beginner* concentrates on VBA programming concepts including variables, conditions, loops, data structures, procedures, file I/O, and object-oriented programming with special topics including SQL and database programming using Microsoft's ADO programming model.

Using Premier Press's *Absolute Beginner* series guidelines, you will learn to program in Access VBA using professional insight, clear explanations, lots of examples, and pictures. Each chapter contains programming challenges, a chapter review, and a complete program that uses chapter-based concepts to construct a fun and easy-to-build application.

To work through this book in its entirety, you should have access to a computer with Microsoft Access installed. The programs in this book were written in Microsoft Office XP, specifically Access 2002. Those readers using older versions of Microsoft Access such as Access 97 or Access 2000 will find that almost all of the VBA programming concepts still apply.

How to Use This Book

To learn how to program a computer, you must acquire a complex progression of skills. If you have never programmed at all, you will probably find it easiest to go through the chapters in order. Of course, if you are already an experienced programmer, it might not be necessary to do any more than skim the earliest chapters. In either case, programming is not a skill you can learn by reading. You'll have to write programs to learn. This book has been designed to make the process reasonably painless.

Each chapter begins with a brief introduction to chapter-based concepts. Once inside the chapter, you'll look at a series of programming concepts and small programs that illustrate each of the major points of the chapter. Finally, you'll put these concepts together to build a complete program at the end of the chapter. All of the programs are short enough that you can type them in yourself (which is a great way to look closely at code), but they are also available on the CD-ROM. Also located at the end of every chapter is a summary that outlines key concepts learned. Use the summaries to refresh your memory on important concepts.

Throughout the book, I'll throw in a few other tidbits, notably the following:

 HINT These are good ideas that experienced programmers like to pass on.

 TRAP There are a few areas where it's easy to make a mistake. I'll point them out to you as we go.

 TRICK These will suggest techniques and shortcuts that will make your life as a programmer easier.

IN THE REAL WORLD

As you examine the games in this book, I'll show you how the concepts are used for purposes beyond game development.

CHALLENGES

At the end of each chapter, I'll suggest some programs that you can write with the skills you've learned so far. This should help you start writing your own programs.

Introduction to Access VBA Programming

This chapter reveals the essentials of Microsoft's VBA language, its integrated development environment, and intimate relationships with event-driven and object-based programming. Throughout the chapter, you will see how chapter-based concepts such as procedures, controls, and statements are applied using numerous examples and screen shots. After reading Chapter 1, you will have acquired the right amount of knowledge and experience for subsequent VBA programming topics and challenges.

Specifically, this chapter covers the following topics:

- **Introduction to Microsoft Access VBA**

- **The Visual Basic for Applications IDE**

- **Accessing objects and their properties**

- **Forms and common controls**

Introduction to Microsoft Access VBA

Introduced over a decade ago, Microsoft Access is a fully functional RDBMS (relational database management system) that has become one of the most powerful programs in the Microsoft Office suite of applications. Part of the *Developer* and *Professional* versions of Office XP, Access 2002 provides beginning database developers an easy-to-use graphical interface and a cost-effective way to learn database fundamentals such as tables, queries, forms, and reports. In addition to traditional relational database capabilities, Access 2002 comes with many Internet-ready features such as Data Access Pages for HTML and support for the Internet and XML.

Like many professional RDBMS, Microsoft Access comes with its own programming language called VBA. VBA, or Visual Basic for Applications, is a subset of Microsoft's popular enterprise programming language Visual Basic. VBA follows the Visual Basic language syntax and comes with many of its common features, such as an integrated development environment (a.k.a. IDE), and many common controls for building professional event-driven and data-driven applications.

Though VBA supports the look and feel of Visual Basic, it is not Visual Basic. A main difference is that Visual Basic allows for the creation of executable programs, whereas VBA does not. Moreover, VBA for Access is specifically designed for Microsoft Access: it has knowledge of and support for the Microsoft Access object model. The concept of an object model is different for each Microsoft Office application. For example, both Microsoft Excel and Microsoft Word support VBA, but each has its own object model that its VBA language supports.

In the first half of this book I will show you how to program in VBA using Access forms and Access's built-in visual Basic environment. During this time, you will become familiar with the most common VBA syntax and programming structures such as conditions, loops, arrays, and functions. With this knowledge, I will introduce you to some of Access's more powerful and advanced features such as ActiveX Data Objects (ADO), SQL, Object Oriented Programming, and Microsoft Office Objects.

Before unlocking the specifics of VBA programming, it's time to discuss a few important concepts such as objects and events.

Understanding Objects

The key to programming in VBA is understanding and using objects. Access VBA supports a multitude of objects, many of which form a hierarchical relationship. In object-based programming, the concept of an object is defined as a noun—a person, place, or thing. Objects have properties, which describe the object, and methods, which perform actions. For example, say I have an object called Person. The Person object contains properties called HairColor, Weight, Height, and Age that describe the object. The Person object also contains methods that describe an action the object can perform such as Run, Walk, Sleep, and Eat. As you can see, understanding the concept of objects is really quite simple!

Many Access VBA objects also contain data structures called collections. In a nutshell, collections are groupings of objects, which you will be introduced to in this chapter. You will learn more about collections in Chapter 11 where I discuss Object Oriented Programming.

As mentioned, Access VBA supports many objects such as the Form object, which is simply a window or dialog box. The Form object contains many properties such as Caption, Moveable, and Visible. Each of these properties describes the Form object and allows VBA programmers to set characteristics of a user's interface. Like the Person object earlier, the Form object contains methods such as Move and Refresh.

Many objects share common characteristics such as properties and methods. To demonstrate, the Label object (which implements the label control) shares many of the Form's properties such as Caption and Visible.

Properties and methods of objects are accessed using the dot operator (period) as demonstrated in the next two VBA statements.

```
Label1.ForeColor = vbBlue

Label1.Caption = "Hello World"
```

Don't worry about the details in the preceding statements for now, but do realize that properties such as ForeColor and Caption belong to the Label1 object and they are accessed using the dot operator (.). I'll discuss this in more detail in sections to come.

The Event-Driven Paradigm

The event-driven paradigm is a powerful programming model that allows programmers to build applications that respond to actions initiated by the user or system. Access VBA includes a number of events that are categorized by the objects they represent. VBA programmers write code in event procedures to respond to user actions such as clicking or system actions such as a form loading.

To demonstrate the event-driven model, consider our Form object that contains many events such as Click, Load, and MouseUp. As seen next, both Click and MouseUp events are triggered by the user performing an action with the mouse.

```
Private Sub Form_Click()
    'write code in here to respond to the user clicking the form
End Sub


Private Sub Form_MouseUp(Button As Integer, _
    Shift As Integer, X As Single, Y As Single)

    'write code in here to respond to the user releasing a mouse button
End Sub
```

I'll discuss the details of these event procedures soon enough. For now, understand that objects have related events, which can be triggered by users. You, the VBA programmer, write code in these event procedures to respond to user actions. Moreover, events can be triggered by the system or by the program itself. For example, the Load event seen next is triggered when a Form object is first loaded into memory.

```
Private Sub Form_Load()
    'write code in here to respond to the form loading into memory
End Sub
```

If you're new to programming, this may seem a bit awkward at first. I promise you, it is really not that difficult. In fact, VBA does a great job of providing much of the detail for you. By the end of this chapter, you will be writing your first Access VBA event-driven programs with ease.

The Visual Basic for Applications IDE

If you've written programs in Visual Basic before, the VBA integrated development environment (IDE) should feel very familiar to you. If not, don't worry—the VBA IDE is user-friendly and easy to learn. For ease of use, I will refer to the VBA integrated development environment as the Visual Basic Editor, or VBE, from now on.

The VBE contains a suite of windows, toolbars, and menu items that provide support for text editing, debugging, file management, and help. Two common methods of access the VBE are forms and code modules. If you haven't done so already, open a new Access database and create a form in Design view as shown in Figure 1.1.

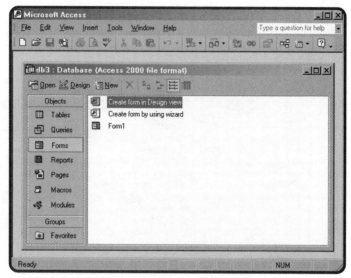

Note that Microsoft Access supplies a number of wizards to guide you through the process of creating tables, forms, reports, and queries. For the most part, I will intentionally shy away from wizards in order to reveal Access's underlying power and functionality.

After adding a form, make sure your form is highlighted (shown in Figure 1.1), then select the Code menu item from the View menu as demonstrated in Figure 1.2.

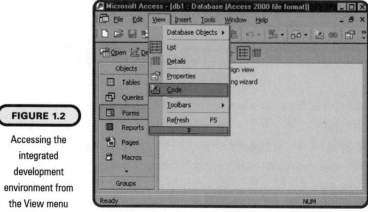

If your Code menu item is not selectable, make sure you've created and selected (highlighted) a form first.

 TRICK An easy shortcut to opening the VBE and alternating between Access and the Visual Basic editor is by pressing Alt+F11.

After selecting the Code menu item, the VBA IDE should open up in a separate window similar to the one shown in Figure 1.3.

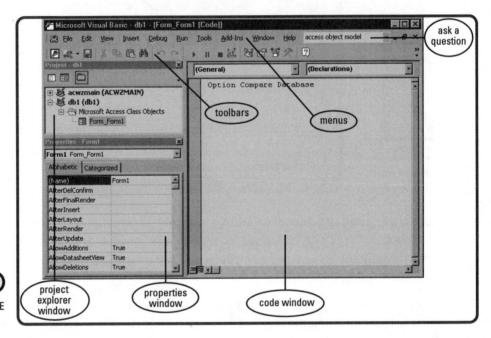

FIGURE 1.3

Opening the VBA IDE for the first time

There are a few IDE components that you should familiarize yourself with right away. Each of the following is shown in Figure 1.3:

- **Toolbars.** Toolbars contain shortcuts to many common functions used throughout your VBA development such as saving, inserting modules, and running your program code. Toolbars can be added from the View menu item.

- **Menus.** Menus in the IDE provide you with many development features such as file management, editing, debugging, and help.

- **Ask a Question.** Part of the Standard toolbar, the Ask a Question feature is a combo box that allows you to easily search for answers to your VBA questions. You can also access VBA's help system through the Help menu or by pressing F1.

- **Project Explorer Window.** The Project Explorer window provides you with a bird's-eye view of all files and components that are used to build your Access VBA programming environment. Notice in Figure 1.3 that my form's name appears under the db1 project and directly beneath the Microsoft Access Class Objects heading. If I had multiple forms in my database, there would be multiple form names under the db1 project. Remember that Microsoft Access stores all components including forms, queries, reports, and modules in a single .mdb file.

- **Properties Window.** The Properties window shows all available properties for the object selected in the list box above. For example, Figure 1.3 shows all of the available properties for the Form1 object. Most importantly, the Properties window allows you to change the values of an object's property during design-time development.

- **Code Window.** The Code window is where you enter your VBA code and find procedures and event procedures for objects using the two list boxes at the top of the Code window.

If you haven't done so yet, explore each of the previously mentioned components and windows so that you are comfortable in navigating the VBE environment.

Introduction to Event Procedures

Procedures are simply containers for VBA code. Access VBA contains four types of procedures:

- Subprocedures
- Function procedures
- Property procedures
- Event procedures

Each type of procedure is designed to accomplish specific tasks. For example, event procedures are designed to catch and respond to user-initiated events such as a mouse click or system-initiated events such as a form loading. In this section I'll concentrate on event procedures, as they are the foundation for an event-driven language such as VBA. In subsequent chapters, you will learn about other types of procedures in detail.

As mentioned, objects such as forms contain methods and properties. They also contain specialized events that are provided for you automatically after the object has been added to your database. VBA takes care of naming your object's events for you. Their naming convention is

ObjectName_EventName

For example, a form added to your Access database called `Form1` will have a number of events including the following:

```
Private Sub Form_Load()

End Sub


Private Sub Form_Unload(Cancel As Integer)

End Sub
```

Notice the naming convention used for each event procedure: the object name followed by the event name, with an underscore in between. Objects and their events are accessed from the VBE code window seen in Figure 1.4.

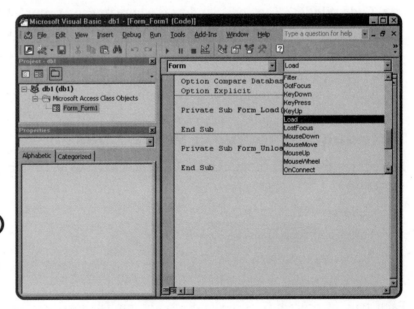

FIGURE 1.4

Selecting objects
and their events in
the VBE code
window

The list box at left in the code window (seen in Figure 1.4) identifies available objects. The list box at right in the code window contains all available events for the object selected in the left list box. Each time you select an event, VBA creates the event shell for you automatically. This saves you from having to manually type each event's beginning and ending procedure statements.

Each procedure in the VBE code window is separated by a horizontal line.

Empty event procedures, such as those seen in Figure 1.4, serve no purpose until you write code in them using VBA statements.

Introduction to VBA Statements

VBA statements are comprised of variables, keywords, operators, and expressions that build a complete instruction to the computer. Every VBA statement falls into one of three categories as follows.

- **Declaration statement.** Creates variables, data types, and procedures.
- **Assignment statement.** Assigns data or values to variables or properties.
- **Executable statement.** Initiates an action such as a method or function.

Most VBA statements fit onto one line, but sometime it is appropriate to continue a VBA statement onto a second or further lines for readability. To split a single VBA statement into multiple lines, VBA programmers use the line continuation character (_). To demonstrate, the following assignment statement uses the continuation character to extend a statement across two lines.

```
Label1.Caption = _
    "This is a single VBA assignment statement split onto two lines."
```

One of the best ways to provide understandable VBA statements is with comments. Comments provide you and other programmers with a brief description of how and why your program code does something. In Access VBA, comments are created by placing a single quote ('), sometimes called a tick mark, to the left of a statement. Comments are also created by placing the keyword *REM* (short for remark) to the left of a statement. The following statements demonstrate both ways of creating VBA comments:

```
' This is a VBA comment using the single quote character.

REM This is a VBA comment using the REM keyword.
```

When a computer encounters a comment, it is ignored and not processed as a VBA statement.

Accessing Objects and Their Properties

Besides the Properties window, Microsoft Access provides a number of ways to access objects and their properties. Each way provides a level of intricacy and detail while providing its own level of performance characteristics. In its simplest form, programmers can simply call the name of an object such as the `Form` object or the name of a control such as a command button directly. This is only applicable when accessing objects and controls that belong to the current scope of a code module. For example, the next VBA assignment statement updates the form's Caption property during the form's Load event:

```
Private Sub Form_Load()
    Form.Caption = "Chapter 1"
End Sub
```

The concept of assignment statements as seen in the preceding event procedure will be explained shortly.

In addition to forms, controls belonging to the current form and scope can be referenced by simply calling their names:

```
Private Sub Form_Load()
    lblSalary.Caption = "Enter Salary"
    txtSalary.Value = "50000.00"
    cmdIncrease.Caption = "Increase Salary"
End Sub
```

There are times, however, when you will need to go beyond the current scope and access forms and controls that do not belong to the current object. There are a number of other reasons for being more specific about what controls you are referencing, such as performance considerations and advanced control access techniques such as enumeration. To accomplish these goals, I'll show you how to access forms and controls using common VBA techniques with the Me keyword prefix and collections such as the Forms collection.

The Forms Collection

Properties of the Form object can be accessed in the VBE code window by simply supplying the form's Access class:

```
Form_Form1.Caption = "updating the form's caption property"
```

Notice the naming convention used in the keyword Form_Form1. When an Access form is created and saved, Microsoft Access refers to it in the VBE as a *Microsoft Access Class* Object with the name Form representing the standard object name with a trailing underscore (_) followed by the individual form's name. Moreover, you can use the form's Access class name to access not only its own properties, but also controls contained on the form. For example, the following VBA assignment statement uses the Access form class name to modify a label's Caption property:

```
Form_Form1.Label1.Caption = "updating the label's caption property"
```

This approach is convenient when working with small VBA projects. There are times, however, when you will want to use a more advanced feature such as the `Forms` collection when working with multiple forms, or multiple controls on a form. Access provides the `Forms` collection for being more specific about which form's `Caption` property you are referencing.

The `Forms` collection contains all open forms in your Access database. To access individual forms in the `Forms` collection, simply supply the `Forms` collection an index or form name as seen in the next statements:

```
'   Using an index to refer to a form in the collection.
Forms(0).Caption = "Chapter 1"


'   Using a form name to reference a form in the collection.
Forms("Form1").Caption = "Chapter 1"
```

TRAP Because form indexes can change, it is considered safer to use the form name when accessing forms in the `Forms` collection.

Notice that when passing the name of the form to the `Forms` collection, you must surround the form name in double quotes. If the form's name contains one or more spaces, you must use brackets ([ ]) to surround the name. After specifying a form in the `Forms` collection, you can use the dot operator to reference the individual form's properties such as `Caption`.

The Me Keyword

To make things more interesting, Access provides the `Me` keyword, which refers to the current object or form within the scope of the VBE code module. More specifically, I can use the `Me` object in place of the Access form class name to access properties, methods, and controls of the current form:

```
Me.Caption = "updating the form's caption property"

Me.lblSalary.Caption = "updating the label's caption property"
```

The `Me` keyword provides a self-documenting feature for VBA programmers in that it explicitly tells the reader what object, property, or form you are referring to.

In addition to the dot operator (.), Microsoft VBA provides the exclamation point (!) identifier for identifying what type of item or object immediately follows:

```
Me!lblSalary.Caption = "updating the label's caption property"
```

Because the dot (.) operator and exclamation mark (!) operator can often be interchanged, it can be confusing to remember which serves what purpose. A general rule of thumb is to use the ! operator prior to accessing an item in a collection. Use the dot operator when referencing a property of a form or control. To keep things simple, however, I will use the dot operator to reference both items in collections and properties of forms and controls.

Assignment Statements

You can assign data to object properties such as the form's Caption property using an assignment operator in a VBA assignment statement. The assignment operator is really a fancy term for the equals (=) sign. However, it's really much more important, as you will soon see. To demonstrate, evaluate the next lines of VBA code, which assign the text "Ouch!" to the Caption property of the Form1 control:

```
Form.Caption = "Ouch!"
```

Or

```
Forms("Form1").Caption = "Ouch!"
```

Or

```
Forms(0).Caption = "Ouch!"
```

Or

```
Me.Caption = "Ouch!"
```

Or

```
Form_Form1.Caption = "Ouch!"
```

A core concept in most programming languages is to understand the difference between data assignment and testing for equality. This is especially important in programming languages such as VBA, which use the same operator.

Specifically, the assignment statement

```
Me.Caption = "Ouch!"
```

reads "the Caption property takes the literal value Ouch!" or "the Caption property gets the literal value Ouch!" Either way, the equals sign in an assignment statement is not testing for equality. In other words, you would never want to read the previous assignment as "the Caption property equals Ouch!" In the next chapter, I will discuss how the equals sign can be used in testing for equality.

Forms and Common Controls

In this section you will continue your investigation into objects, their properties, and events using forms and the following common controls:

- **Form.** A container used to hold other controls and provide a graphical interface for user interaction with data or system management.
- **Image.** A displayable container for pictures in binary formats such as *.bmp*, *.ico*, *.TIF*, *.JPG*, or *.GIF*.
- **Label.** Used for informational purposes such as describing other controls (the text box, for example).
- **Command button.** Used for triggering a click event by the user.
- **Text box.** Provides a common container for user input.

Each of the previously mentioned common controls can be accessed and placed onto your form by clicking once on the control in the Toolbox and clicking once on the form. Access then places the control on your form in a predetermined shape and size. After that, you can resize controls using your left mouse button, or clicking once on the control and then using the *Ctrl* and arrows key simultaneously to resize the control and the *Shift* and arrows keys simultaneously to move the control.

Common Control Naming Conventions

To provide readability and consistency throughout your code, I recommend a naming convention that I myself use called *Hungarian notation* (named after a computer scientist). To apply this notation, simply modify the Name property of each control to use a three-letter prefix (all in lowercase) that indicates the control type followed by a meaningful description. Each word that describes the control (not the prefix) should have its first letter capitalized.

Table 1.1 shows some sample naming conventions for controls discussed in this chapter and throughout this book.

Forms

Forms are to GUI (graphical user interface) programmers what a canvas is to a painter. Essentially, Access forms are graphical controls that act as containers for

TABLE 1.1 COMMON CONTROL NAMING CONVENTIONS

Control	Prefix	Example
Check Box	chk	chkRed
Combo Box	cbo	cboStates
Command Button	cmd	cmdQuit
Form	frm	frmMain
Image	img	imgLogo
Label	lbl	lblFirstName
List Box	lst	lstFruits
Option Button	opt	optMale
Text Box	txt	txtFirstName

other graphical controls such as text boxes, labels, and command buttons. Once built, forms are the graphical interface that provide a window into a database. Behind the scenes, a form is represented by a `Form` object. VBA programmers use the `Form` object to get and set properties of the current graphical form.

Microsoft Access provides an easy-to-use wizard for creating data-bound forms and controls. This "form wizard" works nicely if you already have a table defined and need only the functionality the wizard provides. For simple databases, wizards can be sufficient, but as mentioned earlier, in this book I will stay away from form wizards.

To create a form without a wizard, simply choose to create a form in Design view from the Forms Object window as shown in Figure 1.5.

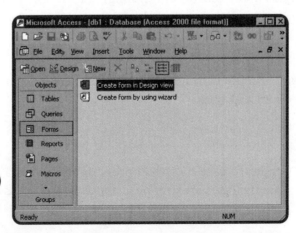

FIGURE 1.5

Choosing to create a form in Design view

After creating a form in Design view, you should see an empty form as demonstrated in Figure 1.6.

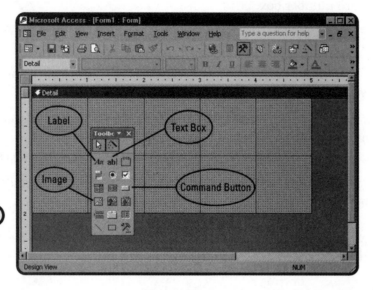

FIGURE 1.6

An empty form created in Design view

Microsoft Access forms are designed to be data driven. Hence, they contain many inherent controls for navigating through database records. After creating a new form and viewing it in Form view (from the View menu), inherent controls (seen in Figure 1.7) can be easily removed by setting the following form properties to no in design time:

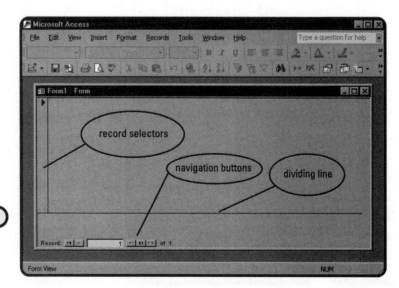

FIGURE 1.7

Inherent form controls seen in Form view

- **DividingLines**. Used to separate sections on a form.
- **NavigationButtons**. Provides access to navigation buttons and a record number box.
- **RecordSelectors**. Record selectors display the unsaved record indicator when a record is being edited in Form view.

Each of these form properties can be set to either **yes** or **no** using the VBE properties window.

After adding a form to your Access database, a Toolbox window (seen in Figure 1.6) containing common controls is now visible. The Toolbox window contains some of Access's more common controls for building graphical interfaces.

If your Toolbox window does not appear, simply select the Toolbox menu item from the View menu.

 The Toolbox window can be docked into the Access parent window by dragging it onto the top, bottom, or left or right side of Access's main window.

VBA programmers and Access form developers can access object properties through the properties window seen in Figure 1.8, or through VBA statements in run time. If you're unable to see the Properties window, choose the Properties menu item from the View menu or simply press F4. Using the list box at the top of the Properties windows (see Figure 1.8), you can easily switch between available control properties during design time.

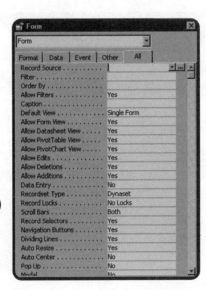

FIGURE 1.8

Accessing control properties during design time with the Properties window

Seen in Table 1.2 are some common form properties.

TABLE 1.2 COMMON FORM DESIGN-TIME PROPERTIES

Property	Description
Caption	Textual description the user can see
BorderStyle	Describes if the user can resize the form's size
ControlBox	Provides access to the form's control box
Moveable	Allows the user to move the form
(Navigation Buttons)	Adds or removes the record navigation buttons
ScrollBars	Allows access to available types of scroll bars
TimerInterval	Determines the interval, in milliseconds, between Timer events

Note that Table 1.2 represents a fraction of the form's properties. Moreover, not all control properties can be accessed or are available with the properties window in design time. This means other properties are available only during run time through VBA statements.

In addition to properties, the form object has many events, which can be accessed via the VBE. The following are some common form events:

- Activate. Occurs when the form becomes the active window
- Click. Activated when a user presses and releases a mouse button over the form
- Close. Occurs when a form has been removed from the computer's screen
- DblClick. Triggered when a user double-clicks the form
- KeyDown. Occurs while the form has the focus and the user presses a key
- KeyPress. Occurs when a user presses a key or key combination that represents an ANSI code while the form has the focus
- KeyUp. Initiated when a user releases a key while the form has the focus
- Load. Occurs when a form is opened
- MouseDown. Occurs when the user presses a mouse button while the form has the focus
- MouseMove. Starts when a user moves the mouse while the form has the focus

- **MouseUp**. Occurs when the user releases a mouse button while the form has the focus
- **Timer**. Starts at regular intervals, which are determined by the form's **TimerInterval** property
- **Unload**. Triggered after a form is closed but prior to the form being removed from the computer's screen

With your knowledge of form properties and events, you can add VBA assignment statements inside of event procedures by accessing the VBE code window and selecting the form object and then an event procedure. To demonstrate, I've inserted a VBA assignment statement (seen next) in the form's **Click** event to update the form's **Caption** property as seen in Figure 1.9.

```
Private Sub Form_Click()
    Forms("Form1").Caption = "Hello World"
```

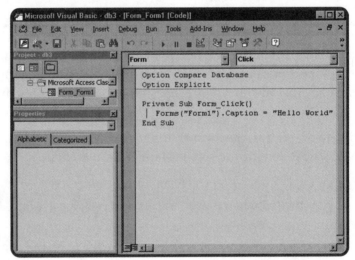

Similarly, I can add a similar VBA assignment statement in another form event called **Load**:

```
Private Sub Form_Load()
    Me.Caption = "Greetings World"
End Sub
```

If you haven't worked with VBA or an event-driven language before, now is a good time to open an Access database and try the preceding VBA event procedures and assignment statements.

To test your VBA code, save your work and switch back to the Access database (Alt+F11) and view your form in Form view (from the Toolbar or View menu).

 TRICK For a potentially better user experience, you can customize your form as the start-up object by selecting the Startup menu item from the Tools menu and changing the Display Form/Page option as revealed in Figure 1.10.

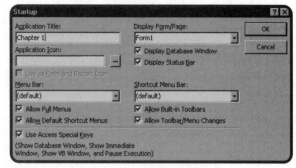

> **FIGURE 1.10**
>
> Customizing startup properties with the Tools dialog window

In addition to changing the startup form in the Tools dialog window, you can choose not to have the database window or status bar displayed at program startup.

Images

Like forms, the image control also acts as a container. More specifically, the image control is a container for binary image files such as *.GIF*, *.bmp*, or *.JPG* file formats.

After adding an image control to your form (refer to Figure 1.6), an Insert Picture dialog window helps you find a picture for display in the image control. Then, the image control's design-time properties can be managed using the Properties window, some of which are listed in Table 1.3.

The image control can be useful for adding artistic flair to your forms and can even help to describe a form's purpose through graphics. Like many other controls, the image control has associated events that describe actions for which you can write code to respond to user actions. The following list includes all of the image control's events:

- Click. Activated when a user presses and releases a mouse button over the image
- DblClick. Triggered when a user double-clicks the image

TABLE 1.3 COMMON IMAGE DESIGN-TIME PROPERTIES

Property	Description
Name	Internal control name
Picture	Describes the image file location
PictureType	Can be set to one of two types, Embedded or Linked. If type is Embedded, the picture becomes part of the Access database file. If type is Linked, Access creates and stores a link to the picture.
SizeMode	Determines how a picture is sized such as Clip, Zoom, or Stretch
SpecialEffect	Applies special object formatting such as Raised, Sunken, Flat, Etched, Shadowed, or Chiseled
Visible	Determines if the user can see the label

- **MouseDown.** Occurs when the user presses a mouse button on an image
- **MouseMove.** Starts when a user moves the mouse over the image
- **MouseUp.** Occurs when the user releases a mouse button on an image from which the mouse button was clicked down

Using properties and events, an image control can be used similarly to that of a command button in responding to Click events.

```
Private Sub Image1_Click()
    Forms("Form1").Caption = "You clicked the apples."
End Sub


Private Sub Image1_MouseDown(Button As Integer, _
    Shift As Integer, X As Single, Y As Single)
    Me.Image1.SpecialEffect = 2
End Sub


Private Sub Image1_MouseUp(Button As Integer, _
    Shift As Integer, X As Single, Y As Single)
    Me.Image1.SpecialEffect = 1
End Sub
```

Figure 1.11 demonstrates the output from the previous Click event procedure.

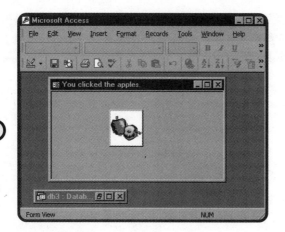

FIGURE 1.11

Using the image control's `Click` event to change a form's `Caption` property

Notice that in the preceding program code, I use three separate events, each with their own VBA assignment statements. In the image `Click` event, I use an assignment statement to change the form's `Caption` property. In `MouseDown` and `MouseUp` events, I change the image's `SpecialEffect` property to make the image behave like a command button (raised and lowered). Valid image-control special effects include the following:

Flat—0

Raised—1

Sunken—2

Etched—3

Shadowed—4

Chiseled—5

Labels

Labels are descriptive entities for other controls. Just as a label on a spice bottle tells you that the bottle contains oregano and not thyme, a text box's label containing the text "first name" tells users to enter their first name into a text box rather than their last name. Labels are not restricted to text boxes. In fact, the label control can be used to describe forms, option buttons, check boxes, and many other controls.

By default, Access text boxes come with labels. You can, however, remove those default labels or add your own free-standing labels using the Toolbox.

Like all Access form common controls, the label control contains many design-time properties, as seen in Table 1.4.

TABLE 1.4   COMMON LABEL DESIGN-TIME PROPERTIES

Property	Description
Name	Internal control name
Caption	Textual description the user can see
Visible	Determines if the user can see the label
BackStyle	Determines normal back style or transparent
BackColor	Determines the back color of the label
ForeColor	Determines the fore color of the label
FontName	The font's name
FontSize	The size of the font displayed in the caption property
TextAlign	Alignment of the text in the caption property

The label control shares the same limited number of built-in event procedures as the image control:

- Click. Activated when a user presses and releases a mouse button over the label
- DblClick. Triggered when a user double-clicks the label
- MouseDown. Occurs when the user presses a mouse button on the label
- MouseMove. Starts when a user moves the mouse while over the label
- MouseUp. Occurs when the user releases a mouse button on the label from which a mouse button was clicked

Labels have a number of interesting and charismatic design-time properties such as BackColor and ForeColor, which can be set during run time using VBA assignment statements. For example, the following program code uses two command-button Click events and the form Load event to alter the Caption property and fore and back colors of a label. Its output can be seen in Figure 1.12.

```
Private Sub cmdBackColor_Click()
    Me.lblChapter1.BackColor = vbBlack
End Sub


Private Sub cmdForeColor_Click()
    Me.lblChapter1.ForeColor = vbYellow
End Sub
```

```
Private Sub Form_Load()
    lblChapter1.Caption = "Chapter 1 - The Label Control"
End Sub
```

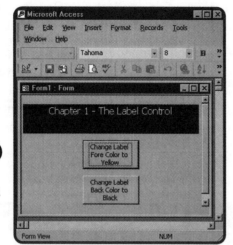

FIGURE 1.12

Modifying label properties with VBA events and assignment statements

 TRAP

The label's **BackColor** property cannot be changed unless the corresponding label's **BackStyle** property is set to **Normal**.

The way I used the **Me** keyword to access the label and its corresponding properties should not be new to you. But what should have caught your attention was what I assigned to the **ForeColor** and **BackColor** properties. Specifically, VBA provides you access to eight color constants:

- vbBlack
- vbRed
- vbGreen
- vbYellow
- vbBlue
- vbMagenta
- vbCyan
- vbWhite

It's important to note that **BackColor** and **ForeColor** properties actually take a number value, which each color constant stores representatively. In addition to using VBA color constants you can assign numbers representing a multitude of colors either by using the **RGB** function or by viewing the **BackColor** or **ForeColor** properties in design time using the properties window.

Command Buttons

With their 3-D appearance, command buttons are one of the most noticeable components of any graphical interface. With their associated click events, command buttons let users dictate much of an application's flow and responses. This type of user interaction sits at the heart of the event-driven paradigm.

As with many other aspects of Microsoft components, Access provides a command-button wizard to aid you in creating a populated and working event procedure. Though somewhat useful, this wizard lacks the power and flexibility programmers need and demand. In a nutshell, select the Cancel option from the Command Button Wizard when adding command buttons to your form.

Table 1.5 shows some of the more common design-time properties and events of the command button.

TABLE 1.5 COMMON COMMAND BUTTON DESIGN-TIME PROPERTIES

Property	Description
Caption	Textual description the user can see
Default	Determines if the command button is the default command on the form
Enabled	Determines if the control is enabled for the user
FontName	The font's name
FontSize	The size of the font displayed in the caption
ForeColor	Determines the fore color of the label
Name	Internal control name
TabIndex	Determines the control's tab order on the form

- Click. Activated when a user presses and releases a mouse button over the label
- DblClick. Triggered when a user double-clicks the label
- Enter. Occurs before the command button actually receives the focus
- Exit. Occurs before the command button actually loses the focus
- GotFocus. Triggered when the command button receives the focus
- LostFocus. Triggered when the command button loses the focus

- **MouseDown**. Occurs when the user presses a mouse button on the label
- **MouseMove**. Starts when a user moves the mouse while over the label
- **MouseUp**. Occurs when the user releases a mouse button on the label from which a mouse button was clicked

You may notice by now that controls including the command button share common properties and events.

A common use of command buttons is to provide the user action or navigational opportunities such as terminating the program with an End or Quit command button. To terminate an Access application, simply supply the **End** keyword as shown in the next command-button **Click** event procedure:

```
Private Sub cmdEnd_Click()
    ' Terminate the program.
    End
End Sub
```

As shown in Figure 1.13, I can use command buttons and event procedures to build a simple light-bulb program.

FIGURE 1.13

Using command buttons and chapter-based concepts to build a simple light-bulb program

```
Private Sub cmdOff_Click()
    Me.cmdOn.Enabled = True
    Me.cmdOn.SetFocus
    Me.cmdOff.Enabled = False
    Me.imgOn.Visible = False
    Me.imgOff.Visible = True
End Sub
```

```
Private Sub cmdOn_Click()
    Me.cmdOff.Enabled = True
    Me.cmdOff.SetFocus
    Me.cmdOn.Enabled = False
    Me.imgOff.Visible = False
    Me.imgOn.Visible = True
End Sub

Private Sub Form_Load()
    Me.cmdOff.Caption = "Off"
    Me.cmdOn.Caption = "On"
    Me.cmdOff.Enabled = False
    Me.imgOn.Visible = False
End Sub
```

In the form Load event, I perform a bit of housekeeping by setting control properties to a desired effect (essentially, light is off). In each command button's Click event I turn the light on or off by continuing to set image and command button properties. Worth noting is the use of the SetFocus method. The SetFocus method must be used in this case to move the focus away from the current control (command button) before I can change its Enabled property. Failure to do this will result in a run-time error.

Text Boxes

There are numerous means for retrieving input from users, but none comes close to the popularity of the text-box control. With the advent of popular GUI languages such as Visual Basic, VBA, and HTML, text boxes have become quite popular with applications ranging from traditional client-server programs to Web-based forms and of course database forms with Microsoft Access.

Text boxes can easily be added to Access forms using the Toolbox window seen in Figure 1.6. After you add a text box in design time, Access automatically adds a label control to the immediate left of the text box. There is good reason for this, as most text boxes require some explanation. And what better venue for a textual description of a text box is there than a label control? If you wish to remove the label from the text box, however, simply click on the text box's associated label once and delete it (Del key or right-click and choose Delete).

As shown in Table 1.6 and the following bulleted list, the text box shares many common properties and events.

TABLE 1.6 COMMON TEXT BOX DESIGN-TIME PROPERTIES

Property	Description
BackColor	Determines the back color of the label
BackStyle	Determines normal back style or transparent
DecimalPlaces	Specifies the number of decimal places Access uses to display numbers
Enabled	Determines if the control is enabled for user interaction
EnterKeyBehavior	Specifies what happens when the Enter key is pressed within a text box
FontName	The font's name
FontSize	The size of the font displayed in the caption
ForeColor	Determines the fore color of the label
Name	Internal control name
ScrollBars	Determines if the text box has scroll bars
TabIndex	Determines the control's tab order on the form
ValidationRule	Determines requirements used for data entered into the text box
ValidationText	Specifies message displayed to user
Visible	Determines if the user can see the text box

- **AfterUpdate**. Occurs after data is changed in the text box
- **BeforeUpdate**. Occurs before data in the control is updated
- **Click**. Activated when a user presses and releases a mouse button over the label
- **DblClick**. Triggered when a user double-clicks the label
- **Enter**. Occurs before the command button actually receives the focus
- **Exit**. Occurs before the command button actually loses the focus
- **GotFocus**. Triggered when the command button receives the focus
- **LostFocus**. Triggered when the command button loses the focus
- **MouseDown**. Occurs when the user presses a mouse button on the label
- **MouseMove**. Starts when a user moves the mouse while over the label
- **MouseUp**. Occurs when the user releases a mouse button on the label from which a mouse button was clicked

Text box controls receive all types of input from users such as dates, time, text, and numbers. VBA programmers (that would be you!) write code in procedures to collect the user input and process it. This may seem trivial, but it's not.

Consider a simple application that requests a user to enter two numbers, after which the user clicks a command button to add the two numbers together. After adding the numbers together, the program should display its output in a label control.

```
Private Sub Command1_Click()
    Label1.Caption = Text1.Value + Text2.Value
End Sub
```

I can use a VBA assignment statement to add the value of both text boxes and assign the result to the Caption property of the label control. Given this fact, why is the output of this VBA statement 55 instead of 10 as revealed in Figure 1.14?

FIGURE 1.14

Retrieving user input
from text boxes

This is an excellent question and best answered by examining the Value property of a text box. The text box's Value property returns or sets the text box's Text property (more on this in a moment). Because the Text property returns a string or textual description of what's inside the text box, the output seen in Figure 1.14 is generated because I've added two strings together ("5" and "5" makes "55").

To accurately process numbers retrieved from text boxes, you use a built-in VBA function called Val. The Val function is simple to use. It takes a string as input and returns a numeric value. The next program statement uses the Val function to correct the previous program's output.

```
Label1.Caption = Val(Text1.Value) + Val(Text2.Value)
```

Notice in this example that each Val function takes a string as input. Specifically, I use two separate Val functions to convert each text box's Value property one at a time on both sides of the addition operation. The strings contained in the Value property are converted to numeric values prior to performing mathematical operations.

Now back to the relationship between the text box's Value and Text properties. If the Text property already contains the contents of the text box, then why use the Value property? Another excellent question. Before I answer, however, look at the following updated code that uses the Text property to add two numbers with output seen in Figure 1.15.

```
Private Sub Command1_Click()
    Label1.Caption = Val(Text1.Text) + Val(Text2.Text)
End Sub
```

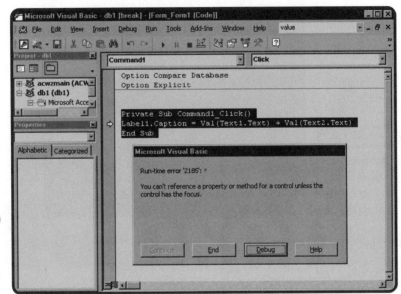

FIGURE 1.15

Attempting to use the Text property to retrieve user input from text boxes

As Figure 1.15 depicts, VBA does not like this approach, but why? The Text property of a text box is only accessible once the text box has the focus—only then is the Text property current or valid. The Value property, however, is the saved value of the text box control regardless of its focus.

To clear the text box of all contents, simply assign an empty string, also known as empty quotes, to the text box's Value property:

```
Me.Text1.Value = ""
```

In subsequent chapters, I will show you much more about text boxes, such as validating and error-proofing user input with validation programming and text-box events.

Chapter Program: Word Art

Seen in Figure 1.16, the program Word Art uses chapter-based concepts such as objects, controls, event procedures, and VBA assignment statements to build a simplistic and easy-to-use text editor.

Note that by setting the text box's `EnterKeyBehavior` property to `True` or `New Line in Field`, the text box allows for multiline text entry. All of the code required to build the Word Art program is seen next.

FIGURE 1.16

Demonstrating chapter-based concepts with the Word Art program

```
Option Compare Database
Option Explicit


Private Sub cmdBackBlack_Click()
    Me.txtEditor.BackColor = vbBlack
End Sub


Private Sub cmdBackBlue_Click()
    Me.txtEditor.BackColor = vbBlue
End Sub


Private Sub cmdBackRed_Click()
    Me.txtEditor.BackColor = vbRed
End Sub
```

```
Private Sub cmdBackWhite_Click()
    Me.txtEditor.BackColor = vbWhite
End Sub


Private Sub cmdForeBlack_Click()
    Me.txtEditor.ForeColor = vbBlack
End Sub


Private Sub cmdForeBlue_Click()
    Me.txtEditor.ForeColor = vbBlue
End Sub


Private Sub cmdForeRed_Click()
    Me.txtEditor.ForeColor = vbRed
End Sub


Private Sub cmdForeWhite_Click()
    Me.txtEditor.ForeColor = vbWhite
End Sub


Private Sub cmdClear_Click()
    ' Clear the contents of the text box and
    ' return focus back to the text box.
    Me.txtEditor.Value = ""
    Me.txtEditor.SetFocus
End Sub


Private Sub cmdEnd_Click()
    ' Terminate the program.
    End
End Sub
```

Chapter Summary

In this chapter, you learned about the Access Visual Basic environment, also known as the Access VBE, objects, properties, event procedures, and VBA statements. Core concepts include the following:

- The Access VBE is made up of smaller windows such as the Code, properties, and Project Explorer windows.

- Design time is when an Access VBA developer creates the graphical interface and sets design-time control properties. Run time is when your Access program is running and your VBA statements are executed.

- Access VBA uses objects and collections such as the Form object and the Forms collection to manage its components during run time with VBA code.

- There are a multitude of ways to access objects and their properties, not only using object names and collections, but also with operators such as the dot operator (.) and exclamation point (!).

- It's common to use the dot operator when accessing properties of an object and the exclamation point when accessing items in a collection.

- Common controls can be added to your forms during design time; each control, including the form, has its own properties and event procedures.

- Properties can be assigned data using VBA assignment statements.

- VBA assignment statements use the assignment operator (=), which reads from right to left. Data on the right of the assignment operator is assigned to the property or variable on the left side of the assignment operator.

In the next chapter, you will continue your investigation into the VBA programming language with beginning data types and variables.

CHALLENGES

1. Using the following controls, try to recreate the graphical interface seen in Figure 1.16.
   - 1 form
   - 3 labels
   - 1 text box
   - 10 command buttons

2. Add a form to your Access database. Using the VBE code window, add code to the form's Load event to update the form's Caption property to your name.

3. Add one label, one text box with an attached label, and a command button to a form. Assign the text "Enter your name:" in the text box's attached label Caption property. In the Click event of the command button, write a VBA assignment statement that takes the user's name and outputs a welcome message in the other label.

4. Improve the Word Art program by adding controls to the user interface that allow the user to modify the text box's font size. Hint: assign valid font size numbers to the text box's FontSize property.

Introduction to Data and Variables

This chapter will establish beginning data concepts such as storage, data retrieval, and assignment, which are paramount in both database systems and programming languages. To understand these concepts, I will discuss Access field types and how you can create your own data storage with variables and VBA data types.

Specifically, this chapter covers the following topics:

- **Understanding data**

- **Database fields**

- **Variables and beginning data types**

Understanding Data

At the lowest computer architecture level, data is represented by electrical states in digital circuits. These states can be translated into binary representations of 0's and 1's, which modern computing systems can understand as machine language. Understanding how data is converted to and from binary codes is beyond the scope of this book. But it is worth noting that, depending on interpretation, binary codes can represent both a character and an integer number. To demonstrate this concept, study Table 2.1.

TABLE 2.1 EXAMPLE BINARY REPRESENTATIONS

Binary Code	Integer Equivalent	Character Equivalent
01100001	97	a
01100010	98	b
01100011	99	c
01100100	100	d

Wow! The information in Table 2.1 should trigger an interesting question in your head, which goes something like this. "If binary codes can represent both characters and numbers, how do I know what type of data I'm working with?" The notion and application of variables help to answer this question. Variables provide a storage mechanism that accurately manages the binary representations for us. For example, if I store data in an Integer variable, I can feel pretty sure that VBA will give me back an integer number. And, if I store data in a String variable, I feel pretty sure that VBA will give me back characters and not a number. Using built-in VBA functions, it is possible to convert numbers to strings (characters) and strings to numbers, but I'll save that discussion for Chapter 5.

Now that you know how data is represented, it's time to find out where and how data is stored. Data can be stored in varying types of media such as volatile memory (also known as random access memory or RAM) and nonvolatile areas such as disk drives. Programmers can easily manage volatile memory areas using variables with languages like VBA. Nonvolatile memory areas such as hard drives are generally managed (stored) in systems such as files or databases like Microsoft Access. This concept is worth repeating in italics. *Data stored in volatile memory areas such as RAM is managed through variables. Data stored in nonvolatile locations such as disks is managed in systems such as Access.*

In this chapter, I will discuss both types of storage.

Database Fields

To store data in Microsoft Access (nonvolatile storage), you should be familiar with tables. Database tables are containers for rows of information. Each table must establish one or more fields. Each field in a database table is assigned a specific data type, and together the fields make up a unique row of data using a primary key.

As revealed in Figure 2.1, creating a table in design view for data storage is quite easy in Microsoft Access.

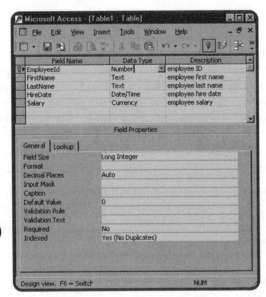

FIGURE 2.1

Building an Access table with fields and data types

Microsoft Access provides a number of common data types for storing information in fields. The most common of these data types are seen in Table 2.2.

TABLE 2.2 COMMON ACCESS FIELD TYPES

Data Type	Description
AutoNumber	An autogenerated number whose values can be incremented or randomly generated. Often used as the table's primary key.
Currency	Used for storing numbers and prevents rounding off during calculations.
Date/Time	Can store dates and/or times in a multitude of formats.
Memo	Used for storing non-numeric data such as strings. The Memo data field can store up to 65,536 characters.
Number	Stores numbers such as integers, singles, and doubles. Number data types are also a good candidate for primary keys.
Text	Used for storing non-numeric data such as strings. The Text data field can store up to 255 characters.
Yes/No	Stores Boolean values such as Yes/No, True/False or On/Off.

TRAP

The Text data type is by default set to a maximum size of 50 characters. Trying to insert data greater than the maximum size allowed in a Text field type will generate a database error. If your Text field storage needs require greater length, you will need to increase its field size attribute during table design. If you require a number of characters greater than 255 (the maximum size allowed in a Text field), you will need to use the Memo field type.

To better understand field types and their use, database developers must understand the data they are working with and how it can be logically grouped or normalized into tables and then separated into appropriate field or data types. This type of database work is commonly referred to as normalization or data modeling.

As an easy exercise, see if you can model some data by matching an Access field type (seen in Table 2.2) with the data needs represented in the following list:

1. An employee's Social Security number
2. The start time of a test
3. The number of employees in a company
4. A varying bonus percentage applied to employee salaries
5. Whether a user is currently logged into a system
6. The addresses of homes

7. The textual contents of a sample chapter

8. An ID generated each time a new user is created

9. The cost of a book

10. A computer's serial number

The correct field types for the previous storage needs are provided at the end of the chapter in Table 2.6.

Variables and Beginning Data Types

Paramount in any programming language is the concept of variables. In a nutshell, variables are pointers to storage locations in memory that contain data. You will often hear variables referred to as containers for data. In reality they are pointers, which represent a memory address that points to a memory location.

Though every variable created is unique (unique memory address), all variables share some common characteristics.

- Every variable has a name.
- Each variable has an associated memory address (hidden in high-level languages such as VBA).
- Every variable has a connected data type such as String, Integer, or Boolean.

Variables in Access VBA must begin with a letter and cannot be longer than 255 characters, nor can they contain periods or spaces. When created, variable names point to a location in memory that can be managed during the execution of your program.

VBA programmers use the `Dim` keyword (short for Dimension) to declare a new variable in what's called a declaration statement:

```
Dim myVariable
```

Once a variable has been declared, VBA reserves space in memory so you can store and retrieve data from its memory location using VBA statements. Simply declaring variables is not the end of the road, however. It is good programming practice to tell VBA what kind of variable you are creating. In other words, a common question to ask yourself is "Will this variable store strings, numbers, Boolean, dates, or object-type data?" VBA provides a number of data types for declaring variables. The more common of these are listed in Table 2.3.

TABLE 2.3 COMMON DATA TYPES IN VBA

Data Type	Storage Size	Range
Boolean	2 bytes	True/False
Currency	8 bytes	−922,337,203,685,477.5808 to 922,337,203,685,477.5807
Date	8 bytes	1 January 100 to 31 December 9999
Double	8 bytes	−1.79769313486231E308 to −4.94065645841247E−324 for negative values and 4.94065645841247E−324 to 1.79769313486232E308 for positive values
Integer	2 bytes	−32,768 to 32,767
Long	4 bytes	−2,147,483,648 to 2,147,483,647
Single	4 bytes	−3.402823E38 to −1.401298E−45 for negative values and from 1.401298E−45 to 3.402823E38 for positive values
String (variable length)	10 bytes + string length	Up to approximately 2 billion (2^{31}) characters
String (fixed length)	length of string	1 to approximately 64K (2^{16}) characters
Variant (with numbers)	16 bytes	Up to range of double
Variant (with characters)	22 bytes + string length	Same as variable length string

By default, VBA initializes your declared variables for you. Specifically, all number-based variables are initialized to zero (0), strings are initialized to empty string (""), and Boolean variables are initialized to False. This may seem trivial, but it is a nice feature that is not offered in every programming language.

To assign a data type to a variable, simply supply a data type name in the variable declaration using the As clause:

```
Dim myName As String
```

With this declaration statement, I've created one variable of String data type called myName. I can now use the myName variable in VBA statements to get and set data inside the reserved memory, which the variable myName points to. This concept is demonstrated in the following statement:

```
myName = "Emily Elizabeth"
```

Notice that when you assign data to string variables, the data on the right-hand side must be enclosed within double quotes. Moreover, VBA programmers can use the concatenation operator (&) to glue two or more strings together. The next few VBA statements reveal VBA string concatenation:

```
Dim myTitle As String

myTitle = "Access VBA " & "Programming for the " & "Absolute Beginner"

Me.Caption = myTitle
```

In the preceding example, I can successfully assign the contents of the `myTitle` variable to the `Caption` property of the form because each store string data types.

Numbers, however, do not require double quotes when used in assignment statements:

```
Dim mySalary As Double

mySalary = 50000.55
myBalance = -457.23
```

 Understanding the difference between string data and string variables is an important concept in beginning programming. Beginning programmers often forget to surround text with double quotes when assigning data to string-based variables or properties. Forgetting to do so can cause compile-time errors.

Study the next program statements and see if anything strikes you as weird:

```
mySalary = 50000.55
Me.Caption = mySalary
```

It's intriguing that I can assign the variable `mySalary` (a `Double`) to a property such as `Caption`, which holds `String` data types. After executing, the value in the `Caption` property is now "50000.55" and not 50000.55.

Many languages, such as C, would not like the preceding assignment statement one bit. This is because many languages require you to convert or cast data of one data type prior to assigning to another variable of different data type. VBA, however, is often helpful and can perform some data conversions for you automatically. Don't count on VBA to always convert data for you successfully, however. In fact, it is good programming practice to always use the `Val` function to convert strings to numbers when performing numeric calculations on string variables or properties.

In addition to variables, most programming languages, including VBA, offer support for constants. Unlike variables, constants retain their data values throughout their scope or lifetime. Constants are useful for declaring and holding data values that will not change during the life of your application. In fact, after they are declared, their value cannot be changed unless they are declared in a standard code module using the `Public` keyword. In VBA, you must use the `Const` statement to declare a constant as revealed in the next statement, which creates a constant to hold the value of pi:

```
Const PI = 3.14
```

For readability, I like to capitalize the entire constant name when declaring constants in my VBA code. This way, they really stick out for you and other programmers who see the constant names among many other variable names and program code.

Option Statements

VBA has a few module-level utility statements known as options that are used for naming conventions, string comparisons, and other internal settings. First, you may have already noticed the `Option Compare Database` statement located in the general declarations area of the VBE code window.

Note: The general declarations area is located at the top of a code module and is considered an area that is outside of any procedure.

Microsoft Access Help defines `Option Compare Database` as follows: "This statement results in string comparisons based on the sort order determined by the locale ID of the database where the string comparisons occur." This statement can be modified to either `Option Compare Binary` or `Option Compare Text` instead of `Option Compare Database`. If your VBE code module does not include an `Option Compare` statement, VBA will default to `Option Compare Binary`, which results in string comparisons based on a character's internal binary representation.

The next option statement, `Option Explicit`, is more important to beginning VBA programmers as it forces you to explicitly declare all variables before you can use them. This is a huge service to even seasoned VBA programmers. Forcing the explicit declaration of variables saves you from an often painful process of misspelling or misrepresenting variables that ultimately lead to program or compile error.

Unless you tell Microsoft Access to make it so, the `Option Explicit` statement may not appear by default in your VBE code module. To have this statement provided in each of your code modules, simply access the Options window from the VBE Tools menu and select the Require Variable Declaration setting as demonstrated in Figure 2.2.

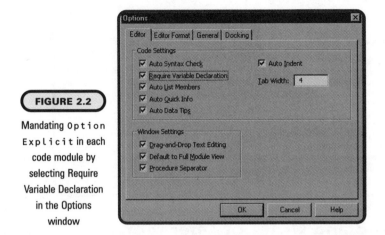

FIGURE 2.2

Mandating `Option Explicit` in each code module by selecting Require Variable Declaration in the Options window

The next option clause is the `Option Base` statement, which is manually typed into the general declarations area of each code module. In a nutshell, the `Option Base` statement defines the lower bounds for arrays. VBA arrays are by default 0-based arrays, but can start at 1 using an `Option Base` statement:

```
Option Base 1
```

I'll discuss arrays and their upper and lower bounds in more detail in subsequent chapters.

Variable Naming Conventions

Depending on the programmer and programming language, there are a number of popular naming conventions for variables. I like to use a single prefix that denotes data type, followed by a meaningful name with first letters capitalized for each word making up the variable name. Table 2.4 lists some common data types with a sample variable name and purpose.

As you program more and see more programming, you will notice many other popular naming conventions. The important note is to use a naming convention and stick with it.

TABLE 2.4 SAMPLE NAMING CONVENTIONS

Data Type	Purpose	Sample Variable Name
Boolean	Determines if a user is logged in	bLoggedIn
Currency	Specifies an employee's salary	cSalary
Date	Employee's hire date	dHireDate
Double	Result of calculation	dResult
Integer	Used for keeping track of a player's score	iScore
Long	Current temperature	lTemperature
Single	Miles traveled on vacation	sMilesTraveled
String	Employee's last name	sLastName
Const	A constant, which holds the current tax rate	TAXRATE

VBA Arithmetic and Order of Operations

It's no secret that programming in any language involves some level of math. Though it's not necessary to be a whiz in calculus, algebra, or trigonometry, it is useful to understand the essential arithmetic operators and order of precedence offered in a given programming language. For basic mathematical operations, VBA supports the operators seen in Table 2.5.

TABLE 2.5 COMMON MATHEMATICAL OPERATORS

Operator	Purpose	Example	Result
+	Addition	dSalary = 521.9 + 204	725.9
-	Subtraction	iPoints = 100 − 20	80
*	Multiplication	dResult = 5 * 213.78	1068.9
/	Division	iResult = 21 / 3	7
^	Exponential	iResult = 2 ^ 3	8

In addition to basic math operations, VBA supports what's known as order of operations using parentheses. Without parentheses, VBA determines order of operations in the following order:

1. Exponents

2. Multiplication and division

3. Addition and subtraction

When VBA encounters a tie between operators, it performs calculations starting from the leftmost operation. To get a better handle on the importance of operator precedence and order of operations, consider the following equation, which calculates a profit:

```
Profit = (price * quantity) - (fixed cost + total variable cost)
```

The next VBA assignment statement implements the preceding equation without parentheses—in other words, without a well-defined order of operations:

```
dProfit = 19.99 * 704 - 406.21 + 203.85
```

The result of this calculation is 13870.6. Now study the next VBA statement, which implements the same equation, this time using parentheses to build a well-defined order of operations:

```
dProfit = (19.99 * 704) - (406.21 + 203.85)
```

Using parentheses to guide my order of operations, my new profit is 13462.9. That's a difference of $407.70 that might have been recorded as inflated profits. Unless you're a programmer for Enron, this is not acceptable bookkeeping software.

Variable Scope

Variable scope is a fancy way of describing how long a variable will hold its data, or in other words its lifetime. VBA supports three types of variable scope.

- Procedure-level scope
- Module-level scope
- Public scope

To create a variable with procedure-level scope, simply declare a variable inside of a procedure:

```
Private Sub Form_Load()

    Dim dProfit As Double
    dProfit = 700.21

End Sub
```

In the preceding form Load event procedure, I declared a Double variable called dProfit that will hold its value so long as the current scope of execution is inside the procedure. More specifically, once program execution has left the form Load procedure, the dProfit variable is initialized back to 0.

If you need to maintain the value of dProfit for a longer period of time, consider using a module-level or public variable. Module-level variables are only available to the current module from where they are declared, but are available to all procedures contained within the same module. Moreover, module-level variables are considered private and can be declared with the keyword Dim or Private in the general declarations area:

```
Dim dRunningTotal As Double ' module-level variable

Private iScore As Integer ' module-level variable
```

You can create public variables that are available to the entire project (all code modules) by declaring a variable using the Public keyword in the general declarations area of a code module:

```
Public bLoggedIn As Boolean
```

Determining variable scope is part of application development. During development, you define all needed variables, their storage type, and their scope. As you will see shortly, the chapter-based program demonstrates these concepts well.

Chapter Program: The Fruit Stand

The Fruit Stand (Figure 2.3) is a simplified data-entry system for a small fruit vendor. It implements many chapter-based concepts such as variables, constants, and VBA statements. Note that the Fruit Stand program does not include error checking to verify correct input. You will learn about error checking and input validation in Chapter 8.

All of the code required to build the Fruit Stand program is seen next.

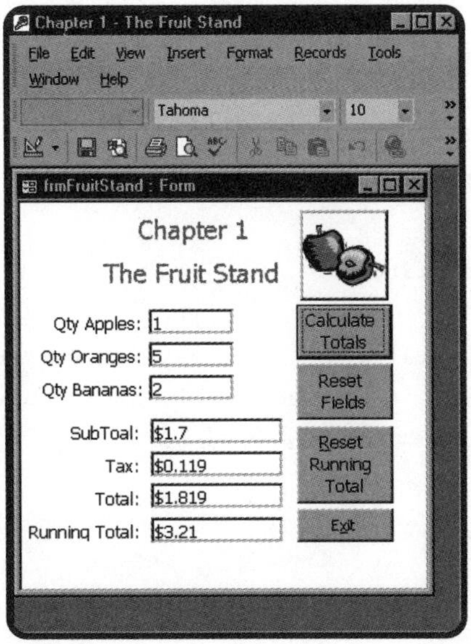

FIGURE 2.3

Demonstrating
chapter-based
concepts with the
Fruit Stand program

```
Option Compare Database
Option Explicit


' declare module level variable and constants
Dim dRunningTotal As Double
Const TAXRATE = 0.07
Const dPricePerApple = 0.1
Const dPricePerOrange = 0.2
Const dPricePerBanana = 0.3


Private Sub cmdCalculateTotals_Click()

    ' declare procedure-level variables
    Dim dSubTotal As Double
    Dim dTotal As Double
    Dim dTax As Double

    ' calculate and apply sub total
    dSubTotal = (dPricePerApple * txtApples.Value) + _
        (dPricePerOrange * txtOranges.Value) + _
        (dPricePerBanana * txtBananas.Value)

    lblSubTotal.Caption = "$" & dSubTotal
```

```vba
        ' calculate and apply tax
        dTax = (TAXRATE * dSubTotal)
        lblTax.Caption = "$" & dTax

        ' calculate and apply total cost
        dTotal = dTax + dSubTotal
        lblTotal.Caption = "$" & dTotal

        ' build and apply running total using module-level variable
        dRunningTotal = dRunningTotal + dTotal
        lblRunningTotal.Caption = "$" & dRunningTotal

End Sub

Private Sub cmdExit_Click()

    End ' terminates the application

End Sub

Private Sub cmdResetFields_Click()

    ' reset application fields
    Me.txtApples.Value = "0"
    Me.txtOranges.Value = "0"
    Me.txtBananas.Value = "0"

    Me.lblSubTotal.Caption = "$0.00"
    Me.lblTax.Caption = "$0.00"
    Me.lblTotal.Caption = "$0.00"

End Sub

Private Sub cmdResetRunningTotal_Click()

    ' reset running total variable and application field
    dRunningTotal = 0
    Me.lblRunningTotal.Caption = "$0.00"
```

```
End Sub

Private Sub Form_Load()

    ' set focus to first text box
    txtApples.SetFocus

End Sub
```

Chapter Summary

In this chapter, you were introduced to data concepts such as storage representation, storage media, variables, and data assignment. More specifically, you learned the following key concepts:

- At the lowest level, data is represented as machine code in binary format (0's and 1's).

- Programmers must know that binary codes can be represented as numbers and characters. To differentiate between the two, programmers use variables and built-in functions to convert data between numbers and characters.

- Data can be stored in two types of formats—volatile memory such as RAM and nonvolatile memory such as disk drives.

- Variables act like containers for data, but are really pointers to memory addresses, which store the data.

- VBA programmers can use the Dim, Public, or Private keywords to declare (create) variables for data storage. Moreover, specific data types are applied to variables during variable declaration such as Integer, Double, String, and Boolean.

- When declared, variables have scope, which determine the life of the data stored in the variable.

- Just as with control properties, data can be assigned to variables using VBA assignment statements using the assignment operator (=).

As promised earlier, Table 2.6 contains the matching Access database field type for each storage need.

TABLE 2.6 MATCHING ACCESS FIELD TYPES

Storage Need	Field Type
An employee's Social Security number	Text
The start time of a test	Date / Time
The number of employees in a company	Number
A varying bonus percentage applied to employee salaries	Number
Whether a user is currently logged into a system	Yes / No
Addresses of homes	Text
The textual contents of a sample chapter	Memo
An id generated each time a new user is created	AutoNumber
The cost of a book	Currency
A computer's serial number	Text

CHALLENGES

1. Using the following controls, try to recreate the graphical interface seen in Figure 2.3.
   - 10 labels
   - 3 text boxes (with attached labels)
   - 1 image control
   - 4 command buttons

2. Build a simple calculator program with an Access form that allows a user to enter numbers in two separate text boxes. The Access form should have four separate command buttons for adding, subtracting, multiplying, and dividing. Write code in each command button's Click event to output the result in a label control.

3. Construct a more advanced calculator program similar to the one found in Microsoft operating systems. A sample GUI is demonstrated in Figure 2.4.

FIGURE 2.4

Microsoft's common calculator accessory

Conditions

In this chapter I will show you how to implement conditions, which allow programmers to build decision-making abilities into their applications using If blocks and Select Case structures. In addition, I will show you how to leverage VBA's built-in dialog boxes and additional controls to enhance your graphical interface and your system's intelligence.

Specifically, this chapter covers the following topics:

- If blocks

- Select case structures

- Dialog boxes

- Common controls continued

If Blocks

A basic component of a high-level language is the ability to construct a condition. Most high-level programming languages offer the If block as a way to evaluate an expression. Before proceeding into If blocks, I will discuss what an expression is in terms of computer programming.

Microsoft's Access Help defines an expression as "A combination of keywords, operators, variables, and constants that yields a string, number, or object. An expression can be used to perform a calculation, manipulate characters, or test data." Moreover, expressions can be used to build conditions, which return a Boolean value of true or false. This is an important concept, so I'll repeat in italics. *Expressions can be used to build conditions that evaluate to true or false.*

VBA programmers can use expressions in an If condition:

```
If (number1 = number2) Then

    Label1.Caption = "number1 equals number2"

End If
```

Known as an If block, the preceding code reads "if the variable number1 equals the variable number2 then assign some text to the Caption property of Label1." This means that the expression inside of the parentheses must evaluate to true for the VBA statement inside of the If block to execute. Note that the parentheses surrounding the expression are not required, but provide readability.

Also note the inclusion of the Then keyword at the end of the If statement. The Then keyword is required at the end of each If statement.

 Always indent VBA statements inside of a condition or loop to provide easy to read code. A common convention is to indent two or three spaces or to use a single tab. Doing so implies that the VBA assignment statement belongs inside of the If block.

But what if the expression does not evaluate to true? To answer this question, VBA includes an Else clause, which catches the program's execution in the event the expression evaluates to false. The If/Else block is demonstrated next.

```
If (number1 = number2) Then

    Label1.Caption = "number1 equals number2"

Else

    Label1.Caption = "number1 does not equal number2"

End If
```

Giving the preceding examples, you might be asking yourself about other possibilities for building simple expressions with operators other than the equals sign. As shown in Table 3.1, VBA supports many common operators to aid in evaluating expressions.

TABLE 3.1 COMMON OPERATORS USED IN EXPRESSIONS

Operator	Description
=	Equals
<>	Not equal
>	Greater than
<	Less than
>=	Greater than or equal to
<=	Less than or equal to

In addition to the `Else` clause, VBA provides the `ElseIf` clause as part of a larger expression. The `ElseIf` clause is one word in VBA and is used for building conditions that may have more than two possible outcomes.

```
If (number1 = number2) Then

    Label1.Caption = "number1 equals number2"

ElseIf (number1 > number2) Then

    Label1.Caption = "number1 is greater than number2"
```

```
ElseIf (number1 < number2) Then

    Label1.Caption = "number1 is less than number2"

End If
```

Notice in the preceding example that the ElseIf clause must include an expression followed by the keyword Then, just like an If condition. In addition, you can use the Else clause to act as a concluding clause in the event that none of the conditions evaluates to true:

```
If (sColor = "red") Then

    Label1.Caption = "The color is red"

ElseIf (sColor = "white") Then

    Label1.Caption = "The color is white"

ElseIf (sColor = "blue") Then

    Label1.Caption = "The color is blue"

Else

    Label1.Caption = "The color is not red, white or blue"

End If
```

Nested If Blocks

There are times when you may need to provide one or more nested conditions inside of another condition. This concept is known as nested conditions and can often require much thought as to the flow of the program.

To exhibit the concept of nested conditions, I'll implement a nested If block, which implements a simple payroll system.

```
If (sEmployeeType = "salary") Then

    ' Employee is paid a salary.
    cPay = cSalary
```

```
Else

    ' Employee is paid hourly wages and has worked 40 or less hours.
    if (iHoursWorked <= 40) Then

        cPay = cHourlyRate * iHoursWorked

    Else

        ' Employee earned overtime, which is time and a half.
        cOverTime = (iHoursWorked - 40) * (cHourlyRate * 1.5)
        cPay = (cHourlyRate * 40) + cOverTime

    End If

End If
```

Because I used indenting techniques, you can easily see that I have a nested **If** block inside of the **Else** block. This nested **If** block is executed only if the first **If** condition evaluates to false. If the first or outer **If** condition evaluates to true, the employee wage is calculated as a salary, after which program control is sent to the outer or last **End If** statement.

Note that without indentation, the preceding nested program code is very difficult to read. Always indent program statements including nested **If** blocks inside of conditions.

Compound If Blocks

So far, you've seen how to build simple and nested conditions using **If** blocks. There is, however, much more to consider if you plan to build more complex decision-making capabilities such as compound conditions into your VBA applications. To build compound expressions, VBA programmers can use the conditional operators **And**, **Or**, and **Not**.

 TRAP Conditional operators such as **And**, **Or**, and **Not** are considered reserved keywords and must be used in an expression. Otherwise, VBA will generate a compile error.

To get a better understanding of the preceding conditional operators, I'll use what's known as truth tables to explain possible scenarios and results for each operator.

A truth table must include inputs and their possible results. Each input can evaluate to either true of false. Using one or more inputs and a corresponding operator, you can build all possible results in a truth table. Remember that regardless of the number of inputs and type of operator, a compound expression will ultimately result in either true or false.

IN THE REAL WORLD

Truth tables are commonly used in mathematic and logic circles such as quantitative analysis, discrete mathematics, and Boolean algebra. Using logical operators, truth tables allow one to evaluate all possible results to prove an outcome.

Table 3.2 demonstrates the truth table for the And operator. The And operator uses two inputs to determine the result for the entire expression.

TABLE 3.2   TRUTH TABLE FOR AND OPERATOR

Input X	Input Y	Result
True	True	True
True	False	False
False	True	False
False	False	False

You can see from the truth table that there is only one occasion when the And operator will generate a true result in an expression (when both inputs are true). As a further demonstration, the next program code implements a compound condition using the And operator.

```
If (sEmployeeType = "salary" And sEmployeeEvalResult <> "poor") Then

    ' Employee is given a 20% bonus.
    cBonusPay = cSalary * .20

End If
```

In the preceding example, the employee is given a 20% bonus only if both conditions are true. If either condition is false, the entire compound condition evaluates to false and the employee is not awarded the bonus.

Seen in Table 3.3, the Or operator has a much different effect based on its inputs. More specifically, the Or operator will always generate a true value providing at least one input is true. The only time a compound condition using the Or keyword will result in a false result is when both inputs are false.

TABLE 3.3 TRUTH TABLE FOR OR OPERATOR

Input X	Input Y	Result
True	True	True
True	False	True
False	True	True
False	False	False

The next block of code demonstrates a compound condition using the Or keyword programmatically.

```
If (sMonth = "June" Or sMonth = "July") Then

    sSeason = "Summer"

End If
```

So long as the variable sMonth is either June or July, the variable sSeason will be set to Summer. Note that only one side of the expression needs to be true for the compound conditions to be true.

The truth table for the Not operator seen in Table 3.4 contains only one input. In a nutshell, the Not operator reverses the value of its input value, such that Not true results in false and Not false results in true. The Not operator is implemented in VBA as seen in the next program block.

TABLE 3.4   TRUTH TABLE FOR NOT OPERATOR

Input X	Result
True	False
False	True

```
If Not(5 = 5) Then

    lblResult.Caption = "true"

Else


    lblResult.Caption = "false"


End If
```

Given the preceding code, what do you think the value of the label's `Caption` property will be? If you said false, you would be correct, but why? To understand, you must look at the result of the inner expression (5=5), which evaluates to true. The `Not` of true is false, which means the statement inside the `If` condition will not execute. Instead, the statement inside the `Else` condition will execute.

Select Case Structures

The `Select Case` structure is another tool for VBA programmers to build conditionals. Specifically, the `Select Case` structure evaluates an expression only once. It's useful for comparing a single expression to multiple values:

```
Select Case sDay
    Case "Monday"
        lblDay.Caption = "Weekday"
    Case "Tuesday"
        lblDay.Caption = "Weekday"
    Case "Wednesday"
        lblDay.Caption = "Weekday"
    Case "Thursday"
        lblDay.Caption = "Weekday"
```

```
    Case "Friday"
        lblDay.Caption = "Weekday"
    Case Else
        lblDay.Caption = "Weekend!"
End Select
```

In this case (excuse the pun) the `Select Case` structure evaluates a string-based variable and uses five `Case` statements to define possible expression values. The `Case Else` statement is used to catch a value in the top expression that is not defined in a `Case` statement. The `Case Else` statement is not required. After code within a `Case` or `Case Else` block is executed, program control is then moved to the `End Select` statement, which is required.

The `Select Case` structure is very flexible. For example, I can simplify the preceding structure by using `Select Case`'s ability to place multiple items in a single statement separated by commas:

```
Select Case sDay
    Case "Monday", "Tuesday", "Wednesday", "Thursday", "Friday"
        lblDay.Caption = "Weekday"
    Case Else
        lblDay.Caption = "Weekend!"
End Select
```

In the following code, the `Select Case` structure also allows you to check for a range of values using the `Is` and `To` keywords:

```
Select Case dTemperature
    Case Is < 32
        lblTemperature.Caption = "Freezing"
    Case 32 To 45
        lblTemperature.Caption = "Cold"
    Case 46 To 69
        lblTemperature.Caption = "Cool"
    Case 70 To 89
        lblTemperature.Caption = "Warm"
    Case Is > 90
        lblTemperature.Caption = "Hot"
End Select
```

Using ranges of values and comparison operators, I can easily build logic into my `Case` statements to determine ranges of temperatures.

Dialog Boxes

Dialog boxes are generally small windows that prompt the user for a response. Dialog boxes can be configured to include one to three command buttons, which provide the user with various options for interaction. In this section, you will learn about two common VBA dialog boxes—the message box and the input box.

Message Box

VBA's `MsgBox` function is a built-in function, which can generate a dialog box. The `MsgBox` function takes five parameters separated by commas as input:

```
MsgBox Prompt, Buttons, Title, HelpFile, Context
```

The only argument required by the `MsgBox` function is the `Prompt` parameter, which is displayed on the dialog box to the user. Though not required, the `Buttons` parameter is very useful. You can specify various VBA constants to customize the available buttons. The most common of these constants are shown in Table 3.5.

TABLE 3.5 BUTTONS SETTINGS

Constant	Value
vbOKOnly (default)	0
vbOKCancel	1
vbAbortRetryIgnore	2
vbYesNoCancel	3
vbYesNo	4
vbRetryCancel	5
vbCritical	16
vbQuestion	32
vbExclamation	48
vbInformation	64

Another useful, but not required, parameter is the `Title` argument, which displays text in the title bar area of the message box. Using these parameters, I can create and display a simple dialog box in the `Click` event of a command button:

```
Private Sub Command1_Click()
    MsgBox "The MsgBox function creates a dialog box.", vbInformation, _
"Chapter 3"
End Sub
```

To successfully use the `Buttons` parameter of the `MsgBox` function, you will want to work with variables and conditions. Specifically, you will need to create a variable that holds the user's response when the user selects a button on the dialog box. This variable will get its value from the result of the `MsgBox` function. That's right—the `MsgBox` function not only creates a dialog box, but also returns a value. This is how VBA programmers determine which button on the dialog box was clicked. The possible return values are described in Table 3.6.

TABLE 3.6 MSGBOX FUNCTION RETURN VALUES

Constant	Value
vbOK	1
vbCancel	2
vbAbort	3
vbRetry	4
vbIgnore	5
vbYes	6
vbNo	7

Remember from Chapter 2 that constants are containers for data that cannot be changed. The built-in VBA constants, such as the ones seen in Tables 3.5 and 3.6, hold integer values. This means that you can use either the constant name or its value directly. To see how this works, examine the next program, which uses the `MsgBox` function, one variable, and a `Select Case` structure to determine what button the user has pressed.

```
Private Sub Command1_Click()

    Dim iResponse As Integer

    ' Display a message box to the user and assign the MsgBoxs return
    ' value to a variable.
    iResponse = MsgBox("Press a button", vbAbortRetryIgnore, "Chapter 3")
```

```
' Determine which button was selected.
Select Case iResponse
   Case vbAbort
      lblResponse.Caption = "You pressed abort."
   Case vbRetry
      lblResponse.Caption = "You pressed retry."
   Case vbIgnore
      lblResponse.Caption = "You pressed ignore."
End Select

End Sub
```

Figures 3.1 and 3.2 demonstrate sample output from the preceding code.

FIGURE 3.1

A multi-button
message box

FIGURE 3.2

Sample output from
selecting a message-
box button

HINT

Linefeed characters can be added in a message-box prompt using the C h r (1 0) function call.

```
MsgBox "This prompt demonstrates how to add a" & _
       " line feed character" & Chr(10) & "in a message box."
```

When using the message-box function in an expression such as

```
iResponse = MsgBox("Press a button", vbAbortRetryIgnore, "Chapter 3")
```

you need to realize that parentheses are required to surround function parameters. Without parentheses, the VBA compiler will complain and prevent further execution. On the other hand, the VBA compiler will not like the use of parentheses when the MsgBox function is used by itself.

```
MsgBox "The MsgBox function creates a dialog box.", _
       vbInformation, "Chapter 3"
```

This is standard operating procedure when working with VBA functions, so it's worth repeating again in italics. *Functions in expressions require the use of parentheses for their parameters, whereas functions outside of expressions or by themselves do not.*

Input Box

The input box also displays a dialog box, but allows a user to input information, hence the name input box. Like the message box, the input box is created with a function call. Specifically, the function InputBox takes seven parameters:

```
InputBox Prompt, Title, Default, XPos, YPos, HelpFile, Context
```

The most common InputBox parameters are Prompt, Title, and Default, where Prompt and Title behave similarly to the same parameters of the message box. The Default argument is used to display default text in the text box area of the input box. Also note that the InputBox function does not have a Buttons parameter. The only required parameter is Prompt.

The InputBox function returns a string data type, so you will need to declare a String variable to capture its return value.

In Figure 3.3, I use an input box to prompt a user with a question.

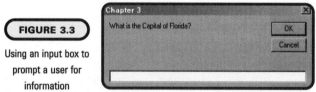

FIGURE 3.3

Using an input box to prompt a user for information

Sample VBA code would look something like the following.

```
Private Sub cmdAskQuestion_Click()

    Dim sResponse As String

    sResponse = InputBox("What is the Capital of Florida?", "Chapter 3")

    If sResponse = "Tallahassee" Then
        lblResponse.Caption = "That is right!"
    Else
        lblResponse.Caption = "Sorry, that is not correct."
    End If

End Sub
```

I can enhance the previous code to ensure the user has pressed the default OK button on the input box prior to validating the user's response. More specifically, if the user presses the Cancel button, a zero-length string is returned by the InputBox function. To check for this, I can use an outer If block as follows:

```
Private Sub cmdAskQuestion_Click()

  Dim sResponse As String

  sResponse = InputBox("What is the Capital of Florida?", "Chapter 3")

  ' Check to see if the user pressed Cancel.
  If sResponse <> "" Then

      If sResponse = "Tallahassee" Then
          lblResponse.Caption = "That is right!"
      Else
          lblResponse.Caption = "Sorry, that is not correct."
      End If

  End If

End Sub
```

Common Controls Continued

As you've already seen, there are a number of common controls available to you in the Toolbox. In this chapter, you learn about a few more that can require the use of conditions. Specifically, I'll discuss the following common controls, seen in Figure 3.4:

- Option group
- Option buttons
- Check boxes
- Toggle buttons

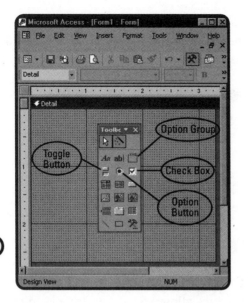

FIGURE 3.4

Common controls
continued

Option Group

The option group control is a container that logically groups controls such as
option buttons, check boxes, and toggle buttons. You've probably read more than
once that I'm against Microsoft wizards. Well, there is one exception. Though not
required, the option group provides a very effective wizard for grouping your controls inside the option group's frame. I like this wizard and find its capabilities
sufficient for groups of option buttons, check boxes, and toggle buttons.

When first adding an option group to your form, Access initiates the Option
Group Wizard. As shown in Figure 3.5, the first step in the wizard is to add label
names for each item in your group. At this stage, it doesn't matter what control
you're using—you're only adding textual descriptions for each item in the group.

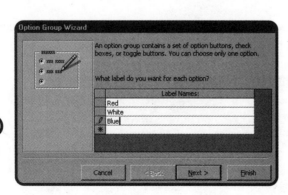

FIGURE 3.5

Adding label names
for each control in
the option group

After you've added all label names and clicked Next, the wizard asks you to choose a default control if one is desired. In Figure 3.6, I've asked the wizard to make my item called "Red" the default control.

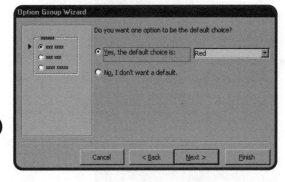

FIGURE 3.6

Selecting a default control

Figure 3.7 depicts the next step in the wizard, where you set values for each option in the group. Option values allow VBA programmers to tell which option the user has selected in the group. The wizard's default values for each option are acceptable.

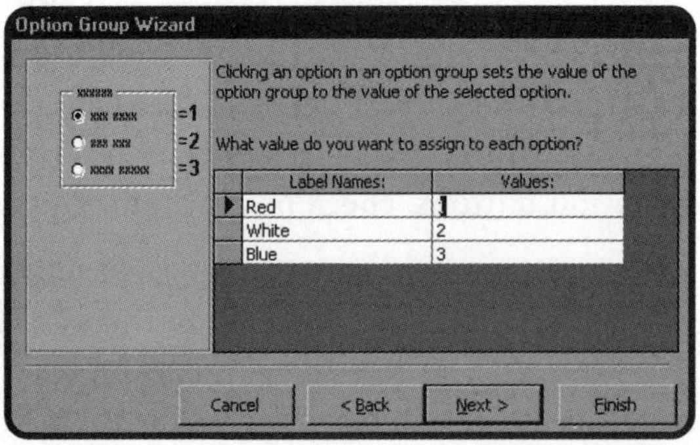

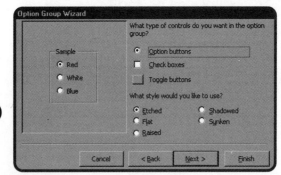

FIGURE 3.7

Providing values for each option

The next wizard screen, displayed in Figure 3.8, allows you to select what type of option controls will be displayed in your option group.

FIGURE 3.8

Choosing an option control type for the option group

The last screen in the wizard (Figure 3.9) prompts you to enter a caption for your option-group frame. This caption is actually a property of a label control that automatically sits at the top of the frame.

FIGURE 3.9

Entering a caption
for the option group's
label

In the next three sections, I will show you specific implementations of option groups.

Option Buttons

Often referred to as radio buttons, option buttons provide a user with a list of selectable choices. Specifically, the user can select only one option at a time. Individual option buttons comprise two controls, a label and option button. Each has its own properties and can be managed during design time or run time.

 After creating an option group either manually or with the Option Group Wizard, you should change the name of each option control to one that contains a meaningful description. This will greatly reduce confusion when working with VBA code.

To determine which option button has been selected in a group, you use the option group's `Value` property. For this to work, each option button must have been assigned a valid and unique number in its `OptionValue` property (set by default in the Option Group Wizard). When a user clicks an option button, the `Value` property is set to the same number as the option button's `OptionValue` property. These concepts are demonstrated in the next program code, which implements the GUI seen in Figure 3.10.

```
Option Compare Database
Option Explicit


Const SALARY = 50000#
Const HOURLYRATE = 7.75
```

```vba
Private Sub cmdCalculatePay_Click()

Dim dOverTime As Double
Dim dNormalPay As Double

If Me.fraEmployeeType.Value = 1 Then

    ' Employee is paid a salary.
    lblPay.Caption = "Your salary is $" & SALARY

Else

    ' Employee is paid by the hour.
    ' Find out if the employee has worked overtime.
    If Val(txtHoursWorked.Value) > 40 Then

        dOverTime = (Val(txtHoursWorked.Value) - 40) * (HOURLYRATE * 1.5)
        dNormalPay = HOURLYRATE * 40
        lblPay.Caption = "Your hourly pay is $" & dNormalPay + dOverTime

    Else

        lblPay.Caption = "Your hourly pay is $" & HOURLYRATE * 40

    End If

End If

End Sub

Private Sub optHourly_GotFocus()
    txtHoursWorked.Enabled = True
    lblPay.Caption = ""
End Sub

Private Sub optSalary_GotFocus()
    txtHoursWorked.Enabled = False
    lblPay.Caption = ""
End Sub
```

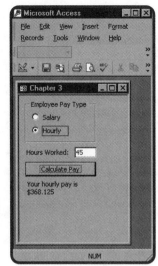

FIGURE 3.10

Using option buttons
to determine an
employee's pay type

Note that the option group is really defined as the name of the frame (an option group is really a frame control). Next, notice that I used the `GotFocus` method of each option button to disable the Hours Worked text box. The `GotFocus` event is triggered whenever the option button receives focus such as clicking.

Check Boxes

When used in an option group, check boxes behave much like option buttons. If you have experience in other graphical languages, you might be surprised to learn that a user can select only one check box at a time when it is located in an option group. This is different behavior from VBA's parent language Visual Basic.

Remember that an option group provides a single selection for any option-based control such as check boxes, option buttons, and toggle buttons.

To use check boxes in a multi-selection facility, you will need to add them manually outside of an option group. In addition, you will need to set each check box's `DefaultValue` property to a unique number during design time.

Implemented in Figure 3.11, the following code demonstrates how one might use checkboxes in a multi-selection capacity.

```
Option Compare Database
Option Explicit


Dim dRunningTotal As Double


Private Sub cmdTotal_Click()
```

```
    dRunningTotal = 0


    If chkTShirt.Value = True Then
        dRunningTotal = dRunningTotal + 9.99
    End If


    If chkBaseballCap.Value = True Then
        dRunningTotal = dRunningTotal + 12#
    End If


    If chkSwimmingTrunks.Value = True Then
        dRunningTotal = dRunningTotal + 24.19
    End If


    If chkSunBlock.Value = True Then
        dRunningTotal = dRunningTotal + 3#
    End If


    If chkSunGlasses.Value = True Then
        dRunningTotal = dRunningTotal + 6.99
    End If


    lblTotal.Caption = "Your total is $" & dRunningTotal


End Sub
```

FIGURE 3.11

Selecting more than one check box at a time

I can use the `Value` property of each check box to determine whether the user has "checked" it. If the check box has been checked, the `Value` property is set to `True`; if not, it is set to `False`.

Toggle Buttons

When used in an option group, toggle buttons serve the same purpose as option buttons and check boxes, which allow a user to select one item at a time.

In the next example (shown in Figure 3.12), I use an option group of three toggle buttons and their `GotFocus` methods to change the `Caption` and `Fore-Color` properties of a label control.

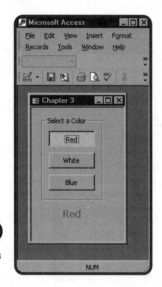

FIGURE 3.12

Using toggle buttons in an option group

```
Private Sub tglRed_GotFocus()
    lblOutput.ForeColor = vbRed
    lblOutput.Caption = "Red"
End Sub


Private Sub tglWhite_GotFocus()
    lblOutput.ForeColor = vbWhite
    lblOutput.Caption = "White"
End Sub


Private Sub tglBlue_GotFocus()
    lblOutput.ForeColor = vbBlue
```

```
        lblOutput.Caption = "Blue"
End Sub
```

Toggle buttons, check boxes, and option buttons all behave similarly when used in an option group. To use one or the other is simply a preference on your part.

Chapter Program: Hangman

Hangman is a game common among school-aged children: a player tries to guess a word or phrase before a figure of a man is hanged (in my case a monster). Each time the player guesses incorrectly, a portion of a body is shown until the body is complete, at which time the game is over. The player wins by guessing the word or phrase before all body parts are shown.

To build the Hangman game, simply construct the graphical interface as seen in Figure 3.13. Note that the graphic of the monster is really six different graphics files, all of which can be found on the CD-ROM. Of course, you could make your own.

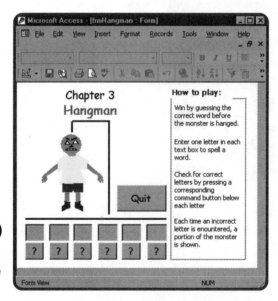

FIGURE 3.13

Using chapter-based concepts to build the Hangman game

The majority of the code to build the Hangman game is located in the `Click` events of the six command buttons, which sit directly below each text box and check for a correct letter, game won, and game lost.

I have yet to discuss user-defined functions and how they can reduce duplicate code, so the program code for the Hangman game is quite long. Hence, the code below contains only one command-button `Click` event to represent game play.

Except for variable and control names, all other command-button Click events look alike. The accompanying CD-ROM contains the entire code for the Hangman game.

```
Option Compare Database
Option Explicit


' Form level variables to track game results.
Dim iCounter As Integer
Dim letter1 As String
Dim letter2 As String
Dim letter3 As String
Dim letter4 As String
Dim letter5 As String
Dim letter6 As String


Private Sub cmdA_Click()

    ' Determine what letter was entered.
    Select Case txtA.Value

        ' Check for both upper and lower case.
        Case "A", "a"

            ' Letter entered was an "A" or "a".
            letter1 = "A"

            ' See if the user has successfully completed the word.
            If (letter1 & letter2 & letter3 & letter4 _
                & letter5 & letter6) = "ACCESS" Then

                    ' User successfully completed the word.
                    ' Inform the user and disable all text boxes.
                    MsgBox "You won!", , "Hangman"
                    txtA.Enabled = False
                    txtC1.Enabled = False
                    txtC2.Enabled = False
                    txtE.Enabled = False
                    txtS1.Enabled = False
                    txtS2.Enabled = False
```

```
        Else

                ' User has not won, but did guess the correct
                ' letter.
                txtA.Enabled = False
        End If

    Case Else

        ' User did not guess the correct letter.
        ' Find an available body part to display.
        If imgLeftLeg.Visible = False Then
           imgLeftLeg.Visible = True
           iCounter = iCounter + 1
        ElseIf imgRightLeg.Visible = False Then
           imgRightLeg.Visible = True
           iCounter = iCounter + 1
        ElseIf imgBody.Visible = False Then
           imgBody.Visible = True
           iCounter = iCounter + 1
        ElseIf imgLeftArm.Visible = False Then
           imgLeftArm.Visible = True
           iCounter = iCounter + 1
        ElseIf imgRightArm.Visible = False Then
           imgRightArm.Visible = True
           iCounter = iCounter + 1
        ElseIf imgHead.Visible = False Then
           imgHead.Visible = True
           iCounter = iCounter + 1
        End If

        ' Find out if the user has lost.
        ' If so, inform them and disable all
        ' text boxes.
        If iCounter = 6 Then
           MsgBox "Sorry, you lost.", , "Hangman"
           txtA.Enabled = False
           txtC1.Enabled = False
           txtC2.Enabled = False
           txtE.Enabled = False
           txtS1.Enabled = False
           txtS2.Enabled = False
```

```
          End If

     End Select

End Sub

Private Sub Form_Load()

    ' Perform some housekeeping
    imgHead.Visible = False
    imgBody.Visible = False
    imgLeftArm.Visible = False
    imgRightArm.Visible = False
    imgLeftLeg.Visible = False
    imgRightLeg.Visible = False

    txtA.Value = ""
    txtC1.Value = ""
    txtC2.Value = ""
    txtE.Value = ""
    txtS1.Value = ""
    txtS2.Value = ""

    txtA.Enabled = True
    txtC1.Enabled = True
    txtC2.Enabled = True
    txtE.Enabled = True
    txtS1.Enabled = True
    txtS2.Enabled = True

    cmdA.Enabled = True
    cmdC1.Enabled = True
    cmdC2.Enabled = True
    cmdE.Enabled = True
    cmdS1.Enabled = True
    cmdS2.Enabled = True

    iCounter = 0

End Sub
```

```
Private Sub cmdQuit_Click()
    ' Quit the game.
    End
End Sub
```

Chapter Summary

This chapter covered the many faces of conditions. You learned how expressions are used to build conditions with `If` and `Select Case` structures. Moreover, you learned how to use conditions to enhance your graphical interface with dialog boxes and option groups. Specifically, the following key concepts were discussed in Chapter 3:

- Expressions can be used to build conditions that evaluate to true or false.
- VBA conditions are built with `If` blocks and `Select Case` structures.
- Compound conditions have two or more sides and are built using the operators `And`, `Or`, and `Not`.
- The `Select Case` structure is useful for checking an expression against a list of values.
- The `Case` statements in a `Select Case` structure can check a single value, multiple values, or a range of values.
- VBA contains the built in functions `MsgBox` and `InputBox` for building dialog boxes.
- The `MsgBox` function returns an integer value, whereas the `InputBox` function returns a string.
- The option group control contains a useful wizard for building groups of option buttons, check boxes, and toggle buttons.
- In an option group, a user can select only one check box, toggle button, or option button at a time.

CHALLENGES

1. Using Figure 3.14 as a guide, construct a simple math quiz that asks a user to answer a math problem. Store the correct answer as a module-level constant and assign the user's answer in a local or procedure-level variable. In the `Click` event of the Check Answer command button, compare the user's response (in variable form) to the module-level constant. Inform the user of the results (correct or incorrect) using the label control. Write code in the `Click` event of the Quit command button to terminate the application.

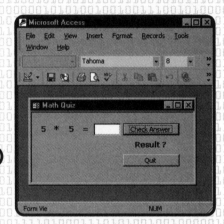

FIGURE 3.14

Sample math quiz
GUI for challenge
number 1

2. Construct another quiz game, this time using an input box to ask the question and return the user's answer. Inform the user of their result in the form of a message box. Remember to check for an empty string (user presses the Cancel button) before checking the user's response.

3. Build upon the Word Art program from Chapter 1 to include four option groups with a mixture of option buttons, check boxes, and toggle buttons. One option group should allow the user to select up to five different font sizes. Another option group will give the user an opportunity to select among three different font weights. The last two option groups will replace the many command buttons that provide choices of foreground and background colors.

4. Enhance the Hangman game to allow the player multiple chances to win. More specifically, display a message box that gives the player a Yes/No option to restart the game only if the game was lost.

Looping Structures

In this chapter I will show you how to build iteration into your programs using VBA looping structures such as Do and For loops. In addition, you will learn some new VBA controls for managing groups of items and how to build random numbers into your programs. Specifically, this chapter covers the following topics:

- Introduction to looping structures

- List and combo boxes

- Random numbers

Introduction to Looping Structures

To loop (or iterate), computers need instructions known as looping structures, which determine such things as how many times a loop's statements will execute and by what condition the loop will exit. Each programming language implements it own version of looping structures, but most languages including VBA support some variation of Do and For loops. Though the syntax of looping structures varies from language to language, looping structures share similar characteristics:

- Loops are logical blocks that contain other programming statements.
- Loops can increment a counter.
- Loops implement a condition by which the loop will exit.
- Many looping structures support conditions at either the top or bottom of the loop.
- Special statements can be used to exit the loop prematurely.

Before looking at specific VBA implementations, I'll discuss some possibilities for looping, some of which may not be so apparent at first. Consider the following list of programming scenarios, each of which requires the use of looping structures:

- Displaying a menu
- Running an autopilot system for a jumbo jet
- Finding a person's name in an electronic phone book
- Controlling a laser-guided missile
- Applying a 5% raise to all employees in a company
- Spinning the wheels in an electronic slot machine

Believe it or not, all of the preceding scenarios have already been implemented by programmers using techniques and concepts similar to the ones I will show you in this chapter.

How many times do you think a loop would iterate for each of the previous items? This is an interesting question. Some scenarios require a predefined number of iterations. For example, if I write a software program to apply a 5% raise to all employees in a company, I can be sure that there will be a limited number of iterations. In other words, the number of times the loop will execute is directly related to the number of employees in the company. Displaying a menu, however, can be a much different scenario. Take an ATM (automated teller machine) menu, for example. After a customer withdraws money from the ATM, should the ATM menu display again for the next customer? Well, you know the answer is yes, but then how many times should that same menu display—for how many customers? The answer is indefinitely. It doesn't happen often, but there are times when a loop needs to be infinite—or in other words, endless.

 TRAP

Infinite loops are created when a loop's terminating condition is never met. You will most likely encounter an intentional or unintentional infinite loop sometime in your programming career.

```
Do While 5 = 5

    MsgBox "Infinite loop"

Loop
```

To break out of an endless loop in VBA, simply try pressing the Esc key or the Ctrl+Break keys simultaneously.

To ensure that loops are not endless, each loop has a condition that must be met for the loop to stop iterating. It's important to note that loops use expressions to build conditions just as an If block or Select Case structure does. Moreover, each loop's condition evaluates to either true or false.

Many times, a loop's exiting condition is determined by a counter that is either incremented or decremented. In VBA, numbers are incremented and decremented using VBA assignment statements. In a nutshell, you must reassign a variable to itself with either an increment or decrement expression:

```
' Increment x by 1
x = x + 1

' Decrement y by 1
y = y - 1
```

After this cursory overview on looping structures, you're now ready to look at some specific VBA implementations. Specifically, you'll learn about the following VBA looping structures:

- Do While
- Do Until

- Loop While
- Loop Until
- For Loops

Do While

The Do While loop uses a condition at the top of the loop to determine how many times statements inside the loop will execute. Because the loop's condition is checked first, it is possible that the statements inside the loop will never execute.

```
Dim x As Integer
Dim y As Integer

Do While x < y

    MsgBox "x is less than y"

Loop
```

In this loop, it's possible that x is less than y, preventing the statement inside the loop from ever executing.

In the Do While loop, the statements are executed so long as the condition evaluates to true. In other words, the loop stops when the condition is false.

In the next example, the Do While loop uses an increment statement to satisfy the condition which allows the loop to iterate five times.

```
Dim x As Integer
Dim y As Integer

x = 0
y = 5

Do While x < y

    MsgBox "The value of x is " & x
    x = x + 1

Loop
```

Knowing that the loop will execute five times, what do you think the value of x will be after the last iteration? The value of x will be 4 after the last iteration. If you're having trouble seeing this, try placing this code in the Click event of a command button so you can step through it one iteration at a time with each click of the command button.

Do Until

Similarly to the Do While loop, the Do Until loop uses reverse logic to determine how many times a loop will iterate.

```
Dim x As Integer
Dim y As Integer


Do Until x > y


    MsgBox "Infinite Loop!"


Loop
```

In the preceding example, the statement inside the loop will execute until x is greater than y. Since there is no incrementing of x or decrementing of y, the loop is infinite.

Note that x being equal to y will not satisfy the condition—in other words, the statement would still execute inside the loop. Only once x is greater than y will the looping process stop.

Now study the following code and determine how many times the loop will iterate and what the value of x will be after the loop terminates.

```
Dim x As Integer
Dim y As Integer


x = 0
y = 5


Do Until x > y


    MsgBox "The value of x is " & x
    x = x + 1


Loop
```

This `Do Until` loop will execute six times, and the value of x after the last iteration is 6.

Loop While

Say I wanted to make sure the statements inside a loop execute at least once despite the loop's condition. The `Loop While` loop solves this dilemma by placing the loop's condition at the bottom of the loop:

```
Dim x As Integer
Dim y As Integer

x = 5
y = 2

Do

    MsgBox "Guaranteed to execute once."

Loop While x < y
```

Because the preceding loop's condition executes last, the statement inside the loop is guaranteed to execute at least once and in this case only once.

Loop Until

Using logic combined from the `Do Until` and `Loop While` loops, the `Loop Until` loop uses a reverse logic condition at the end of its looping structure.

```
Dim x As Integer
Dim y As Integer

x = 5
y = 2

Do

    MsgBox "How many times will this execute?"
    y = y + 1

Loop Until x < y
```

Using an increment statement, this loop's statements will execute four times. More specifically, the loop will iterate until y becomes 6, which meets the loop's exit condition of true.

For Loops

The next and last type of looping structure this chapter investigates is the For loop. The For loop is a very common loop for iterating through a list. It uses a range of numbers to determine how many times the loop will iterate.

```
Dim x As Integer

For x = 1 To 5

    MsgBox "The value of x is " & x

Next x
```

Notice that you are not required to increment the counting variable (in this case variable x) yourself. The For loop takes care of this for you with the Next keyword.

 Though it is common to specify the counting variable after the Next keyword, it is not required. When used by itself, the Next keyword will automatically increment the variable used on the left-hand side of the assignment in the For loop.

Using the For loop, you can dictate a predetermined range for the number of iterations:

```
Dim x As Integer

For x = 10 To 20

    MsgBox "The value of x is " & x

Next x
```

You can determine how the For loop increments your counting variable using the Step keyword. By default, the Step value is 1.

```
Dim x As Integer

For x = 1 To 10 Step 2
```

```
MsgBox "The value of x is " & x
```

```
Next x
```

The preceding `For` loop using the `Step` keyword will iterate five times, with the last value of x being 9.

Though it is common to use number literals on both sides of the `To` keyword, you can also use variables or property values:

```
Dim x As Integer

For x = Val(Text1.Value) To Val(Text2.Value)

    MsgBox "The value of x is " & x

Next x
```

Using the value of two text boxes, I can build a dynamic `For` loop, which obtains its looping range from a user.

List and Combo Boxes

Both list and combo boxes can store a list of items defined in either design time, in run time with VBA, or through a linked database form such as Access. Shown in Figure 4.1, list and combo boxes can be added to your forms using the Toolbox.

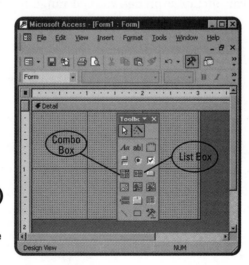

FIGURE 4.1

Viewing the combo and list box from the VBA Toolbox

Microsoft Access provides yet another wizard for adding and binding items to your list and combo boxes. This section, however, will concentrate on building and managing list and combo boxes without a wizard.

 TRICK You can stop Microsoft Access from displaying all control wizards by turning the control wizard off (pressing the wand icon) in the Toolbox.

Whether you are building list and combo boxes manually or through a wizard, there are many properties you must take into account. The most common of these properties are listed in Table 4.1.

TABLE 4.1 COMMON LIST AND COMBO BOX PROPERTIES

Property	Description
ColumnCount	Specifies the number of columns.
ColumnHeads	Determines if the list or combo box has column headings.
ColumnWidths	Determines the width of each column, separated by semicolons. Valid values are 0 (hidden) to 22 inches.
ListCount	Determines the number of rows in the list or combo box. Available only during run time.
ListIndex	Used for identifying the item selected in list or combo box. Available only in run time.
ListRows	Specifies the maximum number of rows to display.
MultiSelect	Specifies whether or not the user can select more than one row at a time.
RowSource	Determines the entries in the list separated by semicolons.
RowSourceType	Used to specify the type of row—Table/Query, Table/View/StoredProc, Value List, Field List, or a Visual Basic function. Works in conjunction with the RowSource property.

In addition to common properties, both list and combo boxes share two important methods for adding and removing items. In VBA they are appropriately called AddItem and RemoveItem.

In the next four subsections, you'll learn the most common approaches for managing items in both list and combo boxes.

Adding Items

Depending on the source, adding items with VBA can be a bit different between list and combo boxes. When used in a straightforward manner, however, both list and combo boxes support the `AddItem` method. Before using the `AddItem` method, you must set your combo or list box's `RowSourceType` property to `Value List`.

 Forgetting to set your list or combo box's `RowSourceType` property to `Value List` will cause a run-time error when using the `AddItem` method.

Seen in Figure 4.2, the next program uses the form `Load` event to execute multiple `AddItem` methods for both a combo and a list box.

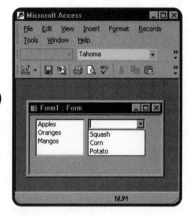

FIGURE 4.2

Using the `AddItem` method to populate a list box with fruit and a combo box with vegetables

```
Private Sub Form_Load()

    lstFruits.AddItem "Apples"
    lstFruits.AddItem "Oranges"
    lstFruits.AddItem "Mangos"

    cboVegetables.AddItem "Squash"
    cboVegetables.AddItem "Corn"
    cboVegetables.AddItem "Potato"

End Sub
```

The `AddItem` method takes two parameters (`Item`, `Index`), the first of which is required.

Many times, loops are used to populate list and combo boxes with static data or table information from a database.

```
Private Sub Form_Load()

    Dim x As Integer

    ' Add 25 items to the list box.
    For x = 1 To 25

        lstFruits.AddItem "The value of x is " & x

    Next x

End Sub
```

So far, adding items have been fairly static. To make things more interesting, you can add items to your list box or combo box based on user input. Before doing so, however, it's fairly common to check for duplicates before adding the item, which the following program and its output in Figure 4.3 demonstrate.

```
Option Compare Database
Option Explicit


Private Sub Form_Load()
```

```
    ' Add preliminary items to the list box.
    lstFruits.AddItem "Apples"
    lstFruits.AddItem "Oranges"
    lstFruits.AddItem "Mangos"

End Sub

Private Sub cmdAddItem_Click()

    Dim iCounter As Integer

    ' Search for a duplicate item.
    ' If none is found, add the item.
    For iCounter = 0 To (lstFruits.ListCount - 1)

        If lstFruits.ItemData(iCounter) = txtInput.Value Then

            MsgBox "Duplicate item. Can't add item."
            Exit Sub ' A duplicate was found, exit this procedure.

        End If

    Next iCounter

    ' No duplicate found, adding the item.
    lstFruits.AddItem txtInput.Value

End Sub
```

A few statements may appear new to you in the preceding program code. First, note the use of the ListCount property in the For loop. The ListCount property contains the number of items in a list or combo box. This number starts at 1, but the lowest number in a list box starts with 0. This is why I subtract 1 from the ListCount property in the For loop statement. To compare what's in the text box to each item in the list box, I can use the list box's ItemData property, which takes an index (in this case the looping variable) as a parameter and passes back the item's value. Last but not least is the presence of the Exit Sub statement. This statement is very common with Visual Basic programmers when needing to exit a procedure prematurely. In my case, I want to exit the procedure prematurely if a duplicate item is found, of course after letting the user know.

If I choose to use a combo box when accepting input from a user, an additional text box control is not needed because the combo box already contains a text box. In reality a combo box is really two controls—a list box and text box. To accept new input from a user with a combo box, your combo box's `LimitToList` property must be set to `No` (default). When retrieving user input from the combo box, work with its `Value` or `Text` properties (similarly to working with a text box).

Removing Items

Removing items from a list or combo box is quite easy. Specifically, you use the `RemoveItem` method, which takes a single parameter called `Index` as a value. Generally speaking, items are removed based on a user's selection. Before removing items, however, it is always a good idea to ensure that a user has selected an item first. To do so, simply check the list or combo box's `ListIndex` property first as the next program demonstrates. Output is seen in Figure 4.4.

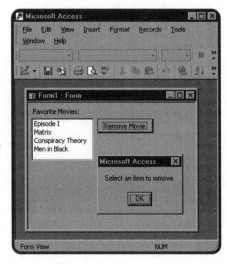

FIGURE 4.4

Checking that an item has been selected before using the `RemoveItem` method

```
Option Compare Database
Option Explicit


Private Sub Form_Load()

    ' Add preliminary items to the list box.
    lstMovies.AddItem "Episode I"
    lstMovies.AddItem "Matrix"
    lstMovies.AddItem "Conspiracy Theory"
    lstMovies.AddItem "Men in Black"
```

```
End Sub

Private Sub cmdRemoveItem_Click()

    ' Has the user selected an item first?
    If lstMovies.ListIndex = -1 Then

        ' The user has not selected an item.
        MsgBox "Select an item to remove."

    Else

        ' The user selected an item, so remove it.
        lstMovies.RemoveItem lstMovies.ListIndex

    End If

End Sub
```

If no items in a list or combo box have been selected, the ListIndex is set to -1. Otherwise the ListIndex contains the index of the currently selected item (starting with index 0 for the first item). This means you can pass the ListIndex property value to the RemoveItem method. This is an efficient and dynamic means of using property values to pass parameters to methods.

Managing Columns

Adding and managing columns with your list and combo boxes is really quite easy. The important rule to remember is that a column header is considered a row or item (index 0) in a list or combo box. This means the header must be treated as an extra item when deleting items or searching for items.

To add and manage columns, you will work with the following properties either in design time or through VBA code in run time.

- ColumnCount. Specifies the number of columns to display.
- ColumnHeads. Determines if the list or combo box has a column header.
- ColumnWidths. Specifies the width of each column separated by semi-colons in inches or centimeters.

Remembering that a column header is treated like another item, a column header is added using the list or combo box's AddItem method. Figure 4.5 demonstrates the visual appearance of columns and a column header.

FIGURE 4.5

Adding columns and
column headers to a
list box

```
Private Sub Form_Load()


    lstBooks.ColumnCount = 3
    lstBooks.ColumnHeads = True
    lstBooks.ColumnWidths = "1.5in;1in;1in"

    lstBooks.AddItem "Title;Author;ISBN"
    lstBooks.AddItem "Access VBA Programming...;Michael Vine;1592000398"
    lstBooks.AddItem "Visual Basic Programming...;Michael Vine;0761535535"
    lstBooks.AddItem "C Language Programming...;Michael Vine;1931841527"
    lstBooks.AddItem "JavaScript Programming...;Andy Harris;0761534105"


End Sub
```

When the `ColumnHeads` property is set to `True`, the first `AddItem` method encountered by VBA is used to populate the column headers. Note that when working with columns, you have to remember to separate each column or column data with semicolons.

Do not confuse the `ColumnHeads` property with the singular version `ColumnHead`. They are different properties belonging to completely different controls.

Random Numbers

One of my favorite beginning programming concepts is random numbers. Random numbers allow you to build a wide variety of applications ranging from encryption to games. In this section, I will show you how to build and use random numbers in your programs using two VBA functions called Randomize and Rnd.

The Randomize function initializes VBA's internal random-number generator. It is only necessary to call this function (no argument required) once during the lifetime of your program. Most often, the Randomize function is executed during startup routines such as a form Load event. Without the Randomize function, the Rnd function will generate random numbers in a consistent pattern, which of course is not really random at all.

The Rnd function takes a number as an argument and returns a Single data type. When used in conjunction with the Randomize function, the Rnd function can generate random numbers. To create a range of Integer-based random numbers, use the following VBA statements:

```
Dim x as Integer

x = Int((10 * Rnd) + 1)
```

The Int function takes a number as argument and converts it to an integer value (whole number). Remember that the Rnd function returns a Single number type, so the Int function is used to convert a decimal number into a whole number. Adding 1 to the result of (10 * Rnd) creates a random number between 1 and 10. Removing the addition of 1 would cause the random number range to be 0 through 10.

One way of utilizing random numbers is through a simulated dice roll. Figure 4.6 reveals the design-time form I used to simulate this. Note that there are eight images, six of which have their Visible property set to False. This way only two dice are visible to the user during run time.

```
Option Compare Database
Option Explicit


Private Sub Form_Load()
    Randomize
End Sub


Private Sub cmdRoll_Click()

    Dim iRandomNumber As Integer
```

```
' Generate random number (die) for die 1.
iRandomNumber = Int((6 * Rnd) + 1)

Select Case iRandomNumber

    Case 1
        imgDie1.Picture = Image1.Picture
    Case 2
        imgDie1.Picture = Image2.Picture
    Case 3
        imgDie1.Picture = Image3.Picture
    Case 4
        imgDie1.Picture = Image4.Picture
    Case 5
        imgDie1.Picture = Image5.Picture
    Case 6
        imgDie1.Picture = Image6.Picture

End Select

' Generate random number (die) for die 2.
iRandomNumber = Int((6 * Rnd) + 1)

Select Case iRandomNumber

    Case 1
        imgDie2.Picture = Image1.Picture
    Case 2
        imgDie2.Picture = Image2.Picture
    Case 3
        imgDie2.Picture = Image3.Picture
    Case 4
        imgDie2.Picture = Image4.Picture
    Case 5
        imgDie2.Picture = Image5.Picture
    Case 6
        imgDie2.Picture = Image6.Picture

End Select

End Sub
```

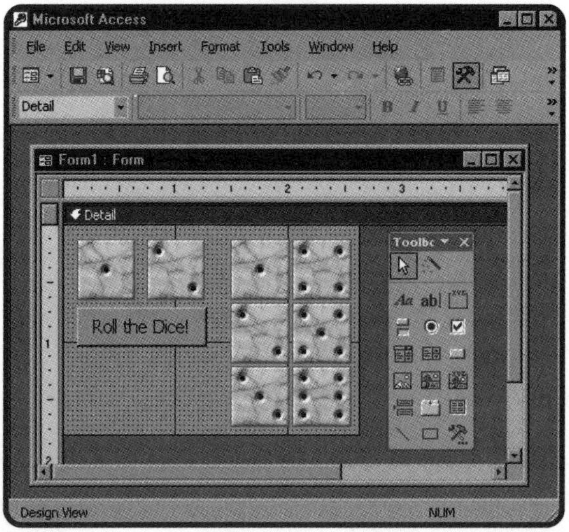

FIGURE 4.6

Using random
numbers and image-
swapping techniques
to emulate rolling of
the dice

To simulate the dice roll, I use the `Click` event of a command button to create a random number ranging from 1 to 6 for each die. After that, I perform a bit of image swapping based on a `Select Case` structure. Image swapping in this case is performed by assigning one `Picture` property to another.

Chapter Program: Math Quiz

The Math Quiz seen in Figure 4.7 is a fun way of learning how to incorporate chapter-based concepts such as loops, random numbers, and list boxes into your VBA applications. Specifically, the Math Quiz prompts a user for the number of math questions she would like to answer. Then, the Math Quiz prompts the user with a predetermined number of addition questions using random numbers between 1 and 100. Stored in the list box (with columns) are each question, the user's response, and the result.

All of the code required to build the Math Quiz is seen next.

```
Option Compare Database
Option Explicit


Private Sub Form_Load()
    Randomize
End Sub


Private Sub cmdRemoveItem_Click()
```

```vb
    ' Determine if an item has been selected first.
    If lstResults.ListIndex = -1 Then
        MsgBox "Select an item to remove."
    Else
        lstResults.RemoveItem lstResults.ListIndex + 1
    End If

End Sub

Private Sub cmdStart_Click()

    Dim sResponse As String
    Dim sUserAnswer As String
    Dim iCounter As Integer
    Dim iOperand1 As Integer
    Dim iOperand2 As Integer

    ' Determine how many math questions to ask.
    sResponse = InputBox("How many math questions would you like?")

    If sResponse <> "" Then

        ' Add header to each column in the list box if one
        ' hasn't already been added.
        If lstResults.ListCount = 0 Then
            lstResults.AddItem "Question;Your Answer;Result"
        End If

        ' Ask predetermined number of math questions.
        For iCounter = 1 To Val(sResponse)

            ' Generate random numbers between 0 and 100.
            iOperand1 = Int(100 * Rnd)
            iOperand2 = Int(100 * Rnd)

            ' Generate question.
            sUserAnswer = InputBox("What is " & iOperand1 & _
                " + " & iOperand2)
```

```
' Determine if user's answer was correct and add an
' appropriate item to the multicolumn list box.
If Val(sUserAnswer) = iOperand1 + iOperand2 Then
    lstResults.AddItem iOperand1 & " + " & _
        iOperand2 & ";" & sUserAnswer & ";Correct"
Else
    lstResults.AddItem iOperand1 & " + " & _
        iOperand2 & ";" & sUserAnswer & ";Incorrect"
End If


    Next iCounter


    End If


End Sub
```

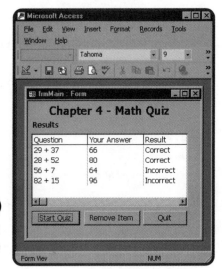

FIGURE 4.7

Using chapter-based concepts to build the Math Quiz game

Chapter Summary

This chapter covered looping structures, list and combo boxes, and random number generation. You specifically learned the following key concepts:

- VBA supports the `Do While`, `Do Until`, `Loop While`, `Loop Until`, and `For` looping structures.

- Looping structures use conditions to determine the number of iterations.

- An infinite or endless loop is caused when the loop's exiting condition is never met.

- List and combo boxes share many common properties and methods.

- To use the `AddItem` method of a list or combo box, the `RowSource-Type` property must be set to `Value List`.

- The `ListIndex` property of a list and combo box can be used to determine which item a user has selected. If no items are selected, the `ListIndex` property is set to −1.

- Columns can be added to list and combo boxes by setting the `Column-Count`, `ColumnHeads`, and `ColumnWidths` properties.

- Columns are managed through run time with VBA or through design time by separating individual columns with semicolons.

- VBA uses the `Randomize` and `Rnd` functions to generate random numbers.

CHALLENGES

1. Place a single command button on a form. Write code in the `Click` event of the command button to display a message box five times using a `Do While` loop. Remember to use a counting variable in the loop's condition, which increments each time the loop iterates.

2. Modify Challenge 1 to use a `For` loop that iterates 20 times with a `Step` value of three (3).

3. Add a combo box and command button to a form. In the form's `Load` event, add three items to the combo box using the `AddItem` method. In the `Click` event of the command button, add input from the combo box's `Value` property (input from the user). Remember to check for duplicate items.

4. Enhance the Math Quiz game to randomize not only numbers but the type of math problem. More specifically, use an additional variable to hold a random number between 1 and 4 where each number represents addition, subtraction, multiplication, or division.

Functions Continued

So far you have learned to use a fair amount of built-in VBA functions such as InputBox and MsgBox, which provide interactive dialog boxes to the user. What you might not know is that VBA provides many more intrinsic or built-in functions for you to use in your programming efforts. Learning how to leverage the power of these built-in functions is all-important in VBA programming and is certainly the key to saving you from unproductive programming time.

To facilitate your learning of VBA functions, this chapter will introduce a number of commonly used function for managing strings, dates, times, and data-conversion efforts. Specifically, you will learn about the following topics:

- String-based functions

- Date/time functions

- Conversion functions

- Formatting functions

String-Based Functions

Someone famous once asked, "What's in a name?" Someone less famous (yours truly) once asked, "What's in a string?" So what is in a string? Well, lots. Strings are key building blocks in any high-level programming language. More specifically, they are data structures themselves, which contain one or more characters. Note that it is also possible for strings to be Null or undefined.

Groupings of characters and/or numbers comprise strings. These groupings of characters can mean different things depending on their use. Many languages, including VBA, provide popular means for parsing, searching, and managing the individual pieces (characters and numbers) that make up strings.

In this section, I will show you how to parse, search, and manage strings using some very popular built-in VBA functions as described in Table 5.1.

TABLE 5.1 COMMON STRING-BASED FUNCTIONS

Function Name	Description
UCase	Converts a string to uppercase
LCase	Converts a string to lowercase
Len	Returns the number of characters in a string
StrComp	Compares two strings and determines if they are equal to, less than, or greater than each other
Right	Determines the specified number of characters from the right side of a string
Left	Determines the specified number of characters from the left side of a string
Mid	Determines the specified number of characters in a string
InStr	Finds the first occurrence of a string within another
Format	Formats a string based on specified instructions

UCase

The UCase function is an easy function to use. It takes a string as a parameter and returns the string in uppercase.

```
Private Sub cmdConvert_Click()

    txtOutput.Value = UCase(txtInput.Value)


End Sub
```

The UCase function can take a string literal, string variable, or property of string type as seen in the previous program with output in Figure 5.1.

FIGURE 5.1

Converting a string
to uppercase using
the UCase function

LCase

The inverse of UCase, the LCase function takes a string parameter and outputs the string in lowercase. Sample code is demonstrated next with output seen in Figure 5.2.

```
Private Sub cmdConvert_Click()

    txtOutput.Value = LCase(txtInput.Value)


End Sub
```

FIGURE 5.2

Converting a string
to lowercase using
the LCase
function

Len

The Len function is a useful tool for determining the length of a string. It takes a string as input and returns a number of Long data type. The Len function's return value indicates the number of characters present in the string parameter. To demonstrate, the next event procedure is used to determine the number of characters in a person's name. Output can be seen in Figure 5.3.

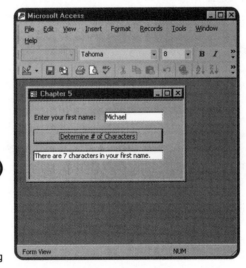

FIGURE 5.3

Using the Len
function to
determine the
number of
characters in a string

```
Private Sub cmdNumberOfCharacters_Click()

    Dim iNumberOfCharacters As Integer

    iNumberOfCharacters = Len(txtFirstName.Value)
```

```
txtOutput.Value = "There are " & iNumberOfCharacters & _
    " characters in your first name."
```

End Sub

StrComp

The StrComp function is useful when comparing the sequence of characters in two strings. The Option Compare statement is used to determine whether binary or textual comparison is done. If a binary comparison is done, characters are treated with case sensitivity. Textual comparisons are not case sensitive.

The StrComp function takes two string parameters and returns one of four numbers as explained in Table 5.2.

TABLE 5.2   OUTPUT VALUES FOR THE StrComp FUNCTION

Return Value	Description
−1	String 1 is less than string 2.
0	Both strings are equal.
1	String 1 is greater than string 2.
Null	One of the strings is Null (undefined).

The next Click event procedure uses the StrComp function to determine the equality of two strings. Figure 5.4 examines sample output from the event procedure.

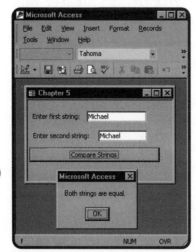

FIGURE 5.4

Using the StrComp to compare two strings for equality

```
Private Sub cmdCompareStrings Click()

    Dim iResult As Integer

    iResult = StrComp(txtFirstString.Value, txtSecondString.Value)

    Select Case iResult

        Case -1
            MsgBox "The first string is less than the second."

        Case 0
            MsgBox "Both strings are equal."

        Case 1
            MsgBox "The first string is greater than the second."

        Case Else
            MsgBox "One or more strings are Null."

    End Select

End Sub
```

Right

The Right function takes two parameters and returns a string containing the number of characters from the right side of a string. The first parameter is the string to be evaluated. The second parameter is a number, which indicates how many characters to return from the right side of the string. Output is shown in Figure 5.5.

```
Private Sub cmdExtract_Click()

    txtOutput.Value = Right(txtInput.Value, 3)

End Sub
```

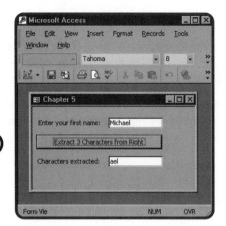

FIGURE 5.5

Extracting three
characters from the
right-hand side of a
string

Left

Working in the opposite direction of the `Right` function, the `Left` function
extracts a predetermined number of characters from the left-hand side of a
string. Like the `Right` function, the `Left` function takes two parameters. The
first parameter is the string to be evaluated. The second parameter is a number,
which indicates how many characters to return from the left side of the string.
Figure 5.6 shows the output.

FIGURE 5.6

Extracting three
characters from the
left-hand side of a
string

```
Private Sub cmdExtract_Click()

    txtOutput.Value = Left(txtInput.Value, 3)

End Sub
```

Mid

The `Mid` function returns a string containing a predetermined number of characters. It takes three parameters, the first two of which are required. The first parameter is the string to be evaluated. The next parameter is the starting position from which characters should be taken. The last parameter, which is optional, is the number of characters to be returned. If the last parameter is omitted, all characters from the starting position to the end of the string are returned.

```
Dim sString As String

Dim sMiddleWord As String


sString = "Access VBA Programming"


sMiddleWord = Mid(sString, 8, 3) ' Returns VBA
```

InStr

The `InStr` function can take up to four parameters and returns a number specifying the starting position of the first occurrence of a string within another string. The required parameters are two strings, where the first string is the string being searched and the second parameter is the string sought after. The optional parameters determine the starting position of the search and the type of string comparison made.

In the next code example, I use both the `Mid` and `InStr` functions to extract a person's last name from a string expression. Output is seen in Figure 5.7.

FIGURE 5.7

Using `Mid` and `InStr` functions to extract one string from another

```
Private Sub cmdClickMe_Click()

    Dim sLastName As String
    Dim startPosition

    ' Search the input string for a space character.
    startPosition = InStr(txtInput.Value, " ")

    ' Extract the last name from the string starting
    ' after the space character.
    sLastName = Mid(txtInput.Value, startPosition + 1)

    MsgBox "Thanks Mr. " & sLastName

End Sub
```

Date/Time Functions

Access VBA contains numerous date/time functions such as `Date`, `Time`, and `Now` for accessing your system's date and time. Specifically, I will show you how to use the following VBA date/time functions:

- `Date`
- `Day`
- `WeekDay`
- `Month`
- `Year`
- `Time`
- `Second`
- `Minute`
- `Hour`
- `Now`

With these functions, you can create date/time stamps, stopwatches, clocks, or custom timer functions.

Date

The `Date` function requires no parameter when executed and returns a `Variant` data type containing your system's current date.

```
MsgBox Date
```

Figure 5.8 demonstrates sample output from the Date function.

Displaying the
current system's
date with the
Date function

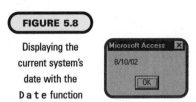

Day

The Day function takes a required date argument (output of the Date function) and returns a whole number between 1 and 31, which represents a day within the current month.

```
Day(Date) ' Returns a number between 1 and 31.
```

WeekDay

The WeekDay function takes two parameters and returns a whole number containing the current day of the week. The first parameter is the date (Date function output), which is required. The second parameter (optional) determines the first day of the week. The default first day of the week is Sunday.

```
WeekDay(Date) ' Returns a number between 1 and 7.
```

Month

The Month function takes a single parameter, which signifies the current date and returns a whole number representing the current month in the year.

```
Month(Date) ' Returns a number between 1 and 12.
```

Year

Much like the preceding date-based functions, the Year function takes a date parameter and returns a whole number representing the current year.

```
Year(Date)
```

Sample output from the Year function is demonstrated in Figure 5.9.

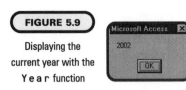

Time

The Time function is another easy-to-use function—it requires no parameters as input and returns a Variant data type with your system's current time.

Figure 5.10 shows a sample return value for the Time function.

```
MsgBox Time
```

FIGURE 5.10

Displaying the
current system time
with the Time
function

When used with other functions and events, the Time function can be quite useful in building many applications. For example, I can use a form's Timer event and TimerInterval property to display the current time updated automatically every second:

```
Private Sub cmdStop_Click()

    ' Stop the Timer event.
    Me.TimerInterval = 0

End Sub


Private Sub Form_Load()

    Me.TimerInterval = 1000 ' 1000 milliseconds = 1 second

End Sub


Private Sub Form_Timer()
```

```
' Update the time every 1 second.
lblTime.Caption = Time
```

```
End Sub
```

Note that setting the form's `TimerInterval` property to 0 stops the `Timer` event from executing.

Second

The `Second` function requires a time parameter (the output from the `Time` function) and returns a whole number from 0 to 59 indicating the current second in the current minute.

```
Second(Time) ' Returns a number from 0 to 59.
```

Minute

Much like the `Second` function, the `Minute` function requires a time parameter (the output from the `Time` function) and returns a whole number from 0 to 59, which indicates the current minute in the current hour.

```
Minute(Time) ' Returns a number from 0 to 59.
```

Hour

The `Hour` function takes a required time parameter and returns a whole number between 0 and 23, which represents the current hour according to your system's time.

```
Hour(Time) ' Returns a number from 0 to 23.
```

Now

The `Now` function incorporates results from both `Date` and `Time` functions. It takes no parameters and returns a `Variant` data type indicating the system's current date and time, respectively.

```
MsgBox Now
```

Sample output from the `Now` function can be seen in Figure 5.11.

FIGURE 5.11

Displaying the
current system date
and time with the
N o w function

Conversion Functions

Conversion functions are very powerful as they allow programmers to convert data from one type to another. Access VBA supports many types of conversion functions. Many common uses for data conversion involve converting strings to numbers and numbers to strings. To explore the application of data conversion, I will discuss the conversion functions found in Table 5.3.

TABLE 5.3 COMMON VBA CONVERSION FUNCTIONS

Function	Description
Val	Converts recognized numeric characters in a string as numbers
Str	Converts a recognized number to a string equivalent
Chr	Converts a character code to its corresponding character
Asc	Converts a character to its corresponding character code

Val

The Val function takes a string as input and coverts recognizable numeric characters to a number data type. More specifically, the Val function stops reading the string when it encounters a non-numeric character. The following are some sample return values:

```
Val("123") ' Returns 123

Val("a123") ' Returns 0

Val("123a") ' Returns 123
```

Str

The Str function takes a number as argument and converts it to a string representation with a leading space for its sign (positive or negative). An error occurs in the Str function if a non-numeric value is passed as a parameter.

```
Str(123) ' Returns " 123"

Str(-123) ' Returns "-123"
```

Chr

You may remember from earlier chapters that data can take many forms. Specifically, numbers can represent both numbers and characters. This means it is up to the programmer to determine how data is stored (variables and data types) and presented (formatting and conversion functions).

Many programming languages including VBA support the concept of character codes. Character codes are numbers, which represent a single character. For example, the character "A" is represented by the character code 65, and the character "a" (lowercase letter A) is represented by the character code 97.

 Appendix A contains a table of VBA's most common character codes.

To convert a character code to its corresponding character, VBA programmers use the Chr function. The Chr function takes a single character code as a parameter and returns the corresponding character.

Figure 5.12 demonstrates a simple program that can convert a character code to its corresponding character:

```
Private Sub cmdConvert_Click()

    txtOutput.Value = Chr(txtInput.Value)


End Sub
```

Note that character codes also represent numeric characters and nonprintable characters such as space, tab, and linefeed.

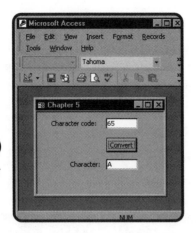

FIGURE 5.12

Converting character
codes to characters
with the C h r
function

Asc

The A s c function works as the inverse of the C h r function. It takes a single character as input and converts it to its corresponding character code. Sample output
from the A s c function can be seen in Figure 5.13.

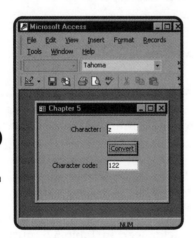

FIGURE 5.13

Using the A s c
function to convert a
character to its
corresponding
character code

```
Private Sub cmdConvert_Click()


    txtInput.Value = Asc(txtOutput.Value)


End Sub
```

Formatting

It is often necessary to format data to a specific need. For example, you may want to display a date in long format, or a number with a thousands separator, or numbers as a currency or percentage. Each of these scenarios and many more can be accomplished with a single VBA function called `Format`.

The `Format` function takes up to four parameters:

```
Format(expression, format, firstDayOfWeek, firstWeekOfYear)
```

Table 5.4 describes each of the Format function's parameters in detail.

TABLE 5.4 FORMAT FUNCTION PARAMETERS

Parameter	Description
expression	An expression to format. Required.
format	A valid user-defined or named expression format. Optional.
firstDayOfWeek	A VBA constant, which specifies the fist day of the week. Optional.
firstWeekOfYear	A VBA constant, which specifies the first week of the year. Optional.

In the next three sections, I will show you how to use the `Format` function to format strings, numbers, and dates and times.

Formatting Strings

There are five characters that can be used to build user-defined strings using the `Format` function. Each format character seen in Table 5.5 must be enclosed in quotes when passed as a format expression argument in the `Format` function.

Note that placeholders are displayed from right to left unless an exclamation mark character is present in the format expression. Consult Microsoft Visual Basic Help for more information on the *Format* function and format expressions.

```
Format("hi there", ">") ' Returns "HI THERE"
```

```
Format("Access VBA Programming", "<") ' Returns "access vba programming"
```

TABLE 5.5 STRING FORMATS

Format Character	Description
@	Displays a character or space as a placeholder.
&	Displays a character or nothing as a placeholder.
<	Formats all characters in lowercase.
>	Formats all characters in uppercase.
!	Placeholders are filled left to right.

Formatting Numbers

Numbers can be displayed with user-defined formatting expressions. The Format function supports a multitude of formatting characters (used in the format argument of the Format function) for numbers as Table 5.6 reveals.

TABLE 5.6 NUMBER FORMATS

Format Character	Description
0	Displays a digit or zero as a placeholder.
#	Displays a digit or nothing as a placeholder.
.	A placeholder that determines how many digits are displayed to the left and right of the decimal.
%	Places the percentage character at the location where it appears in the format expression. Multiplies the number by 100.
,	Separates thousands from hundreds using the comma character.
E- E+ e- e+	Specifies scientific formatting.
- + $ ( )	Specifies a literal character.
\\	Displays a single backslash.

```
s = Format(12345.6, "$##,##00.00") ' Returns $12,345.60


s = Format("12345.6", "00.0") ' Returns 12345.6


s = Format("10", "0.0%")   ' Returns 1000.0%
```

Formatting Date and Time

One of the most common reasons to format data is to display dates and times. The
Format function supports many named (VBA-defined) and user-defined formatting expressions for customizing the display of your dates and times.

Table 5.7 describes many date and time formatting options.

Shown in Figure 5.14 are sample outputs in a list box from formatting dates and
time with the Format function as follows:

```
Private Sub Form_Load()

    lstFormatDateTime.AddItem Format(Date, "d/m/yy")
    lstFormatDateTime.AddItem Format(Date, "dd/mm/yyyy")
    lstFormatDateTime.AddItem Format(Date, "dddd")
    lstFormatDateTime.AddItem Format(Time, "h:m:s")
    lstFormatDateTime.AddItem Format(Time, "hh:mm:ss AM/PM")
    lstFormatDateTime.AddItem Format(Now, "c")

End Sub
```

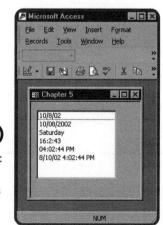

FIGURE 5.14

Using the Format
function and user-
defined expressions
to format date and
time

TABLE 5.7   DATE AND TIME FORMATS

Format Character	Description
:	Separates time in hours, minutes, and seconds
/	Separates dates in day, month, and year
d	Day displayed as a number without a leading zero
dd	Day displayed as a number with a leading zero
ddd	Day displayed as an abbreviation
dddd	Day displayed with the full name
ddddd	Complete date displayed in short format (m/d/yy)
dddddd	Complete date displayed in long format (mmm dd, yyyy)
w	Day of the week displayed as a number (1 starts on Sunday)
ww	Week of the year displayed as a number
m	Month displayed as a number without a leading zero
mm	Month displayed as a number with a leading zero
mmm	Month displayed as an abbreviation
mmmm	Month displayed with full name
q	Quarters in year displayed as a number
y	Day of the year is displayed as a number
yy	Year displayed in 2-digit format
yyyy	Year displayed in 4-digit format
h	Hour displayed without leading zeros
Hh	Hour displayed with leading zeros
N	Minute displayed without leading zeros
Nn	Minute displayed with leading zeros
S	Second displayed without leading zeros
Ss	Second displayed with leading zeros
ttttt	Time displayed with hour, minute, and second
AM/PM	Displays uppercase AM or PM using 12-hour clock
am/pm	Displays lowercase AM or PM using 12-hour clock
A/P	Displays an uppercase A or P using 12-hour clock
a/p	Displays a lowercase A or P using 12-hour clock
c	Displays the date as ddddd and time as ttttt

Chapter Program: Secret Message

The Secret Message program uses built-in VBA functions to build a fun encryption program. More specifically, the Secret Message program uses string-based functions such as Len and Mid and conversion functions Asc and Chr to encrypt and decrypt messages. Figures 5.15 and 5.16 depicts sample input and output from the Secret Message program.

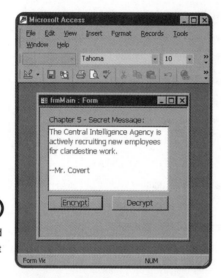

FIGURE 5.15

Using chapter-based concepts to decrypt a message

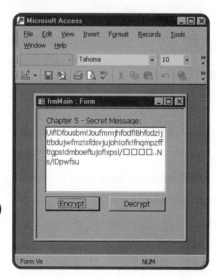

FIGURE 5.16

Using chapter-based concepts to encrypt a message

All of the code required to build the Secret Message program is shown next.

```
Option Compare Database
Option Explicit

 Private Sub cmdDecrypt_Click()

    Dim sDecryptedMessage As String
    Dim sDecryptedCharacter As String
    Dim iCounter As Integer

    If txtMessage.Value <> "" Then

        ' Iterate through each encrypted character in the message.
        For iCounter = 1 To Len(txtMessage.Value)

            ' Convert one encrypted character at a time to its
            ' equivalent character code.
            sDecryptedCharacter = Asc(Mid(txtMessage.Value, iCounter, 1))

            ' Convert the character code (shifted by -1) back
            ' to a character.
            sDecryptedCharacter = Chr(sDecryptedCharacter - 1)

            ' Add the decrypted character to the new decrypted message.
            sDecryptedMessage = sDecryptedMessage + sDecryptedCharacter

        Next iCounter

        ' Display the decrypted message.
        txtMessage.Value = sDecryptedMessage

    End If

End Sub

Private Sub cmdEncrypt_Click()

    Dim sEncryptedMessage As String
    Dim sEncryptedCharacter As String
```

```
Dim iCounter As Integer

If txtMessage.Value <> "" Then

    ' Iterate through each character in the message.
    For iCounter = 1 To Len(txtMessage.Value)

        ' Convert one character at a time to its equivalent
        ' character code.
        sEncryptedCharacter = Asc(Mid(txtMessage.Value, iCounter, 1))

        ' Convert the character code (shifted by 1) back
        ' to a character.
        sEncryptedCharacter = Chr(sEncryptedCharacter + 1)

        ' Add the encrypted character to the new encrypted message.
        sEncryptedMessage = sEncryptedMessage + sEncryptedCharacter

    Next iCounter

    ' Display the encrypted message.
    txtMessage.Value = sEncryptedMessage

End If

End Sub
```

Chapter Summary

This chapter introduced you to some of VBA's more common functions for managing strings, dates, and time. Moreover, you learned how to leverage the power of formatting and how to covert between various data types. You specifically learned about the following key concepts:

- String case can be managed with UCase and LCase functions.
- Strings can be extracted from other strings using functions such as Left, Right, and Mid.
- Strings can be searched and compared with VBA functions InStr and StrComp, respectively.

- VBA supports a multitude of functions such as `Date`, `Time`, and `Now` for displaying dates and/or times.
- Forms have a `Timer` event, which can be triggered automatically and regularly using the form's `TimerInterval` property.
- Data is represented by both numbers and characters using character codes. VBA uses the `Chr` and `Asc` functions to convert between character codes and characters.
- Data is easily formatted for string, number, and date/time display using VBA's `Format` function.

CHALLENGES

1. Using the `Right` function, write code the `Click` event of a command button to output the last seven characters in the string "Access VBA Programming".

2. Using a form's `Timer` event and `TimerInterval` property, build a stopwatch with one label control and two command buttons. Use the `Format` function, `Time` function, and format expression "Ss" to display seconds only.

3. Create a word search game that allows a user to view a string of characters for a predetermined amount of time (say 5 to 10 seconds—build a timer to accomplish this). After time is up, hide the string of characters and prompt to user to enter one or more words they saw in the string. For example, the string of characters "keoixakaccessqcinmsboxeamlz" contains the words "access" and "box." Use the `InStr` function to determine whether the user's guess is contained in the word search string.

4. Build a form with one text box and one command button. Allow the user to enter multiple lines into the text box. In the `Click` event of the command button, use a `For` loop and the `Len` function to iterate through each character in the text box. Every time a space character is found, increment a procedure-level variable. After the loop has completed, output the number of spaces found in a message box.

Code Reuse, Modules, and Advanced Form Concepts

I n this chapter I will show you how to build your own procedures, including function procedures that can return values. I will show you how to better manage your user-defined procedures in standard code modules and how you can leverage advanced forms through VBA with the D o C m d object.

Specifically, I will discuss the following topics in detail:

- Code reuse

- Standard modules

- Advanced form concepts

Code Reuse

Remember that Visual Basic and VBA are event-driven programming languages. This means VBA programmers could easily duplicate work when writing code in two or more event procedures. For example, consider a bookstore application that contains three different windows where a user could search for a book by entering a book title and clicking a command button. As a VBA programmer, you could easily write the same code in each command-button `Click` event. This approach is demonstrated in the next three event procedures.

```
Private Sub cmdSearchFromMainWindow_Click(BookTitle As String)

    ' Common code to search for a book based on book title.

End Sub


Private Sub cmdSearchFromHelpWindow_Click(BookTitle As String)

    ' Common code to search for a book based on book title.

End Sub


Private Sub cmdSearchFromBookWindow_Click(BookTitle As String)

    ' Common code to search for a book based on book title.

End Sub
```

The program statements required to search for a book could be many lines long, and these are needlessly duplicated in each event procedure. To solve this problem, you could build your own user-defined procedure called `SearchForBook`, which implements all the required code only once to search for a book. Then, each event procedure need only call `SearchForBook` and pass in a book title as a parameter.

To remove duplicate code, I must first build the `SearchForBook` user-defined procedure:

```
Public Sub SearchForBook(sBookTitle As String)

    ' Search for a book based on book title.

End Sub
```

Instead of duplicating the search statements in each `Click` event, I need only call the `SearchForBook` subprocedure, passing it a book title:

```
Private Sub cmdSearchFromMainWindow_Click()

    SearchForBook(txtBookTitle.Value)

End Sub

Private Sub cmdSearchFromHelpWindow_Click()

    SearchForBook(txtBookTitle.Value)

End Sub

Private Sub cmdSearchFromBookWindow_Click()

    SearchForBook(txtBookTitle.Value)

End Sub
```

This new approach eliminates duplicate code, logic, and waste by creating what's known as code reuse. Specifically, code reuse is the process by which programmers pull out commonly used statements and put them into unique procedures or functions, which can be referenced from anywhere in the application.

Code reuse will make your life as a programmer much easier and more enjoyable. It is an easy concept to grasp and is really more applied than theoretical. In the world of VBA, code reusability is implemented as subprocedures and function procedures. Programmers create user-defined procedures for problems that need frequently used solutions. In the next sections, I will show you how to accomplish code reuse by building your own user-defined subprocedures and function procedures.

Introduction to User-Defined Procedures

In Chapter 5, you learned how to use built-in VBA functions (also known as procedures). You may have wondered how those functions were implemented or built. In this section, you will learn how to build your own functions using user-defined procedures. Access VBA supports three types of procedures: subprocedures, function procedures, and property procedures. I will specifically discuss subprocedures and function procedures while saving property procedures for Chapter 11 when I discuss Object Oriented Programming.

IN THE REAL WORLD

The main difference between subprocedures and procedure functions is that subprocedures do not return values. Many other programming languages such as C or Java simply refer to a procedure that returns no value as a void function.

Though different in implementation and use, both subprocedures and function procedures share some similar characteristics such as beginning and ending statements, executable statements, and incoming arguments. The main difference between the two revolves around a return value. Specifically, subprocedures do not return a value, whereas function procedures do.

User-defined procedures are added to your Visual Basic code modules manually or with a little help from the Add Procedure dialog box. To access the Add Procedure dialog box, open your VBE (Visual Basic Environment) and make sure the code window portion has the focus. Then, select the Procedure menu item from the Insert menu as demonstrated in Figure 6.1.

 The Procedure menu item will show as unavailable (disabled) if the code window in the VBE does not have the focus.

Seen in Figure 6.2, the Add Procedure dialog box allows you to name your procedure and select a procedure type and scope. If you select "All Local variables as Statics," your procedure-level variables will maintain their values through your program's execution.

After creating your procedure, the Add Procedure dialog box tells VBA to create a procedure shell with beginning and ending statements as shown in Figure 6.3.

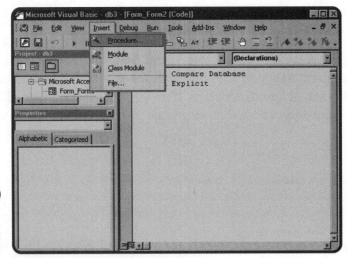

FIGURE 6.1

Accessing the Add Procedure dialog box from the Insert menu

FIGURE 6.2

Adding a procedure with the Add Procedure dialog box

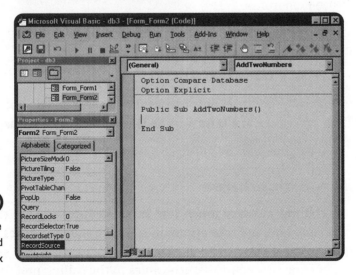

FIGURE 6.3

An empty procedure created with the Add Procedure dialog box

Subprocedures

Subprocedures must have a `Sub` statement and corresponding `End Sub` statement. They can contain executable Visual Basic statements such as declaration and assignment statements. Subprocedures can take arguments such as variables, constants, and/or expressions. If no arguments are provided, the beginning `Sub` statement must contain an empty set of parentheses:

```
Public Sub DisplayCurrentTime()

    MsgBox "The time is " & Time

End Sub
```

The next subprocedure implements adding two numbers, which are passed in as arguments.

```
Public Sub AddTwoNumbers(iNumber1 As Integer, iNumber2 As Integer)

    MsgBox "The result of " & iNumber1 & " and " & iNumber2 & _
            " is " & iNumber1 + iNumber2

End Sub
```

When executed by itself, the `AddTwoNumbers` procedure requires no parentheses surrounding its parameter list:

```
AddTwoNumbers 4, 6
```

When used in an assignment statement, however, the comma-separated parameter list must be enclosed in parentheses:

```
lblOutput.Caption = AddTwoNumbers(4, 6)
```

Note again that subprocedures only execute statements and do not return a value to the calling procedure. If a return value is required, consider using a function procedure (discussed next).

Function Procedures

Function procedures are very much like subprocedures in that they consist of Visual Basic statements and take arguments. Unlike subprocedures, function procedures begin with a `Function` statement and end with an `End Function` statement. Function procedures return values to the calling procedure by assigning a value to the function name:

```
Public Function MultiplyTwoNumbers(dNumber1 As Double, dNumber2 As Double)

    MultiplyTwoNumbers = dNumber1 * dNumber2

End Function
```

The `MultiplyTwoNumbers` function procedure takes two arguments and assigns the result of their multiplication to the function name, thereby returning the result to the calling function:

```
lblResult.Caption = MultiplyTwoNumbers(6, 9)
```

To be more dynamic, I could pass `Value` properties of two text boxes directly in as arguments:

```
lblResult.Caption = MultiplyTwoNumbers(Val(txtNumber1.Value), _
    Val(txtNumber2.Value))
```

To ensure that the `MultiplyTwoNumbers` function receives numbers (doubles) as arguments, I use the `Val` function inside the parameter list to convert strings to numbers.

Arguments and Parameters

The words arguments and parameters are often used in the same context. Really they are different in purpose and definition. Microsoft Visual Basic Help defines an argument as "a constant, variable, or expression passed to a procedure" and a parameter as a "variable name by which an argument passed to a procedure is known within the procedure." To summarize, an argument is the actual data passed to the procedure by the caller, whereas the parameter is the container or variable that holds the argument. Confusing I'm sure, but know there is technically a difference between the two words.

Many programming languages, including VBA, allow arguments to be passed either by value or by reference. When arguments are passed by value, VBA makes a copy of the original variable's contents and passes the copy to the procedure. This means that the procedure can't modify the original contents of the argument, only the copy.

To pass arguments by reference, you will need to preface the parameter name with the `ByVal` keyword as shown in the `Increment` procedure below.

```
Private Sub cmdProcess_Click()

    Dim iNumber As Integer

    iNumber = 1

    Increment iNumber

    MsgBox "The value of iNumber is " & x

End Sub

Public Sub Increment(ByVal x As Integer)

    x = x + 5

End Sub
```

Looking at the code window in Figure 6.4, you can see that it is not required to give the argument the same name as the variable passed in.

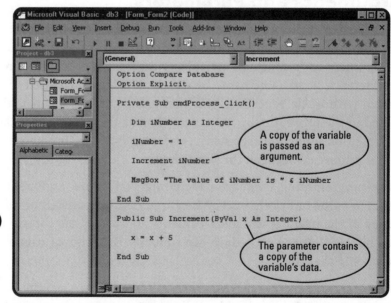

As Figure 6.5 reveals, the Increment procedure was unable to modify the original contents of the iNumber variable. To modify the variable's contents, you must send the argument by reference.

FIGURE 6.5

Passing arguments
by value does not
allow the called
procedure to modify
the argument's
original value

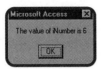

TRAP

When not used in assignment statements, argument lists can't be enclosed in parentheses. Keep in mind that Visual Basic will not always produce a run-time error when parentheses are used and yet not required. Instead Visual Basic may simply pass the argument incorrectly, producing unexpected results.

Arguments passed by reference send the procedure a reference to the arguments memory location. In a nutshell, a memory address is sent to the procedure when arguments are passed by reference. This means the procedure is able to modify the original data. Passing arguments by reference is the default argument behavior in VBA. Passing arguments by reference is the most efficient means of passing arguments to procedures—efficient because only a reference (memory address) to the argument is passed, not the data itself.

To pass arguments by reference, simply preface the argument name using the ByRef keyword or use no preface keyword at all.

```
Private Sub cmdProcess_Click()

    Dim iNumber As Integer

    iNumber = 1

    Increment iNumber

    MsgBox "The value of iNumber is " & iNumber

End Sub


Public Sub Increment(ByRef x As Integer)

    x = x + 5

End Sub
```

Arguments are passed by reference automatically. It is not necessary to preface the argument name with the B y R e f keyword.

Passing the i N u m b e r variable by reference allows the I n c r e m e n t procedure to modify the argument's value directly as shown in Figure 6.6.

FIGURE 6.6

Passing arguments
by reference allows
the called procedure
to modify the
argument's original
value

Standard Modules

Access VBA supports two types of modules, class modules and standard modules. Class modules are directly related to an object such as a form or report. Form class modules contain event procedures for the associated controls and objects. Standard modules, however, have no association with an object. They store a collection of variables and user-defined procedures, which can be shared among your Access programs.

You can add a standard module either from the Microsoft Access window or through the Visual Basic environment as seen in Figures 6.7 and 6.8, respectively.

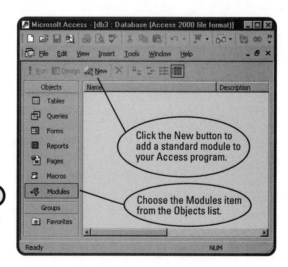

FIGURE 6.7

Adding a standard
module from the
Access window

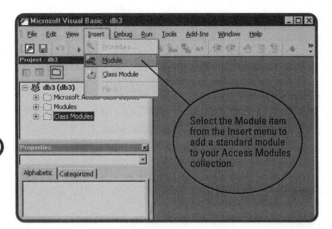

Select the Module item from the Insert menu to add a standard module to your Access Modules collection.

FIGURE 6.8

Adding a standard module from the Visual Basic environment

To see how you could utilize a standard module, I've revised the Secret Message program from Chapter 5. Specifically, I added one standard module and two public functions called `Encrypt` and `Decrypt`. Using public functions allow me to reuse the code in these functions from anywhere in my application.

To move the encrypt and decrypt functionality from event procedures to functions, I first create the function shells using the Add Procedure dialog box. Next, I add a string parameter to both functions. This argument is passed into each function when called. Moreover, the parameter called `sMessage` replaces the hard-coded text-box value from the previous version of Secret Message. All occurrences of the text-box name are replaced with the parameter name. This is truly code reuse, as I can now call these function and pass my message from anywhere in my Access application. The last required change is to assign the function's desired output to the function's name.

The enhanced Secret Message program code is shown next.

```
Option Compare Database
Option Explicit


Public Function Decrypt(sMessage As String)

    Dim sDecryptedMessage As String
    Dim sDecryptedCharacter As String
    Dim iCounter As Integer

    For iCounter = 1 To Len(sMessage)
```

```
            sDecryptedCharacter = Asc(Mid(sMessage, iCounter, 1))
            sDecryptedCharacter = Chr(sDecryptedCharacter - 1)
            sDecryptedMessage = sDecryptedMessage + sDecryptedCharacter


    Next iCounter


    ' Assign decrypted message to function name.
    Decrypt = sDecryptedMessage


End Function


Public Function Encrypt(sMessage As String)


    Dim sEncryptedMessage As String
    Dim sEncryptedCharacter As String
    Dim iCounter As Integer


    For iCounter = 1 To Len(sMessage)


        sEncryptedCharacter = Asc(Mid(sMessage, iCounter, 1))
        sEncryptedCharacter = Chr(sEncryptedCharacter + 1)
        sEncryptedMessage = sEncryptedMessage + sEncryptedCharacter


    Next iCounter


    ' Assign encrypted message to function name.
    Encrypt = sEncryptedMessage


End Function
```

With my Encrypt and Decrypt functions implemented in a standard module, I simply need to call them and pass the Value property from the text box. After the function call is executed, the function's return value is assigned back to the text box's Value property.

```
Option Compare Database
Option Explicit


Private Sub cmdDecrypt_Click()
    ' Call the Decrypt function passing the encrypted
    ' message as an argument. Assign function's result
```

```
    ' to the text box's Value property.
    If txtMessage.Value <> "" Then
        txtMessage.Value = Decrypt(txtMessage.Value)
    End If
End Sub


Private Sub cmdEncrypt_Click()
    ' Call the Encrypt function passing the plain text
    ' message as an argument. Assign function's result
    ' to the text box's Value property.
    If txtMessage.Value <> "" Then
        txtMessage.Value = Encrypt(txtMessage.Value)
    End If
End Sub
```

You should understand that the changes made to the Secret Message program are transparent to the user. In other words, the use of user-defined functions and standard modules does not change the way the user interacts with the program, nor does it change the program's functionality. The important concept is that the changes were made to provide a more modular, componentized program, which implements code reuse through user-defined procedures and modules. These changes benefit you and fellow programmers.

Advanced Form Concepts

In this section, you will investigate some new form concepts such as the DoCmd object, which performs Access functionality within VBA, and how to logically group controls onto pages using the Access Tab control.

The DoCmd Object

The DoCmd object is very popular with Access VBA programmers. It has many methods, which allow you to run Access utilities from within VBA. Utilities such as opening and closing forms, setting property values of controls, and executing Access menu items can all be performed with the DoCmd object. For example, to open and show one form from a command-button Click event, simply call the DoCmd's OpenForm method:

```
Private Sub cmdShowHelp_Click()

    DoCmd.OpenForm "frmHelp"

End Sub
```

Notice that it is not necessary to preface the form name with the class object name `Form`. In fact, doing so will cause a Visual Basic run-time error as demonstrated in Figure 6.9.

```
Private Sub cmdShowHelp_Click()

    DoCmd.OpenForm "Form_frmHelp" ' Causes a VB run-time error.

End Sub
```

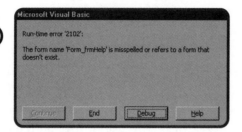

FIGURE 6.9

Prefacing a form's name with the `Form` class name causes a VB run-time error

If the form is already open, the `DoCmd` object simply sets the focus to the form.

You can use the `DoCmd`'s `Close` method to close an open form. If the form is already closed, nothing happens.

The `Close` method requires at least two parameters to close a form:

```
Private Sub cmdCloseHelp_Click()

    DoCmd.Close acForm, "frmHelp"

End Sub
```

The first parameter in the `Close` method is an object type constant (`acForm`), which tells the `DoCmd` object that you want to close a form. The next argument is the object name, which in this case is the name of a form.

It is often helpful to make your users aware of a lengthy process such as updating or searching for records in a database. Most application developers change the user's mouse pointer to an hourglass to let a user know that the system is busy working on something. Specifically, you can change a mouse pointer to an hourglass using the `DoCmd`'s `Hourglass` method as demonstrated in the next two event procedures:

```
Private Sub cmdHourGlassOff_Click()

    DoCmd.Hourglass False

End Sub

Private Sub cmdHourGlassOn_Click()

    DoCmd.Hourglass True

End Sub
```

The `Hourglass` method takes a `Boolean` value of either `True` or `False`. Sending a `True` value to the `Hourglass` method turns the mouse pointer into an hourglass. After your processing is complete, remember to set the mouse icon back to a pointer by passing `False` to the `Hourglass` method.

Another common use of the `DoCmd` object is the `RunCommand` method, which initiates an Access menu or toolbar command from within VBA. Each built-in Access toolbar and menu item has an associated VBA constant, which can be accessed from the `DoCmd`'s `RunCommand` method. For example, the following `Click` event initiates Access's print preview action for the associated form:

```
Private Sub cmdPrintPreview_Click()

    DoCmd.RunCommand acCmdPrintPreview

End Sub
```

In short, the `DoCmd` object contains many useful and powerful methods for leveraging the power of Access within VBA. Consult the Visual Basic Help system from within the VBE for more information on the `DoCmd` object and its methods.

Working with the Tab Control

The Tab control is an advanced control, which allows you to logically group controls onto separate pages or tabs on a single form. The Tab control is part of the common controls collection in Access and can be found in the Toolbox as shown in Figure 6.10.

There are many common customizations you may want to make when building a tab control on your form, as described in Table 6.1.

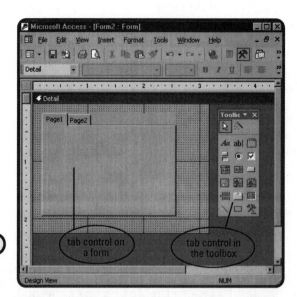

FIGURE 6.10

Finding and using
the Tab control

TABLE 6.1 COMMON TAB CONTROL CUSTOMIZATIONS

Customization	Description
Add or delete tabs	Right-click the Tab control and select Insert or Delete Page to add or delete tabs.
Change tab order	Right-click the Tab control and select Page Order to change the page tab order.
Multi-row tabs	To allow multiple rows of tabs, change the `MultiRow` property in the Tab control properties window to Yes or No.
Tabs or command buttons	Change the `Style` property in the Tab control properties window to Tabs, Buttons, or None.
Tab height	Choose a value for the `TabFixedHeight` property. A value of 0 will be high enough to accommodate its contents.
Tab width	Choose a value for the `TabFixedWidth` property. A value of 0 will be wide enough to accommodate its contents.
Font properties	Change property values for `FontName`, `FontSize`, `FontWeight`, `FontItalic`, or `FontUnderline`. Modifying these values changes font properties for all tabs in the tab control.
Determine tab caption	Enter text in the `Caption` property for each tab in the Tab control.
Add pictures	Each tab can contain a picture next to its caption. Select the ellipsis (...) button next to the Picture property in the properties window.

After customizing your tab control, simply click on a tab to add controls to that page only.

Each page in a tab control contains its own event procedures such as `Click`, `DblClick`, `MouseDown`, `MouseMove`, and `MouseUp`.

```
Private Sub Page1_Click()

    MsgBox "You clicked page 1."

End Sub
```

You may find the tab control useful when you want one form with multiple pages.

Chapter Program: Memory Overload

Seen in Figure 6.11, the Memory Overload program utilizes code reuse through standard modules and user-defined procedures to build a fun and interactive game. I used a Tab control on the Memory Overload form to separate out logical groupings of controls such as game play (Memory Overload), rules (Game Rules), and game information (About).

FIGURE 6.11

Using chapter-based concepts to build the Memory Overload game

There are two modules in the Memory Overload program, the form class module and a standard code module. Most of the code for the form class module lies within four command-button `Click` events. These `Click` events are initiated by users as they attempt to recreate the order and colors of the images shown. For brevity's sake, I've only included one of these command-button Click events. You can find the entire source code for the Memory Overload game on the accompanying CD-ROM.

```
Option Compare Database
Option Explicit


Private Sub cmdBlack_Click()


    ' Increment the number of user attempts.
    iUserAttempts = iUserAttempts + 1


    If iUserAttempts <= 5 Then


        ' Assign the color selected to the current user sequence.
        If sUserSequence1 = "" Then
            sUserSequence1 = "black"
        ElseIf sUserSequence2 = "" Then
            sUserSequence2 = "black"
        ElseIf sUserSequence3 = "" Then
            sUserSequence3 = "black"
        ElseIf sUserSequence4 = "" Then
            sUserSequence4 = "black"
        Else
            sUserSequence5 = "black"
        End If


        If iUserAttempts = 5 Then
            ' User has no more attempts left, see if they have won.
            If DidUserWin = True Then
                MsgBox "You won!"
            Else
                MsgBox "Sorry, you lost."
            End If
            ' Disable command buttons.
            EnableDisableCommandButtons "disable"
        End If


    End If


End Sub
```

```
' Remainder of color Click events can be found on the CD ROM.

Private Sub Form_Load()

    Randomize

    ' Initialize game variables and properties.
    InitializeGame

    ' Disable command buttons.
    EnableDisableCommandButtons "disable"

End Sub

Private Sub cmdQuit_Click()

    End

End Sub

Private Sub cmdStart_Click()

    ' Initialize game variables and properties.
    InitializeGame

    VisibleInvisibleBoxes "visible"

    ' Assign random color to image controls.
    StartGame

End Sub

Private Sub Form_Timer()

    iTime = iTime - 1
    lblTimer.Caption = iTime

    If lblTimer.Caption = "0" Then

        VisibleInvisibleBoxes "invisible"
```

```
    MsgBox "Time is up. Use the command buttons to " & Chr(10) & _
    "select the colors in their original sequence."

    Me.TimerInterval = 0

    ' Enable command buttons.
    EnableDisableCommandButtons "enable"

    lblTimer.Caption = "Memory Overload"

  End If

End Sub
```

I've grouped and placed many user-defined subprocedures and function procedures in my standard module. The procedures contained in the standard module represent common program functionality which is referenced many times by different procedures. I've limited the code shown in the StartGame procedure to save space, though the remainder of this procedure is fairly repetitive. Essentially, it uses random numbers and Select Case structures to assign a random color to each box. The complete program code for the standard module is provided on the accompanying CD-ROM.

```
Option Compare Database
Option Explicit

' Declare global variables.
Public iUserAttempts As Integer
Public iTime As Integer

Public sUserSequence1 As String
Public sUserSequence2 As String
Public sUserSequence3 As String
Public sUserSequence4 As String
Public sUserSequence5 As String

Public sGameSequence1 As String
Public sGameSequence2 As String
Public sGameSequence3 As String
Public sGameSequence4 As String
Public sGameSequence5 As String
```

```vb
Public Sub InitializeGame()

    ' Initialize public variables.
    iUserAttempts = 0
    iTime = 5

    sUserSequence1 = ""
    sUserSequence2 = ""
    sUserSequence3 = ""
    sUserSequence4 = ""
    sUserSequence5 = ""

    sGameSequence1 = ""
    sGameSequence2 = ""
    sGameSequence3 = ""
    sGameSequence4 = ""
    sGameSequence5 = ""

    ' Assign white back color to each box.
    Form_frmMain.box1.BackColor = vbWhite
    Form_frmMain.box2.BackColor = vbWhite
    Form_frmMain.box3.BackColor = vbWhite
    Form_frmMain.box4.BackColor = vbWhite
    Form_frmMain.box5.BackColor = vbWhite

End Sub

Public Sub StartGame()

    Dim iRandomNumber As Integer

    Form_frmMain.TimerInterval = 1000

    ' Generate a random color for each box and assign a
    ' corresponding value to each game sequence variable.
    ' Color assignments are 1=black, 2=red, 3=yellow, 4=blue

    ' Assign random color to box 1.
    iRandomNumber = Int((4 * Rnd) + 1)
    Select Case iRandomNumber
```

```
        Case 1
            Form_frmMain.box1.BackColor = vbBlack
            sGameSequence1 = "black"
        Case 2
            Form_frmMain.box1.BackColor = vbRed
            sGameSequence1 = "red"
        Case 3
            Form_frmMain.box1.BackColor = vbYellow
            sGameSequence1 = "yellow"
        Case 4
            Form_frmMain.box1.BackColor = vbBlue
            sGameSequence1 = "blue"
    End Select

    ' Remainder of procedure code for each image can be found on the CD ROM

End Sub

Public Function DidUserWin()

    ' Return a Boolean value that determines if the user
    ' has won the game. This function is only called after
    ' the game is over.

    If (sUserSequence1 = sGameSequence1) And _
       (sUserSequence2 = sGameSequence2) And _
       (sUserSequence3 = sGameSequence3) And _
       (sUserSequence4 = sGameSequence4) And _
       (sUserSequence5 = sGameSequence5) Then

        DidUserWin = True

    Else

        DidUserWin = False

    End If

End Function
```

```
Public Sub EnableDisableCommandButtons(sOption As String)

    If sOption = "enable" Then
        Form_frmMain.cmdBlack.Enabled = True
        Form_frmMain.cmdBlue.Enabled = True
        Form_frmMain.cmdRed.Enabled = True
        Form_frmMain.cmdYellow.Enabled = True
    Else
        Form_frmMain.cmdStart.SetFocus
        Form_frmMain.cmdBlack.Enabled = False
        Form_frmMain.cmdBlue.Enabled = False
        Form_frmMain.cmdRed.Enabled = False
        Form_frmMain.cmdYellow.Enabled = False
    End If

End Sub


Public Sub VisibleInvisibleBoxes(sOption As String)

    If sOption = "visible" Then

        Form_frmMain.box1.Visible = True
        Form_frmMain.box2.Visible = True
        Form_frmMain.box3.Visible = True
        Form_frmMain.box4.Visible = True
        Form_frmMain.box5.Visible = True

    Else

        Form_frmMain.box1.Visible = False
        Form_frmMain.box2.Visible = False
        Form_frmMain.box3.Visible = False
        Form_frmMain.box4.Visible = False
        Form_frmMain.box5.Visible = False

    End If

End Sub
```

Chapter Summary

This chapter discussed how to leverage the power of code reuse through standard modules and user-defined procedures. You also learned how to manage your forms with VBA through the DoCmd object and how to organize logical groups of items onto multiple pages on a single form using the Tab control.

Specifically, you learned about the following key concepts:

- Code reuse is implemented as user-defined subprocedures and function procedures.
- Function procedures return a value; subprocedures do not.
- Both subprocedures and function procedures can take one or more arguments.
- Arguments are the data passed into procedures. Parameters are the variables inside the procedure, which represent the argument data.
- Arguments can be passed by value and by reference.
- Arguments passed by value contain a copy of the original data. This prevents the procedure from modifying the original data.
- Arguments passed by reference contain a reference to the variable's memory address. The procedure can modify the original data.
- Arguments are passed by reference automatically.
- Standard modules are used to group commonly used user-defined procedures together.
- The DoCmd object has many methods for managing forms with VBA and performing other Access functionality such as running menu and toolbar commands and changing the mouse pointer to an hourglass.
- The Tab control contains customizable tabs for grouping controls onto pages.
- Each page on a tab control contains its own event procedures.

CHALLENGES

1. Build a form with two text boxes that receive numbers as input and one command button that displays a message box containing the larger of the two numbers. Specifically, write code in the `Click` event of the command button to display the result of a user-defined function called `FindLargestNumber` in a message box. Write code in the `FindLargestNumber` function to determine the larger number. Pass both numbers (text-box values) as arguments.

2. Microsoft Access comes with a Switchboard Manager, which can be found under the Tools/Database Utilities menu structure. The Switchboard Manager provides a navigational window of sorts for users to access forms, reports, and other functionalities in your Access application.

   In this challenge, create your own Switchboard manually by adding at least three forms to your Access application. Make one of the forms your Switchboard by placing command buttons on it for every other form you've added (excluding your Switchboard form). In the `Click` event of each command button, write code using the `DoCmd` object to open the appropriate form. Place a command button on all non-Switchboard forms that allows the user to navigate back to the Switchboard using the `DoCmd` object.

3. Modify the Memory Overload game to include levels of difficulty. To do so, add a fourth tab called Options to the Tab control. On this page, add an option group to allow a user to select one out of many levels of difficulty. Provide a brief description of how your difficulty is implemented—for example, more or fewer images, or possibly more or less time allowed to memorize colors and sequences.

Advanced Data Types

In this chapter I will show you how to build advanced data types, which use collections of related data using the following data structures.

- Arrays

- User-defined types

Arrays

Arrays are one of the first data structures learned by beginning programmers. Not only common as a teaching tool, arrays are frequently used by professional programmers to store like data types as one variable. In a nutshell, arrays can be thought of as a single variable, which contains many elements. Moreover, VBA arrays share many common characteristics:

- Elements in an array share the same variable name.
- Elements in an array share the same data type.
- Elements in an array are accessed with an index number.

As noted above, elements in an array share the same variable name and data type. Individual members in an array are called elements and are accessed via an index. Just like any other variable, arrays occupy memory space. To explain further, an array is a grouping of contiguous memory segments, as demonstrated in Figure 7.1.

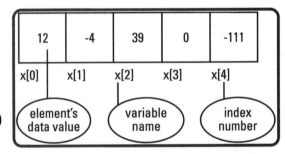

FIGURE 7.1

A five-element array

Notice that the five-element array in Figure 7.1 starts with index 0. This is an important concept to remember, so it's worth repeating in italics. *Unless otherwise stated, elements in an array begin with index number zero.* With that said, there are five array elements in Figure 7.1, starting with index 0 and ending with index 4.

TRAP

A common programming error is not accounting for the zero-based index in arrays. This programming error is often called the off-by-one error. Errors like this are generally not caught during compile time, but rather at run time when a user or your program attempts to access an element number of an array that does not exist. For example, if you have a five-element array and your program tries to access the fifth element with index number 5, a run-time program error will ensue. This is because the last index in a five-element array is index 4.

Single-Dimension Arrays

Using the keywords `Dim`, `Static`, `Public`, and `Private`, arrays are dimensioned (created) just like any other variable.

 HINT Unless `Option Base 1` is specified or dimensioned with an explicit range, arrays by default begin with a zero base index.

```
Dim myIntegerArray(5) As Integer ' Creates six Integer elements.

Dim myVariantArray(10) ' Creates eleven Variant elements.

Dim myStringArray(1 to 7) As String ' Creates seven String elements.
```

In the declarations above, the number of elements in an array is determined during array declaration using a either a number or a range of numbers surrounded by parentheses. A nice feature of VBA is its ability to initialize variables for us. Specifically, VBA initializes number-based array elements to 0 and string-based array elements to "" (empty string).

Individual elements in an array are accessed via an index:

```
lblArrayValue.Caption = myStringArray(3)
```

To further demonstrate, I can use a `For` loop to access all items in an array as shown in the next `Click` event procedure, which initializes a `String` array and then adds the array contents to a list box.

```
Private Sub cmdPopulateListBox_Click()

    ' Declare a seven element String array.
    Dim myStringArray(1 To 7) As String

    Dim x As Integer

    ' Initialize array elements.
    For x = 1 To 7

        myStringArray(x) = "The value of myStringArray is " & x

    Next x

    ' Add array contents to a list box.
    For x = 1 To 7
```

```
        lstMyListBox.AddItem myStringArray(x)


    Next x


End Sub
```

VBA provides two array-based functions called **LBound** and **UBound** for determining an array's upper and lower bounds. The **LBound** function takes an array name and returns the array's lower bound. Conversely, the **UBound** function takes an array name and returns the array's upper bound. These functions are demonstrated in the next **Click** event procedure.

```
Private Sub cmdPopulateListBox_Click()


    ' Declare an eleven element Integer array.
    Dim myIntegerArray(10) As Integer


    Dim x As Integer


    ' Initialize array elements using LBound and UBound functions
    ' to determine lower and upper bounds.
    For x = LBound(myIntegerArray) To UBound(myIntegerArray)


        myIntegerArray(x) = x


    Next x


    ' Add array contents to a list box.
    For x = LBound(myIntegerArray) To UBound(myIntegerArray)


        lstMyListBox.AddItem myIntegerArray(x)


    Next x


End Sub
```

Two-Dimensional Arrays

Two-dimensional arrays are most often thought of in terms of a table or matrix. For example, a two-dimensional array containing four rows and five columns creates 20 elements, as seen in Figure 7.2.

```
Dim x(3,4) As Integer ' Creates a two dimensional array with 20 elements.
```

	Column 0	Column 1	Column 2	Column 3	Column 4
Row 0	x(0,0)	x(0,1)	x(0,2)	x(0,3)	x(0,4)
Row 1	x(1,0)	x(1,1)	x(1,2)	x(1,3)	x(1,4)
Row 2	x(2,0)	x(2,1)	x(2,2)	x(2,3)	x(2,4)
Row 3	x(3,0)	x(3,1)	x(3,2)	x(3,3)	x(3,4)

Row Index   Column Index

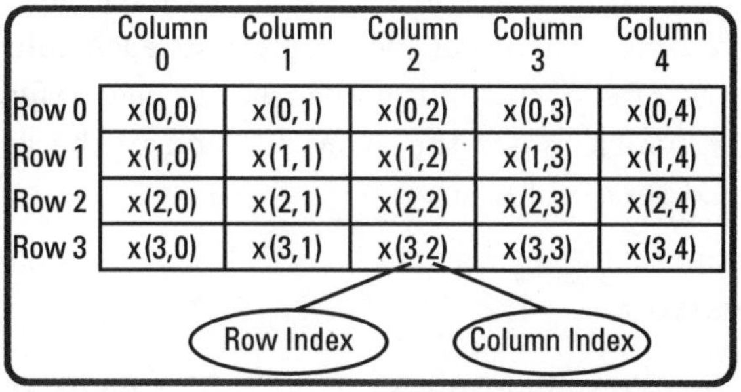

FIGURE 7.2

A two-dimensional array with 20 elements

The first index (also known as a subscript) in a two-dimensional array represents the row in a table. The second index or subscript in a two-dimensional array represents the table's column. Together, both subscripts specify a single element within an array.

A nested looping structure is required to iterate through all elements in a two-dimensional array:

```
Private Sub cmdInitializeArray_Click()

    ' Create a 20 element two dimensional array.
    Dim x(3, 4) As Integer

    Dim iRow As Integer
    Dim iColumn As Integer

    ' Loop through one row at a time.
    For iRow = 0 To 3

        ' Loop through each column in the row.
        For iColumn = 0 To 4

            ' Populate each element with the result of
            ' multiplying the row and column.
            x(iRow, iColumn) = iRow * iColumn

        Next iColumn

    Next iRow

End Sub
```

As shown in the previous `Click` event, the outer `For` loop is used to iterate through one column at a time. Each time the outer loop is executed, a nested `For` loop is executed five times. The inner loop represents each column (in this case five columns) in a row. After each column in a row has been referenced, the outer loop executes again, which moves the array position to the next row and the inner loop to the next set of columns.

Dynamic Arrays

Arrays are useful when you know ahead of time how many elements you will need. But what if you don't know how many array elements your program requires? One way to circumvent this problem is by creating a huge array that will most definitely hold any number of elements you throw at it. I don't recommend this, however. When arrays are declared (created), VBA reserves enough memory to hold data for each element. If you're guessing on the number of elements required, you're most certainly wasting memory needlessly. A more professional way of solving this dilemma is with dynamic arrays.

If you've worked in other programming languages such as C, you might be cringing about the thought of dynamic arrays implemented with linked lists. You will be relieved to learn that VBA makes building and working with dynamic arrays very easy.

When your program logic uses dynamic arrays, it can size and resize your array while the application is running. To create a dynamic array, simply eliminate any references to subscripts or indexes in the array declaration:

```
Dim iDynamicArray() As Integer ' Dynamic array.
```

Leaving the parentheses empty tells VBA that your array will be dynamic.

To set the number of elements in a dynamic array, use the `ReDim` keyword:

```
Private Sub cmdDynamicArray_Click()

    Dim iDynamicArray() As Integer
    Dim sUserResponse As String

    sUserResponse = InputBox("Enter number of elements:")

    ' Set number of array elements dynamically.
    ReDim iDynamicArray(sUserResponse)
```

```
MsgBox "Number of elements in iDynamicArray is " & _
    UBound(iDynamicArray) + 1
```

```
End Sub
```

Using the ReDim keyword above, I can set my array size after the program is running. The only problem with this approach is that each time the ReDim statement is executed, all previous element data is lost. To correct this, use the Preserve keyword in the ReDim statement as follows:

```
Private Sub cmdIncreaseDynamicArray_Click()

    Dim sUserResponse As String

    sUserResponse = InputBox("Increase number of elements by:")

    ' Set number of array elements dynamically, while
    ' preserving existing elements.
    ReDim Preserve iDynamicArray(UBound(iDynamicArray) + sUserResponse)

    MsgBox "Number of elements in iDynamicArray is now " & _
        UBound(iDynamicArray) + 1
```

```
End Sub
```

To preserve current elements while increasing a dynamic array, you must tell VBA to add elements to the array's existing upper bound. This can be accomplished using the UBound function, as demonstrated in the previous Click event procedure cmdIncreaseDynamicArray.

TRAP The Preserve keyword allows to you to change a dynamic array's upper bound only. You cannot change a dynamic array's lower bound with the Preserve keyword.

Passing Arrays as Arguments

Passing an array to a function or subprocedure is not as difficult in VBA as one might think. There are a couple of rules you must follow, however, to ensure a valid argument pass.

To pass all elements in an array to a procedure, simply pass the array name with no parentheses. Next, you must define the parameter name with an empty set of parentheses, as the next two procedures demonstrate:

```
Private Sub cmdPassEntireArray_Click()

    Dim myArray(5) As Integer

    HowMany myArray

End Sub

Private Sub HowMany(x() As Integer)

    MsgBox "There are " & UBound(x) & " elements in this array."

End Sub
```

To pass a single element in an array, it is not necessary to define the parameter name as an array. Rather, simply pass one array element as a normal variable argument:

```
Private Sub cmdPassArrayElement_Click()

    Dim myArray(5) As Integer

    CheckItOut myArray(3)

End Sub

Private Sub CheckItOut(x As Integer)

    MsgBox "The parameter's value is " & x & "."

End Sub
```

Passing arrays and elements of arrays as arguments is that easy.

User-Defined Types

User-defined types are commonly referred to as structures in other programming languages such as C. User-defined types are collections of one or more related elements, which can be of different data types. User-defined types must be declared at the module level (also known as the general declarations area) in a standard module (not a form class module). Programmers can leverage user-defined types to group like variables as one, much as a record in a database does.

Type and End Type Statements

User-defined types are created with the `Type` and `End Type` statements at the module level. More specifically, user-defined types must be declared outside of any procedure in a standard module. To demonstrate, I created a user-defined type called `EmployeeData`:

```
Type EmployeeData

    EmployeeLastName As String
    EmployeeFirstName As String
    EmployeeID As Integer
    EmployeeSalary As Currency
    EmployeeHireDate As Date

End Type
' ...is the same as
Public Type EmployeeData

    Dim EmployeeLastName As String
    Dim EmployeeFirstName As String
    Dim EmployeeID As Integer
    Dim EmployeeSalary As Currency
    Dim EmployeeHireDate As Date

End Type
```

 It is not necessary to use the `Dim` keyword when declaring variables (members) inside a user-defined type.

Note that declaring a user-defined type does not instantiate or create a variable, nor does it reserve any space in memory. The declaration of a user-defined type simply provides VBA with a blueprint when variables of your user-defined type are created.

By default user-defined types are public, though they can be declared using the keyword `Private`, which makes them available only to the current module from where they are created.

```
' Available only in the current module.
Private Type BookData
```

```
    Title As String
    ISBN As String
    Author As String
    Publisher As String
    PublishDate As Date
    Price As Currency


End Type
```

Declaring Variables of User-Defined Type

As mentioned, declaring a user-defined type does not create a variable, but rather defines a template for VBA programmers to use later. To create variables of your user-defined types, define a user-defined type in a standard module. Then, you can create variables of your type at module level.

```
Option Compare Database
Option Explicit


' Define user defined type in a standard module.
Type BookData


    Title As String
    ISBN As String
    Author As String
    Publisher As String
    PublishDate As Date
    Price As Currency


End Type


' Create variable of user defined type in a standard module (general
' declarations area).
Dim myFavoriteBook As BookData ' Declare 5 element array of BookData Type
```

Because user-defined types are public by default, you can create type variables in other modules such as form class modules:

```
Private Sub cmdEnterBookData_Click()


    Dim myCookingBook As BookData ' Declare one variable of BookData Type


End Sub
```

Managing Elements

Once a variable has been declared as a user-defined type, you can use it much like any other variable. To access elements within type variables, simply use the dot notation to assign and retrieve data, as the next program demonstrates.

```
Private Sub cmdEnterBookData_Click()

    Dim myBook As BookData ' Declare one variable of BookData Type

    myBook.Title = txtTitle.Value
    myBook.ISBN = txtISBN.Value
    myBook.Author = txtAuthor.Value
    myBook.Publisher = txtPublisher.Value
    myBook.PublishDate = txtPublishDate.Value
    myBook.Price = txtPrice.Value

    MsgBox myBook.Title & " has been entered."

End Sub
```

Sample output from the preceding program code can be seen in Figure 7.3. Note that a public user-defined type must have already been created in a standard module.

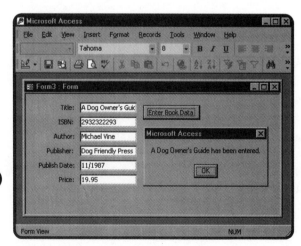

FIGURE 7.3

Accessing elements in a variable of user-defined type

Remember that user-defined types can be thought of as rows in a database table, in that both table rows and user-defined types maintain a grouping of like elements of one or more data types. So far, you have only seen how to create a single variable of user-defined type (analogous to a single row in a database). To create multiple variables of the same user-defined type (much like multiple rows in a database), simply create an array of user-defined type, as shown in the next program.

```
Option Compare Database
Option Explicit


Dim myBooks() As BookData ' Declare dynamic array of BookData Type
Dim currentIndex As Integer


Private Sub cmdAddNewBook_Click()

    ' Add one array element to the dynamic array.
    ReDim Preserve myBooks(UBound(myBooks) + 1)

    ' Clear text boxes
    txtTitle.Value = ""
    txtISBN.Value = ""
    txtAuthor.Value = ""
    txtPublisher.Value = ""
    txtPublishDate.Value = ""
    txtPrice.Value = ""


End Sub


Private Sub cmdEnterBookData_Click()

    myBooks(UBound(myBooks)).Title = txtTitle.Value
    myBooks(UBound(myBooks)).ISBN = txtISBN.Value
    myBooks(UBound(myBooks)).Author = txtAuthor.Value
    myBooks(UBound(myBooks)).Publisher = txtPublisher.Value
    myBooks(UBound(myBooks)).PublishDate = txtPublishDate.Value
    myBooks(UBound(myBooks)).Price = txtPrice.Value

    MsgBox myBooks(UBound(myBooks)).Title & " has been entered."


End Sub


Private Sub cmdNext_Click()
```

```
If currentIndex <= UBound(myBooks) Then

    If currentIndex < UBound(myBooks) Then
      ' Increment index.
      currentIndex = currentIndex + 1
    End If


    txtTitle.Value = myBooks(currentIndex).Title
    txtAuthor.Value = myBooks(currentIndex).Author
    txtISBN.Value = myBooks(currentIndex).ISBN
    txtPublisher.Value = myBooks(currentIndex).Publisher
    txtPublishDate.Value = myBooks(currentIndex).PublishDate
    txtPrice.Value = myBooks(currentIndex).Price


End If


End Sub


Private Sub cmdPrevious_Click()


If currentIndex >= 1 Then

    If currentIndex > 1 Then
      ' Decrement index.
      currentIndex = currentIndex - 1
    End If


    txtTitle.Value = myBooks(currentIndex).Title
    txtAuthor.Value = myBooks(currentIndex).Author
    txtISBN.Value = myBooks(currentIndex).ISBN
    txtPublisher.Value = myBooks(currentIndex).Publisher
    txtPublishDate.Value = myBooks(currentIndex).PublishDate
    txtPrice.Value = myBooks(currentIndex).Price


End If


End Sub


Private Sub Form_Load()
```

```
' Add one array element to the dynamic array.
ReDim myBooks(1)


currentIndex = 1
```

```
End Sub
```

As seen in Figure 7.4, I can traverse through my variable array of user-defined type using an `Integer` variable called `currentIndex`. I use this variable to maintain the current index of the array as I move next and previous through the array. Moreover, I can use dynamic array techniques to add elements of `BookData` type to my array variable.

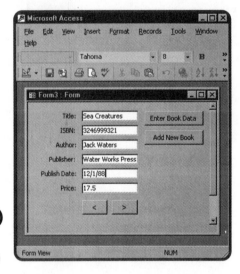

FIGURE 7.4

Managing an array of user-defined type

Chapter Program: Dice

The chapter program Dice is an easy-to-build game and fun to play. Mimicking basic poker rules, the player rolls the dice (presses a command button) and hopes for either three of a kind (worth 10 points) or, better yet, four of a kind (worth 25 points).

The game uses random number techniques to simulate a roll. To create the graphical effect of changing images, I use basic image-swapping techniques, as Figure 7.5 reveals.

During game play, the player does not see the static images of the dice, as demonstrated in Figure 7.6.

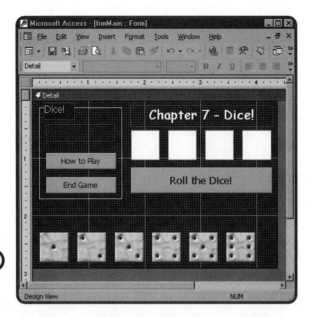

FIGURE 7.5

The Dice game during design time

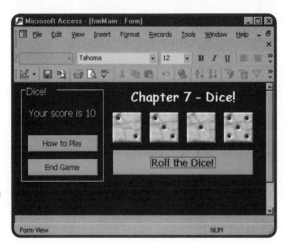

FIGURE 7.6

The Dice game during run time

Using chapter-based concepts such as arrays allows for quick and streamlined development of the Dice game. All VBA code required to build the program is shown next.

```
Option Compare Database
Option Explicit

Dim iScore As Integer
Dim iCurrentHand(3) As Integer
```

```vba
Private Sub cmdQuit_Click()
    End
End Sub

Private Sub cmdRoll_Click()

    Dim x As Integer
    Dim iRandomNumber As Integer

    ' Reset current hand.
    For x = 0 To 3
        iCurrentHand(x) = 0
    Next x

    ' Generate a random number between 1 and 6
    iRandomNumber = Int((6 * Rnd) + 1)

    ' Assign random number to die.
    Select Case iRandomNumber
        Case 1
            imgSlot1.PictureData = imgDice1.PictureData
        Case 2
            imgSlot1.PictureData = imgDice2.PictureData
        Case 3
            imgSlot1.PictureData = imgDice3.PictureData
        Case 4
            imgSlot1.PictureData = imgDice4.PictureData
        Case 5
            imgSlot1.PictureData = imgDice5.PictureData
        Case 6
            imgSlot1.PictureData = imgDice6.PictureData
    End Select

    ' Store the random number as part of the player's hand.
    iCurrentHand(0) = iRandomNumber

    ' Generate the next random number between 1 and 6
    iRandomNumber = Int((6 * Rnd) + 1)

    ' Assign random number to die.
    Select Case iRandomNumber
```

```
        Case 1
            imgSlot2.PictureData = imgDice1.PictureData
        Case 2
            imgSlot2.PictureData = imgDice2.PictureData
        Case 3
            imgSlot2.PictureData = imgDice3.PictureData
        Case 4
            imgSlot2.PictureData = imgDice4.PictureData
        Case 5
            imgSlot2.PictureData = imgDice5.PictureData
        Case 6
            imgSlot2.PictureData = imgDice6.PictureData
End Select


' Store the random number as part of the player's hand.
iCurrentHand(1) = iRandomNumber


' Generate the next random number between 1 and 6
iRandomNumber = Int((6 * Rnd) + 1)


' Assign random number to die.
Select Case iRandomNumber
        Case 1
            imgSlot3.PictureData = imgDice1.PictureData
        Case 2
            imgSlot3.PictureData = imgDice2.PictureData
        Case 3
            imgSlot3.PictureData = imgDice3.PictureData
        Case 4
            imgSlot3.PictureData = imgDice4.PictureData
        Case 5
            imgSlot3.PictureData = imgDice5.PictureData
        Case 6
            imgSlot3.PictureData = imgDice6.PictureData
End Select


' Store the random number as part of the player's hand.
iCurrentHand(2) = iRandomNumber


' Generate the next random number between 1 and 6
iRandomNumber = Int((6 * Rnd) + 1)
```

```vba
    ' Assign random number to die.
    Select Case iRandomNumber
        Case 1
            imgSlot4.PictureData = imgDice1.PictureData
        Case 2
            imgSlot4.PictureData = imgDice2.PictureData
        Case 3
            imgSlot4.PictureData = imgDice3.PictureData
        Case 4
            imgSlot4.PictureData = imgDice4.PictureData
        Case 5
            imgSlot4.PictureData = imgDice5.PictureData
        Case 6
            imgSlot4.PictureData = imgDice6.PictureData
    End Select

    ' Store the random number as part of the player's hand.
    iCurrentHand(3) = iRandomNumber

    ' Check the player's hand.
    DetermineCurrentHand iCurrentHand

End Sub

Public Sub DetermineCurrentHand(a() As Integer)

    ' Look for valid hands worth points.
    ' Valid hands with points are:
    '     3 of a kind - 10 points
    '     4 of a kind - 25 points

    Dim iCounter As Integer

    ' Holds the four possibilities of a win for each possible die.
    Dim iNumbers(1 To 6) As Integer

    ' Count the number of occurrences for each die.
    For iCounter = 0 To 3
        Select Case a(iCounter)
            Case 1
                iNumbers(1) = iNumbers(1) + 1
```

```
            Case 2
                iNumbers(2) = iNumbers(2) + 1
            Case 3
                iNumbers(3) = iNumbers(3) + 1
            Case 4
                iNumbers(4) = iNumbers(4) + 1
            Case 5
                iNumbers(5) = iNumbers(5) + 1
            Case 6
                iNumbers(6) = iNumbers(6) + 1
        End Select
    Next iCounter


    ' Determine if player has four of a kind.
    If iNumbers(1) = 4 Or iNumbers(2) = 4 Or iNumbers(3) = 4 Or _
        iNumbers(5) = 4 Or iNumbers(6) = 4 Then

        MsgBox "Four of a kind! 25 points!"
        iScore = iScore + 25
        lblScore.Caption = "Your score is " & iScore
        Exit Sub


    End If


    ' Player did not have a four of a kind, see if they
    ' have three of a kind.
    If (iNumbers(1) = 3 Or iNumbers(2) = 3 Or iNumbers(3) = 3 Or _
        iNumbers(5) = 3 Or iNumbers(6) = 3) Then

        MsgBox "Three of a kind! 10 points!"
        iScore = iScore + 10
        lblScore.Caption = "Your score is " & iScore
        Exit Sub


    End If


End Sub


Private Sub Command22_Click()
```

```
MsgBox "Dice! Version 1.0" & Chr(13) & "Developed by Michael Vine." & _
    Chr(13) & Chr(13) & _
    "Roll the dice and win points with four of a kind (25 points), " & _
    Chr(13) & _
    "and three of a kind (10 points).", , "Chapter 7 - Dice!"

End Sub


Private Sub Form_Load()
    Randomize
    lblScore.Caption = "Your score is " & iScore
End Sub
```

Chapter Summary

This chapter covered some of VBA's more advanced data types such as arrays and user-defined types. You specifically learned about the following key topics:

- Arrays are used to store groupings of like data types as one variable.
- An array is a grouping of contiguous memory segments.
- Variables in an array are called elements.
- Each variable in an array shares the same name.
- Elements in an array are accessed via an index.
- VBA arrays are zero-based by default.
- Arrays are created just like other variables using the keywords Dim, Static, Public, and Private.
- Two-dimensional arrays are often thought of in terms of a table or matrix.
- Two looping structures (one of which is nested) are required to iterate through each element in a two-dimensional array.
- Dynamic arrays can be created and managed using the ReDim and Preserve keywords.
- Arrays can be passed as arguments to procedures.
- User-defined types are commonly referred to as structures.
- User-defined types are groupings of like information, which can be of different data types.
- User-defined types are created using the Type and End Type statements.

- User-defined types must be declared in a standard module in the general declarations area (outside of any procedure).
- Variables of user-defined type are analogous to rows in a database.

CHALLENGES

1. Create a one-dimensional string-based array with five elements. Assign five different names to the array. Use a For loop to iterate through each of the array elements, displaying the names in a message box.

2. Declare a user-defined type called HomeData with elements Street-Address, City, State, SquareFootage, LotSize, and SalePrice in a standard module. Create a form with six text boxes to add values to each variable type element. In the general declarations area of the form, create a variable of HomeType to store the user entered value. Add two command buttons to the form. In one command button's Click event, store the data entered into the form into your variable type. In the other command-button Click event, display each element's value in a message box.

3. Enhance the Dice game using one or more of the following recommendations:

- Look for two of a kind and two pair in a player's hand.

- Enhance the Dice game to play against the computer. After both the player and computer have rolled the dice, determine who has the best hand.

- Enhance the Dice game to allow for holding. Use logic similar to that of poker, which allows a player to hold certain cards and draw others.

Debug Windows, Input Validation, File Processing, and Error Handling

This chapter will teach you techniques for preventing run-time errors through input validation and error handling. You will learn how to debug your VBA program code using common Visual Basic Environment debugging windows. In addition, I will show you how VBA manages file I/O. Specifically, this chapter will cover:

- **Debugging**

- **Input validation**

- **Error handling**

- **File processing**

Debugging

Sooner or later, all programmers seek the holy grail of debugging. The holy grail of debugging is different for each programming language. VBA programmers are very lucky–the Visual Basic Environment provides a multitude of debugging facilities not found in many other programming environments. As a programming instructor and lecturer, I've often encouraged my Visual Basic students to use the VBE debugging facilities not only to debug programs, but to see how the program flows, how variables are populated, and how and when statements are executed. In other, less friendly languages, programmers must take for granted the order in which their statements are executed. In VBA, you can actually step through your application one statement at a time. You can even go back in time to re-execute statements, as I'll show you a little later on.

In this section, I will show you how to leverage each of the following VBE debugging facilities:

- Break statements
- Immediate window
- Locals window
- Watch window

Stepping through Code

By now you should be fairly comfortable with the design-time and run-time environments. Moreover, you may have discovered the break mode environment. As a refresher, the next bulleted list reviews each type of Access VBA environment.

- **Design time** is the mode by which you add controls to containers (such as forms) and write code to respond to events.
- The **run-time** environment allows you to see your program running the same way a user would. During run time you can see all your Visual Basic code, but you cannot modify it.
- **Break mode** allows you to pause execution of your Visual Basic program (during run time) to view, edit, and debug your program code.

The VBE allows you to step through your program code one line at a time. Known as stepping or stepping into, this process allows you to graphically see what line of code is currently executing as well as values of current variables in scope.

> ## In the Real World
>
> Debugging can be one of the most challenging processes in software development, and unfortunately it's sometimes very costly. In a nutshell, debugging is the process by which programmers identify, find, and correct software errors. There are three common types of bugs in software. **Syntax errors** are the most common form of software bugs. They are caused by misspellings in the program code and are most commonly recognized by the language's compiler. Syntax errors are generally easy to fix. The next type of bug is called a **run-time error**. Run-time errors occur once the program is running and an illegal operation occurs. These errors generally occur because the programmer has not thought ahead of time to capture them (e.g., "file not found," "disk not ready," or "division by zero"). Run-time errors are most often easy to find and sometimes easy to fix. The last common type of bug, and the most difficult to identify and fix, is known as the **logic error**. Logic errors are not easily identified, as they don't necessarily generate an error message. Logic errors are the result of wrong logic implemented in the program code.

Using function keys or menu items, you can navigate through program code with ease. For example, once in break mode, you can press the F8 key to skip to the next line.

During break mode, it is also possible to step over a procedure without having to graphically execute the procedure's statements one at a time. Known as procedure stepping or stepping over, this process can be accomplished during break mode by pressing Shift+F8 simultaneously.

There are times when you may wish to skip ahead in program code to a predetermined procedure or statement. The VBE provides this functionality through the use of breakpoints.

Breakpoints

Breakpoints can be inserted into your Visual Basic procedures during design time or break mode, as seen in Figure 8.1.

To create a breakpoint, simply click in the left-hand margin of the code window at the program statement where you wish program execution to pause. When your program's execution reaches the statement where a breakpoint has been placed, program execution will pause. To continue execution to the next breakpoint,

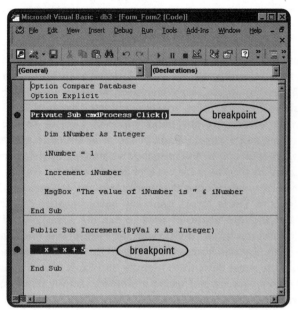

FIGURE 8.1

Inserting breakpoints
on program
statements

simply press F5. To continue program execution one statement at a time, with or without a breakpoint, press the F8 key.

Breakpoints cannot be placed on empty lines or variable declarations.

There are occasions when you will want to go back in time and re-execute a particular program statement without having to halt the entire program and rerun it.

Believe it or not, the VBE provides a facility for traveling back in time while in break mode. To do so, simply click the yellow arrow in the left-hand margin of the code window (seen in Figure 8.2) and drag it to a previous program statement.

The arrow seen in Figure 8.2 is the current line of execution. Using your mouse, you can move the arrow to other valid lines of execution.

Immediate Window

During testing or debugging, it is not always desirable to change the values of variables and properties by modifying program code. A safer way of testing program code is through the use of the Immediate window. The Immediate window can be used during design time or break mode. Most popular in break mode, the Immediate Window can be accessed by pressing CTL+G or through the View menu.

FIGURE 8.2

Going back in time to
re-execute program
statements while in
break mode

The Immediate window allows you to verify and change the values of properties
and/or variables, as shown in Figure 8.3.

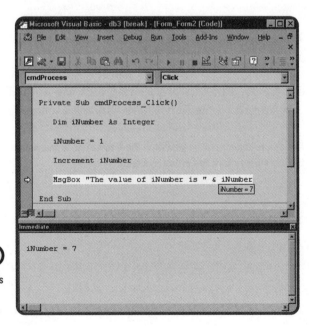

FIGURE 8.3

Changing a variable's
value through the
Immediate window

Interestingly, you can type statements that do not directly correspond with your current programs execution. For example, in Figure 8.4, I entered the expression

```
print 25 + 25
```

into the Immediate window.

FIGURE 8.4

Using the `print` keyword to display results in the Immediate window

After I press the Enter key, the Immediate window produces the result of my expression, in this case 50. The keyword `print` tells the Immediate window to print the expression's result to the Immediate window's screen.

HINT

You can re-execute a statement in the Immediate window by moving the cursor to the statement's line and pressing Enter.

Locals Window

The Locals window, a friendly companion to any VBA programmer, provides valuable information about variables and control properties in current scope.

Accessed from the View menu group, the Locals window (seen in Figure 8.5) not only supplies information on variables and properties, but also allows for the changing of control property values.

To change a property or variable's value using the Locals window, simply click the item in the Value column and type a new variable or property value.

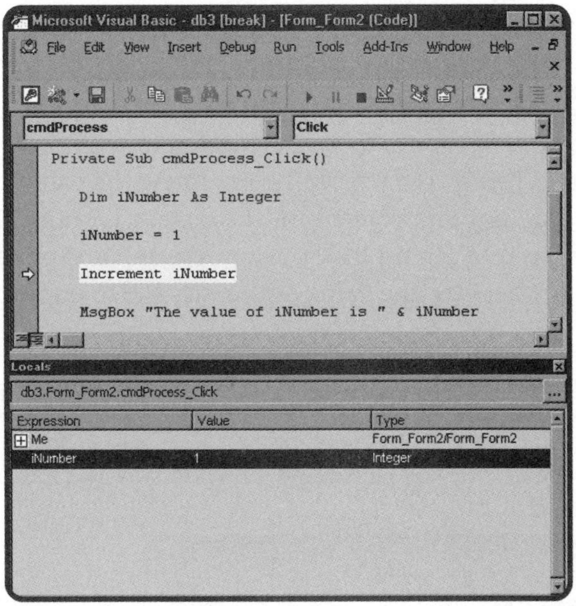

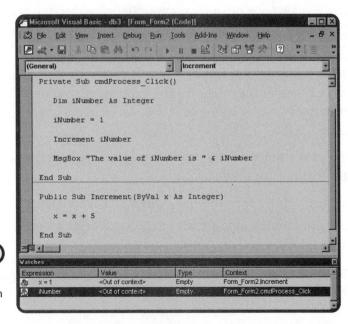

FIGURE 8.5

The Locals window
provides information
on variables and
control properties in
current scope

Watch Window

In addition to breakpoints, the Watch window can aid you in troubleshooting or
debugging program code. Accessed from the View menu item, the Watch window
can track values of expressions and break when expressions are true or have been
changed. In a nutshell, the Watch window keeps track of Watch expressions, as
seen in Figure 8.6.

FIGURE 8.6

Tracking Watch
expressions through
the Watch window

A basic Watch expression allows you to graphically track the value of an expression throughout the life of a program. Moreover, you can create a Watch expression that pauses program execution when an expression has been changed or is true.

For example, let's say that you know a bug occurs in your program because the value of a variable is being set incorrectly. You know the value of the variable is changing, but you do not know where in the code it is being changed. Using a Watch expression (seen in Figure 8.6), you can create an expression that pauses program execution whenever the value of the variable in question changes.

Though Watch Expressions can be created from within the Watch window, it is much easier to create them by right-clicking a variable or property name in the Code window and choosing "Add Watch."

Figure 8.7 shows the dialog box that appears when you add a watch.

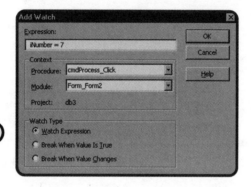

FIGURE 8.7

Adding a watch
expression

The Add Watch dialog box provides many options for creating watch expressions. Essentially, creating a watch expression with the Add Watch dialog box is broken into three parts: Expression, Context, and Watch Type.

An **expression** is a variable, property, function call, calculation, and/or combination of valid expressions. By default, the expression's value is the name of the variable or property you're trying to watch. An example of an expression can be seen in Figure 8.7.

The **Context** is the scope of the variable or property being watched. There are three values that are displayed:

- **Procedure.** Defines the procedure where the expression will be evaluated.
- **Module.** Defines the module where the variable or property resides.
- **Project.** Displays the name of the current project.

The **Watch Type** determines how Visual Basic responds to the expression:

- **Watch Expression.** Displays the Watch expression and expression value in the Watch window.
- **Break When Value Is True.** Visual Basic breaks program execution when the value of the Watch expression is true.
- **Break When Value Changes.** Visual Basic breaks program execution when the value of the expression changes.

Input Validation

Input validation is a great place to begin learning about error handling and bug fixing. This is because a good portion of program errors come from unexpected user input or responses.

For example, what do you think would happen if a user entered a letter or character as an operand into a math quiz game? A better question would be, "How do I prevent a user from entering a letter into a text box intended for numbers?" What about a game that prompts a user for a level—would testing that the input is a number be enough? Probably not, as most games have only a few levels, so you would also need to test for a range of numbers. In a nutshell, the art of input validation depends on a talented programmer with enough foresight to prevent errors before they happen. In Microsoft Access, developers can create input validation for forms, tables and queries with an input mask. In this section, I'll show you how to build input validation using VBA.

IsNumeric

Sometimes preventing input errors can be as easy as determining whether a user has entered a number or a string. There are times when you may wish the user to enter his or her name, or maybe you are looking for a number such as their age. Either way, Visual Basic provides the `IsNumeric` function for testing such scenarios.

The `IsNumeric` function takes a variable or expression as a parameter and returns a `Boolean` value of `True` if the variable or expression is a number and `False` if it is not.

```
Private Sub cmdCheckForNumber_Click()

    If IsNumeric(txtNumbersOnly.Value) = False Then

        MsgBox "Enter numbers only please."
```

```
        Else

            MsgBox "Thank you for entering numbers."

        End If

    End Sub
```

In the example above, you can see that by testing the Value of the text box with the IsNumeric function, I want the user to enter a number. If the IsNumeric function returns the Boolean value of False, I know that the user has entered something other than a number.

Conversely, you could use the IsNumeric function to check for a string value. Simply change the conditional expression in the If statement:

```
Private Sub cmdCheckForNumber_Click()

    If IsNumeric(txtStringDataOnly.Value) = True Then

        MsgBox "Enter string data only please."

    Else

        MsgBox "Thank you for entering non-numeric data."

    End If

End Sub
```

HINT Remember that VBA treats an empty text box as an empty string value (""), which is not NULL, nor is it a number.

When testing for numeric or non-numeric data, it is also common to test for an empty text box, as the next procedure demonstrates.

```
Private Sub cmdCheckForNumber_Click()

    If txtStringDataOnly.Value = "" Then

        MsgBox "Please enter a string value into the text box."
        Exit Sub
```

```
    End If

    If IsNumeric(txtStringDataOnly.Value) = True Then

        MsgBox "Enter string data only please."

    Else

        MsgBox "Thank you for entering non-numeric data."

    End If

End Sub
```

Here's an interesting question: Why do you think it's necessary for me to use the Exit Sub statement in the first If condition? It's because VBA treats an empty string ("") as non-numeric. This means that if I didn't exit the procedure in the first If condition, the user might see two error messages in both the first and second If conditions.

Checking a Range of Values

You may find at times that testing a value for a particular data type (such as number or string) is not enough to prevent input errors. Sometimes it is necessary to check for a range of values. For example, you may wish to prompt a user to enter a number from 1 to 100. Or, maybe you want a person to pick a letter from *a* to *z*.

As you will see, testing for a range of values involves a little more thought from the programmer. Specifically, your first thought should be to know, or get to know, the range or ranges needing to be tested. Are the ranges numeric or character based? Testing ranges of values with numbers or strings uses the same programming constructs, consisting of compound conditions.

Let's take the 1 to 100 example I mentioned earlier. As seen below, I continue to use the IsNumeric function as part of the overall testing for a range of numbers (1 to 100):

```
Private Sub cmdCheckRange_Click()

    If IsNumeric(txtInput.Value) = True Then

        If Val(txtInput.Value) >= 1 And Val(txtInput.Value) <= 100 Then
```

```
        MsgBox "You entered a number between 1 and 100."

    Else

        MsgBox "Your number is out of range."

    End If

  Else

    MsgBox "Please enter a number from 1 to 100."

  End If

End Sub
```

Testing for a range of letters (characters) is not much different, if you remember that all characters (letters or numbers) can be represented with ANSI values. For example, let's say I want a user to enter a letter in the range of *a* through *m* (including both upper- and lowercase letters within the range). I can still use the IsNumeric function to help me out, but I will need to perform some additional tests:

```
Private Sub cmdCheckRange_Click()

  If IsNumeric(txtInput.Value) = False Then

    If Asc(UCase(txtInput.Value)) >= 65 And _
       Asc(UCase(txtInput.Value)) <= 77 Then

        MsgBox "You entered a letter between a and m."

    Else

        MsgBox "Your letter is out of range."

    End If

  Else

        MsgBox "Please enter a letter between a and m."
```

```
    End If
```

```
End Sub
```

In the preceding code, I'm looking for the `IsNumeric` function to return a `False` value, which means the input was not a number. Next I use the `Asc` function, which converts a character to its corresponding ANSI value.

Using compound conditions, I specifically look for an ANSI range between 65 and 77, the numbers that represent the capital letters *A* and *M*. You may also notice that I used the function `UCase` in association with the `Asc` function. The `UCase` function converts lowercase letters to uppercase letters. If I didn't convert the characters to uppercase, I would have needed to check for the lowercase letters as well (ANSI numbers 97 to 109).

Error Handling

Whenever your program interacts with the outside world, you should provide some form of error handling to counteract unexpected inputs or outputs. One way of providing error handling is to write your own error-handling routines.

Error-handling routines are the traffic control for your program. Such routines can handle any kind of programming- or human-generated errors you can think of. They should not only identify the error, but try to fix it, or at least give the program or interacting human a chance to do so.

To begin error handling in a procedure, use the `On Error GoTo` statement to signify that you are going to use an error-handling routine:

```
On Error GoTo ErrorHandler
```

This statement can go anywhere in your procedure, but should be placed toward the top, generally right after any procedure-level variable declarations.

`ErrorHandler` is the name I've chosen for my error-handling routine. Error-handling routines can be given any name—`ErrorBin`, `ErrorBucket`, or whatever you like.

Once an error handler has been declared, errors generated in the procedure will be directed to the error-handling routine, as seen in the example below.

```
Public Function Verify_Input() As Boolean
```

```
On Error GoTo ErrorHandler
```

```
    'get Input from user

    Exit Function

ErrorHandler:

    MsgBox ("An error has occurred.")
    Resume


End Function
```

It is customary to execute the Exit Function or Exit Sub statements before
program execution enters the error-handling routine. Without these statements,
a procedure that executes without errors will execute the error handler as well.
That's an important note, so I'll repeat it again in italics. *Without an Exit clause, a
procedure that executes without errors will execute the error handler as well.*

The error handler begins by calling the name of the error handler followed by a
colon. Within the error handler, you write code to respond to the error. In the
example above, I simply use a message box to report that an error has occurred.

The Resume keyword takes program execution back to the statement where the
error occurred. Note that there are three possible ways for returning program
control to the procedure:

- **Resume**
- **Resume Next**
- **Resume Label**

By itself, the keyword **Resume** returns program control to where the error occurred.

The **Resume Next** statement returns program control to the statement after the statement where the error occurred.

The **Resume Label** statement returns program control to a predetermined line number, as seen below.

```
Public Function Verify_Input() As Boolean

    On Error GoTo ErrorHandler

    'get Input from user

    BeginHere:

    Exit Function

ErrorHandler:

    MsgBox ("An error has occured.")
    Resume BeginHere:

End Function
```

Generally speaking, message boxes are good ways to let a user know an error has occurred. However, knowing that an error has occurred is not enough; the user also needs to know what caused the error, and what the options for resolving the error are.

In the next section you will learn how to identify specific and custom errors using the **Err** object.

The Err Object

When a user encounters an error in your program, he or she should be provided with a clear, precise description of the problem and resolution. The **Err** object provides VBA programmers with an accessible means of finding or triggering Microsoft Windows–specific errors.

Essentially the Err (error) object maintains information about errors that occur in the current procedure. This information is stored in the form of properties. The most common of the Err's properties are:

Description. Contains a description of the current error

Number. Contains the error number of the current error (0 to 65,535)

Source. Contains the name of the object that generated the error

Table 8.1 contains a just a few of VBA's more common error numbers and descriptions. For more error numbers and descriptions, consult Microsoft Access's help system.

TABLE 8.1 COMMON ERROR NUMBERS AND DESCRIPTIONS

Error Number	Error Description
11	Division by zero
53	File not found
61	Disk full
71	Disk not ready
76	Path not found

In the next program example, I use an error handler to check for division by zero.

```
Private Sub cmdDivide_Click()

    On Error GoTo ErrorBin

    MsgBox "Result is " & Val(txtOperand1.Value) / Val(txtOperand2.Value)

    Exit Sub

ErrorBin:

    MsgBox "Error Number " & Err.Number & ", " & Err.Description

    Resume Next

End Sub
```

There may be times when an error occurs in your program that is similar to that of a given `Err` description, but does not trigger the specific `Err` number. The ability to trigger errors can be achieved through the `Err` object's `Raise` method.

The `Raise` method allows you to trigger a specific error condition, thus displaying a dialog box to the user. The `Raise` method takes a number as a parameter. For example, the following statement triggers a "Disk not ready" dialog box:

```
Err.Raise 71
```

Besides providing descriptive error messages, error handling prevents many unwanted problems for your users. In other words, error handling may prevent your program from crashing. Users expect an error for division by zero, but they don't expect division by zero to crash their applications.

The Debug Object

The Debug object is quite common with many VBA and Visual Basic programmers for troubleshooting problems by sending output to the Immediate window.

The `Debug` object has two methods, `Print` and `Assert`. The `Print` method prints the value of its parameter and sends it to the Immediate window as shown in Figure 8.8.

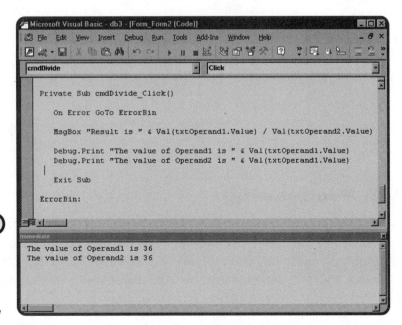

FIGURE 8.8

Using the `Print` method of the `Debug` object to send output to the Immediate window

The `Assert` method conditionally breaks program execution when the method is reached. More specifically, the `Assert` method takes an expression as a parameter, which evaluates to a `Boolean` value. If the expression evaluates to `False`, the program's execution is paused. Otherwise, program execution continues. The next procedure demonstrates the use of the `Assert` method.

```
Private Sub cmdDivide_Click()

    Dim passedTest As Boolean

    On Error GoTo ErrorBin

    If Val(txtOperand2.Value) = 0 Then
        passedTest = False
    Else
        passedTest = True
    End If

    Debug.Assert passedTest ' Conditionally pause program execution.

    MsgBox "Result is " & Val(txtOperand1.Value) / Val(txtOperand2.Value)

    Exit Sub

ErrorBin:

    MsgBox "Error Number " & Err.Number & ", " & Err.Description

    Resume Next

End Sub
```

File Processing

You're probably aware that Access is a database. But really, what is a database? The dictionary defines a database as "a collection of data arranged for easy retrieval." Certainly Microsoft Access implements this definition. But did you know that you, too, can build your own database? Well, yes, you can—and you can do it with file I/O and a little help from this chapter.

Within VBA there are many techniques for building and managing file I/O routines. File I/O (short for input/output) is the approach taken by programmers to manage data stored in files. Data files that you create can be viewed and edited through Microsoft text editors such as Notepad.

Most data files that you will work with are built upon a common foundation, much like a database. The data files you will learn about in this chapter share the following relationships and building blocks:

- **File.** A collection of data, which stores records and fields.
- **Record.** A row of related data that contains one or more fields, separated by a space, tab, or comma.
- **Field.** An attribute in a record, which is the smallest component in a data file.

An example data file is shown in Figure 8.9. The `trivia.dat` data file is used in the chapter-based program. It has five records, with each record containing three fields separated by commas (also called a comma-delimited file).

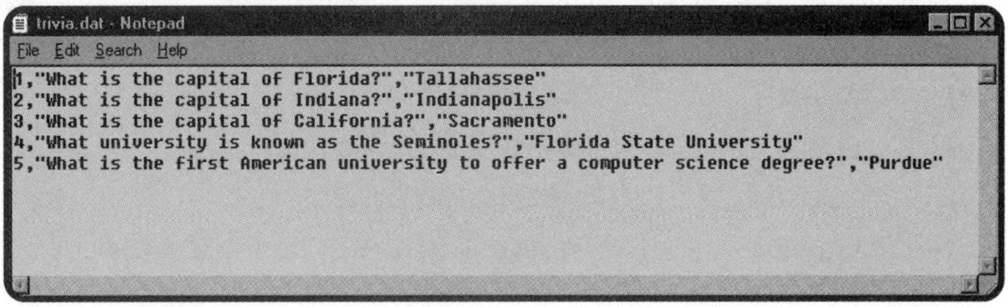

FIGURE 8.9

A sample data file

In the sections to come, I will show you how to build and manage your own data files using sequential file access.

About Sequential File Access

Data files created with sequential file access have records stored in a file one after another in sequential order. When you access data files with sequential file access, records must be read in the same order in which they were written to the file. In other words, if you wish to access the 20th record in a data file, you must first read records 1 to 19.

Sequential file access is useful and appropriate for small data files. If you find that your sequential file access program is starting to run slowly, you may wish to change file access to a relational database management system such as Microsoft Access.

Opening a Sequential Data File

The first step in creating or accessing a data file is to open it. Microsoft provides an easy-to-use facility for opening a data file through the `Open` function:

```
Open "Filename" For {Input | Output | Append} As #Filenumber [Len =
Record Length]
```

The `Open` function takes three parameters. `Filename` describes the name of the file you wish to open or create. `Input\Output\Append` is a selection list from which you pick one to use. `#Filenumber` is a number from 1 to 511 that is used for referencing the file. `Len` is an optional parameter that can control the number of characters buffered.

The sequential access modes are shown in Table 8.2.

TABLE 8.2 SEQUENTIAL ACCESS MODES

Mode	Description
Input	Used for reading records from a data file
Output	Writes records to a data file
Append	Writes or appends records to the end of a data file

I use the `Open` method below to create a new file for output called quiz.dat.

```
Open "quiz.dat" For Output As #1
```

TRICK The `Filename` attribute can contain paths in addition to file names. For example, if you wanted to create employee records in a file named `employee.dat` on a floppy diskette, you could use the following syntax:

```
Open "a:\employee.dat" For Output As #1
```

The result of the `Open` function varies depending on the initial action chosen. If the `Input` parameter is chosen, the `Open` function searches for the file and creates a buffer in memory. If the file is not found, VBA generates an error.

HINT A buffer is an area of storage where data is temporarily stored.

If the file specified is not found, a new file is created using the Filename parameter as the file name.

Note that the Output mode always overwrites an existing file.

Once a data file has been successfully opened, you can then read from it, write to it, and close it.

Reading Sequential Data from a File

If you want to read records from a data file, you must use the Input parameter with the Open function:

```
Open "quiz.dat" For Input As #1
```

Once the file is opened for input, use the Input function to retrieve fields from the file:

```
Input #Filenumber, Fields
```

The Input function takes two parameters, the #Filenumber and a list of fields. For example, if you wanted to read the first record in a data file called quiz.dat (assuming quiz.dat contains three fields for each record) you could use the following program statements:

```
Dim liQuestionNumber as Integer
Dim lsQuestion as String
Dim lsAnswer as String
Open "quiz.dat" For Input As #1
Input #1, liQuestionNumber, lsQuestion, lsAnswer
```

Notice that I pass three variables as the field list to the Input function. These variables will hold the contents of the first record found.

By now, you may be thinking, "So far, so good, but how do I read all records in a data file?" The answer involves something new and something old. First, you will have to use a loop to search through the data file. Second, your loop's condition should use the EOF function.

The EOF (End of File) function tests for the end of the data file. It takes a file number as a parameter and returns a True Boolean value if the end of the file is found or False if the end of file has not been reached.

To test for the end of file, the EOF function looks for an EOF marker that is placed at the end of a file by the Close function. I'll discuss closing data files later in the chapter.

```
Dim liQuestionNumber as Integer
Dim lsQuestion as String
Dim lsAnswer as String
Open "quiz.dat" For Input As #1
Do Until EOF(1)
   Input #1, liQuestionNumber, lsQuestion, lsAnswer
   List1.AddItem "Question number:   " & liQuestionNumber & lsQuestion
Loop
```

The above loop iterates until the EOF function returns a True value. Inside the loop, each record is read one at a time. After a record is read, the Print method of a picture box control is used to output two of the fields (liQuestionNumber and lsQuestion) for display.

Writing Sequential Data to a File

In order to write data to a sequential file, you will want to use either the Output mode, which creates a new file for writing, or the Append mode, which writes records to the end of a data file:

```
Open "quiz1.dat" For Output As #1

Open "quiz.dat" For Append As #1
```

After opening a file for writing, you can use the Write function to write records:

```
Write #Filenumber, Fields
```

The Write function takes two parameters, #Filenumber and a list of fields. The #Filenumber denotes the file number used in the Open function and the Fields parameter is a list of strings, numbers, variables, and/or properties that you want to use as fields.

For example, if I wanted to create a data file and write quiz records to it, I could use the following syntax:

```
Open "quiz.dat" For Output As #1
Write #1, 1, "Is Visual Basic an Event Driven language?", "Yes"
```

I could also use variable names for my fields list:

```
Write #1, liQuestionNumber, lsQuestion, lsAnswer
```

Either way, VBA outputs numbers as numbers and strings as strings surrounded with quotation marks.

Closing Data Files

As you may have guessed, closing a data file is an important part of file processing. Specifically, closing a data file performs the following operations:

- Writes the EOF marker
- When using the Output or Append mode, writes records to the physical file in the sequential order in which they were created
- Releases the file number and buffer for memory conservation

To close a data file, simply use the Close function after all file processing has completed.

```
Close #FileNumber
```

The Close function takes the file number as its only parameter. For example, to close the file quiz.dat after writing one record, I could use the Close function:

```
Open "quiz.dat" For Output As #1
Write #1, 1, "Is Visual Basic an Event Driven language?", "Yes"
Close 1
```

If the Close function is used without any parameters, it closes all open sequential data files.

Error Trapping for File Access

Error trapping is almost always a must when dealing with file I/O. Why? Well, have you ever tried to access your floppy diskette from Windows Explorer, only to get an error message because there is no floppy diskette in the drive? Or, what if the diskette is in the drive, but the file is not found—or better yet, the file is there, but it's corrupt?

As you will see, there are all types of potential errors when dealing with data files and file input/output. Your best bet is to plan ahead and create error-trapping or error-handling routines. In fact, it would be safe to promote error trapping in any procedure that opens, writes, reads, appends, or closes files.

An adequate facility for capturing file I/O errors is to use VBA's Err object. The Err object contains preexisting codes for various known errors such as "file not found," "disk not ready," and many more that can be used to your advantage.

Here's an error-handling routine for a quiz game that uses the Err object to check for specific errors when the game attempts to open a file in the form Load event:

```
Private Sub Form_Load()

    On Error GoTo ErrorHandler:
```

Like any other error-handling routine, I start my procedure off by declaring an error-handling label with an `On Error GoTo` statement.

```
    BeginHere:
```

You can actually put unique labels throughout your code as I've done above with the `BeginHere:` label. Labels can serve useful purposes so long as you keep their existence minimal and easy to follow. As you will see later in the code, I choose the `BeginHere:` label as a good starting point in this procedure.

```
    Open "quiz.dat" For Input As #1
    Exit Sub
```

After opening the sequential data file, the procedure is exited, providing no errors have occurred.

```
ErrorHandler:
    Dim liResponse As Integer
```

But, if an error does occur in opening the file, my guess is that it will be one of the following error conditions (error codes). You can see below that I'm using the `Select Case` structure to check for specific `Err` object codes. If an error code is found, the user is prompted with an opportunity to fix the problem. If the user decides to retry the operation, the program resumes control back to the `BeginHere:` label.

```
    Select Case Err.Number

        Case 53

            'File not found
            liResponse = MsgBox("File not found!", vbRetryCancel, "Error!")

            If liResponse = 4 Then 'retry
                Resume BeginHere:
            Else
                cmdQuit_Click
            End If

        Case 71
```

```
            'Disk not ready
            liResponse = MsgBox("Disk not ready!", vbRetryCancel, "Error!")

            If liResponse = 4 Then 'retry
              Resume BeginHere:
            Else
              cmdQuit_Click
            End If

        Case 76

            liResponse = MsgBox("Path not found!", vbRetryCancel, "Error!")

            If liResponse = 4 Then 'retry
              Resume BeginHere:
            Else
              cmdQuit_Click
            End If

        Case Else

            MsgBox "Error in program!", , "Error"
            cmdQuit_Click

    End Select

End Sub
```

Chapter Program: Trivial Challenge

The Trivial Challenge program, shown in Figure 8.10, is a fun game that uses chapter-based techniques and concepts. Specifically, I used data files, sequential file access, and error handling to build the Trivial Challenge game. The program code for the game is broken into two separate code modules. The standard module contains a public user-defined type, which will be used to store and manage quiz components such as question numbers, the question, the answer, and the user's response. Most of the program code is in the form class module where the game's logic is managed.

All of the code required to build the Trivial Challenge game is revealed next.

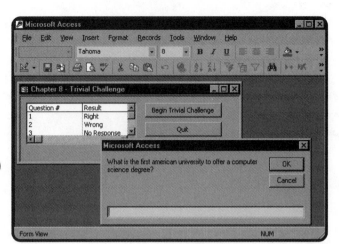

FIGURE 8.10

Using chapter-based
concepts to build the
Trivial Challenge
program

The following is the module code to define a public user-defined type:

```
Option Compare Database
Option Explicit


Public Type Trivia

    QuestionNumber As Integer
    Question As String
    Answer As String
    UserReponse As String


End Type
```

Shown next is the form class module code for building the remainder of the Trivial Challenge game:

```
Option Compare Database
Option Explicit


' Declare dynamic array of Triva type.
Dim myTrivia() As Trivia


Private Sub cmdBegin_Click()

    Dim x As Integer

    ClearListBox
```

```
    ' Prompt the user with trivia questions.
    For x = 1 To UBound(myTrivia)

        myTrivia(x).UserReponse = InputBox(myTrivia(x).Question)

        ' Determine if the user's response was right, wrong or empty.
        If LCase(myTrivia(x).UserReponse) = LCase(myTrivia(x).Answer) Then

            lstResults.AddItem myTrivia(x).QuestionNumber & ";" & "Right"

        Else

            If myTrivia(x).UserReponse = "" Then
                ' User did not respond (pressed Cancel on input box).
                lstResults.AddItem myTrivia(x).QuestionNumber & _
                    ";" & "No Response"
            Else
                lstResults.AddItem myTrivia(x).QuestionNumber & ";" & "Wrong"
            End If

        End If

    Next x

End Sub

Private Sub Form_Load()

    ' Create initial element in dynamic array.
    ReDim myTrivia(1)

    ' Add header to each column in the list box if one
    ' hasn't already been added.
    If lstResults.ListCount = 0 Then
        lstResults.AddItem "Question #;Result"
    End If

    ' Load trivia questions into memory.
    LoadTrivia
```

```vba
End Sub


Public Sub ClearListBox()

   Dim x As Integer

   ' Clear list box
   For x = 1 To (lstResults.ListCount - 1)
       lstResults.RemoveItem lstResults.ListCount - 1
   Next x

End Sub

Public Sub LoadTrivia()

   On Error GoTo ErrorHandler

   ' Open file for sequential input using the application's current path.
   Open Application.CurrentProject.Path & "\" & _
        "trivia.dat" For Input As #1
   ' Read all records until end of file is reached.
   ' Store each question and answer in a user defined type.
   Do While EOF(1) = False

      ' Read trivia data into variables.
      Input #1, myTrivia(UBound(myTrivia)).QuestionNumber, _
      myTrivia(UBound(myTrivia)).Question, _
          myTrivia(UBound(myTrivia)).Answer

      ' Print debug data to the immediate window.
      'Debug.Print myTrivia(UBound(myTrivia)).QuestionNumber, _
      myTrivia(UBound(myTrivia)).Question, _
          myTrivia(UBound(myTrivia)).Answer

      If EOF(1) = False Then

         ' Increment dynamic array for each next trivia question.
         ReDim Preserve myTrivia(UBound(myTrivia) + 1)

      End If
```

```
    Loop

    ' Close the sequential file.
    Close #1

    Exit Sub

ErrorHandler:

        MsgBox "Error number " & Err.Number & Chr(13) & _
                Err.Description

End Sub

Private Sub lstResults_Click()

    ' Display the selected question back to the user.
    If lstResults.ListIndex = -1 Then
        Exit Sub
    End If

    MsgBox myTrivia(lstResults.ListIndex + 1).Question

End Sub
```

Chapter Summary

This chapter discussed debugging, input validation, error handling, and file processing with sequential file access. Specifically, this chapter covered the following key concepts:

- Debugging is the process by which programmers identify, find, and correct software errors.

- Software bugs are generally grouped into one of three categories: syntax errors, run-time errors, and logic errors.

- The Visual Basic Environment includes many debugging features such as breakpoints, the Immediate window, the Locals window, and the Watch window.

- Breakpoints are used to pause program execution.

- The Immediate window can be used to ascertain variable and property values.

- Variable and property values can be altered in the Immediate window.
- Variable and property values within scope can be viewed and managed in the Locals window.
- Watch expressions can be created and managed in the Watch window.
- Input validation generally involves checking for numeric or non-numeric data entered by the user. Moreover, programmers can use input validation to check for a range of numbers or characters.
- VBA programmers often use the `Err` and `Debug` objects to aid in debugging and error handling.
- The `Err` object contains properties for discerning what the current error number and error description are.
- The `Debug` object contains methods commonly used in conjunction with the Immediate window for pausing program execution and displaying program output.
- VBA error-handling routines are initiated using the `On Error GoTo` statement.
- There are three possible ways to return program control to the procedure using the keywords `Resume`, `Resume Next`, and `Resume Label`.
- Data files contain records and fields.
- In VBA, file processing can be achieved with sequential file access using the `Open`, `Write`, `Input`, and `Close` methods.
- Error handling should always be incorporated into file-processing routines.

CHALLENGES

1. Build a form with one text box and one command button. The text box should receive the user's name. In the `Click` event of the command button, write code to validate that the user has entered non-numeric data. Test your program by entering numeric data into the text box.

2. Build a form with one text box and one command button. The text box should receive a number between 1 and 10. In the `Click` event of the command button, write code to validate that the data entered is a number and that it is in the range of 1 to 10.

3. Create a data file called `friends.dat`. Insert a few records into the `friends.dat` file. The record layout should look similar to

   "111-222-3333", "Michael", "Massey"

   where the first field is a phone number, the second field is a friend's first name, and the last field is a friend's last name.

4. Create a form that allows a user to view all records in the `friends.dat` file. Populate a list box on the form with the phone numbers and names of friends. Remember to use error handling when opening the `friends.dat` file.

5. Create a form that allows a user to enter more friends into the `friends.dat` file. Retrieve friend information from the user with text boxes on the form. Remember to use the `Append` option when opening the `friends.dat` file and use error handling accordingly.

CHAPTER

Introduction to Database Languages

In this chapter I will show you how to use common database languages such as SQL for querying and managing databases without the help of Access wizards. If you're new to database languages such as SQL, consider this chapter a prerequisite for Chapters 10 and 11. Even if you've worked with SQL before, you may find this chapter a refreshing account of SQL syntax and common functionality.

Specifically, you will learn about the following database languages:

- Structured query language

- Data definition language

Introduction

Most databases, including Microsoft Access, incorporate one or more data languages for querying information and managing database entities. The most common of these data languages are **data manipulation languages** such as **SQL (structured query language)** and **data definition languages**. Most of these database languages follow a standard convention used by many database vendors, including Microsoft, Oracle, and IBM. Each manufacturer, however, incorporates its own proprietary language-based functions and syntax. Database languages for Microsoft Access are no exception. The moral of this story is to beware of database-specific syntax when working with SQL and data definition languages from one relational database to another.

To work through the examples in this chapter, I will use Microsoft's sample database called `Northwind.mdb`. The Northwind sample database comes with each installation of Microsoft Access.

Shown in Figure 9.1 is Microsoft's Northwind database.

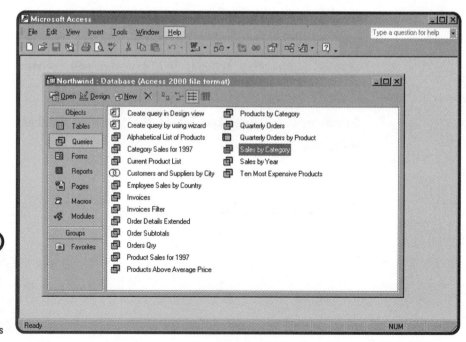

FIGURE 9.1

Looking at the Queries window of the Northwind database reveals many Access queries

After opening the Queries window in the Northwind database, you can see that the Access developers at Microsoft have created many queries. Figure 9.2 looks at a specific query detail in the Northwind database called *Alphabetical List of Products*.

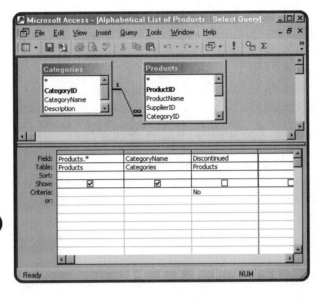

FIGURE 9.2

Detail view for a Microsoft Access query

Building queries in Microsoft Access is much like the experience of building tables and forms in Access. Essentially, Microsoft provides wizards and graphical interfaces for building everything, including queries as seen in Figure 9.2. But, what's really under the hood of Microsoft's query-building interface? Figure 9.3 reveals SQL as the underlying engine behind Access queries.

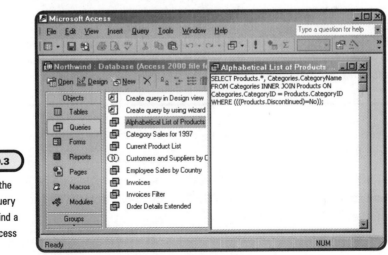

FIGURE 9.3

Uncovering the structured query language behind a Microsoft Access query

To access the SQL window, select a query and then press the Design button. Once the query is seen in Design mode, select the SQL View item from the View menu. You can also access the SQL View menu item when creating a new query.

 HINT Note that the SQL View menu item is only available when a query is in Design mode.

Working with an existing database such as Microsoft's Northwind will prove to be an excellent opportunity to learn and practice SQL queries.

Structured Query Language

SQL (structured query language) is a data manipulation language used for querying relational databases such as Microsoft Access. It uses natural-language syntax for querying, computing, sorting, grouping, joining, inserting, updating, and deleting data in a relational database.

SQL itself is not considered to be a full-fledged programming language like VBA. In this author's mind, a real programming language must at minimum contain facilities for creating variables, as well as structures for conditional logic branches and iteration through loops. Regardless, SQL is a powerful language for asking the database questions also known as queries.

> ### IN THE REAL WORLD
>
> Pronounced sequel, SQL was originally developed by IBM researchers in the 1970s. It has become the de facto database manipulation language for many database vendors. For database users, mastering SQL has become a highly sought-after skill set in the information technology world. Most persons who master the SQL language have no trouble finding well-paid positions.

To provide readability in the sections to come, I will use a new syntax nomenclature for SQL.

- All SQL commands and reserved language keywords will be in uppercase. For example, SELECT, FROM, WHERE, and AND are all SQL commands and reserved keywords.

- Even though Microsoft Access is not a case-sensitive application, table and column names used in SQL statements will use the same case as defined in the database. For example, a column defined as `EmployeeId` will be spelled as `EmployeeId` in the SQL query.

- Table and column names that contain spaces must be enclosed in brackets. For example, the column name `Customer Number` must be contained in SQL as [Customer Number]. Failure to do so will cause errors or undesired results when executing your queries.

- A query can be written on a single line. For readability, I break SQL statements into logical blocks on multiple lines. For example, instead of

```
SELECT [Order Details].OrderID, Sum(CCur([UnitPrice]*[Quantity]*(1-
[Discount])/100)*100) AS Subtotal FROM [Order Details] GROUP BY
[Order Details].OrderID;
```

I will provide readability by logically breaking the query into multiple lines like

```
SELECT [Order Details].OrderID,
       Sum(CCur([UnitPrice]*[Quantity]*(1-[Discount])/100)*100)
    AS Subtotal
  FROM [Order Details]
GROUP BY [Order Details].OrderID;
```

Simple Select Statements

To retrieve information from a relational database, SQL provides the simple `SELECT` statement. A simple `SELECT` statement takes the following form:

```
SELECT ColumnName, ColumnName
  FROM TableName;
```

The `SELECT` clause is used to identify one or more column names in a database table or tables. After identifying the columns in the `SELECT` clause, you must tell the database which table or tables the columns live in using the `FROM` clause. It is customary in SQL to append a semicolon (;) after the SQL statement to indicate the statement's ending point.

To retrieve all rows in a database table, the wildcard character (*) can be used:

```
SELECT *
  FROM Employees;
```

You can execute SQL queries in Access in one of a couple of ways. You can simply save your query, return to the Queries window, and double-click your newly saved query. Or, leaving your SQL View window open, select the Datasheet View item from the View menu. Another way to execute your SQL queries is to select the Run item from the Query menu or click the red exclamation mark (!) on the Toolbar. Either way, the results from the preceding query running against the Northwind database are shown in Figure 9.4.

Employee ID	Last Name	First Name	Title	Title Of C	Birth Date	Hire Date	Address
1	Davolio	Nancy	Sales Representative	Ms.	08-Dec-1968	01-May-1992	507 - 20th Ave. E.
2	Fuller	Andrew	Vice President, Sales	Dr.	19-Feb-1952	14-Aug-1992	908 W. Capital Way
3	Leverling	Janet	Sales Representative	Ms.	30-Aug-1963	01-Apr-1992	722 Moss Bay Blvd.
4	Peacock	Margaret	Sales Representative	Mrs.	19-Sep-1958	03-May-1993	4110 Old Redmond Rd.
5	Buchanan	Steven	Sales Manager	Mr.	04-Mar-1955	17-Oct-1993	14 Garrett Hill
6	Suyama	Michael	Sales Representative	Mr.	02-Jul-1963	17-Oct-1993	Coventry House
7	King	Robert	Sales Representative	Mr.	29-May-1960	02-Jan-1994	Edgeham Hollow
8	Callahan	Laura	Inside Sales Coordinator	Ms.	09-Jan-1958	05-Mar-1994	4726 - 11th Ave. N.E.
9	Dodsworth	Anne	Sales Representative	Ms.	02-Jul-1969	15-Nov-1994	7 Houndstooth Rd.

FIGURE 9.4

Viewing the results of a simple query

The Datasheet window shown in Figure 9.4 displays the result set returned from the SQL query.

HINT

A result set is a common phrase used to describe the result or records returned by a SQL query.

Sometimes it is not necessary to retrieve all columns in a query. To streamline your query, supply specific column names separated by commas in the `SELECT` clause:

```
SELECT LastName, FirstName, Title
    FROM Employees;
```

In the query above, I ask the database to retrieve only the last names, first names, and titles of each employee record. Output is shown in Figure 9.5.

TRAP

Microsoft Access allows users to create table and column names with spaces. Use brackets ([ ]) to surround table and column names with spaces in SQL queries. Failure to do so can cause errors when running your queries.

You can change the order in which the result set displays columns by changing the column order in your SQL queries:

```
SELECT Title, FirstName, LastName
    FROM Employees;
```

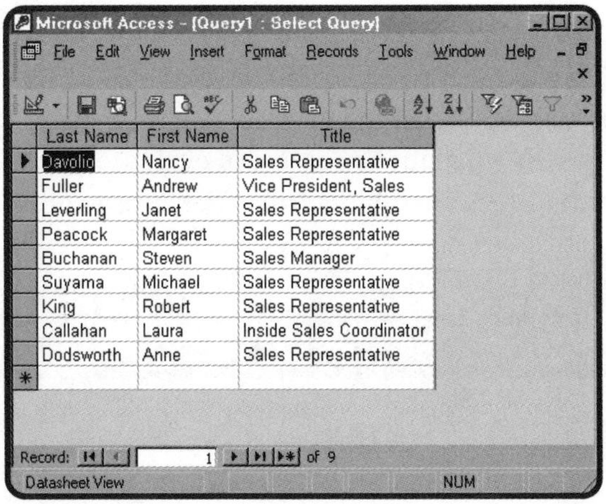

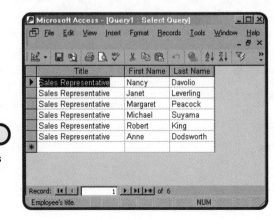

FIGURE 9.5

Specifying individual column names in a SQL query

Changing the order of column names in a SQL query does not alter the data returned in a result set, but rather its column display order.

Conditions

SQL queries allow basic conditional logic for refining the result set returned by the query. Conditions in SQL are built using the WHERE clause:

```
SELECT Title, FirstName, LastName
  FROM Employees;
 WHERE Title = ' Sales Representative';
```

In the query above, I use a condition in the WHERE clause to eliminate rows returned by the query where the employee's title equals Sales Representative. Output from this query is seen in Figure 9.6.

FIGURE 9.6

Using conditions in the WHERE clause to refine the result set

Note that textual data such as 'Sales Representative' in the WHERE clause's expression must always be enclosed by single quotes.

SQL conditions work much like the conditions you've already learned about in Access VBA, in that the WHERE clause's condition evaluates to either true or false. You can use the operators seen in Table 9.1 in SQL expressions.

TABLE 9.1 CONDITIONAL OPERATORS USED IN SQL EXPRESSIONS

Operator	Description
=	Equals
<>	Not equal
>	Greater than
<	Less than
>=	Greater than or equal to
<=	Less than or equal to

To demonstrate conditional operators, the next query returns the rows in the Products table where the value for units in stock is less than or equal to 5. Output is seen in Figure 9.7.

```
SELECT  *
  FROM Products
 WHERE UnitsInStock <= 5;
```

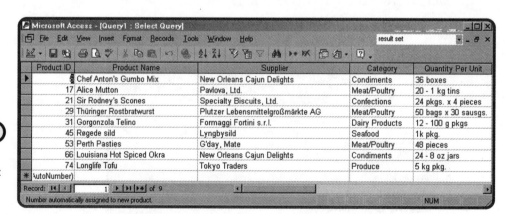

FIGURE 9.7

Refining the products result set with conditional operators

Note that it is unnecessary and in fact prohibited to surround numeric data with single quotes.

SQL queries also can contain compound conditions using the keywords AND, OR, and NOT. The next two SQL queries demonstrate the use of compound conditions in the WHERE clause.

```
SELECT   *
  FROM Products
WHERE UnitsInStock < 5 AND UnitPrice > 10;
```

```
SELECT   *
  FROM Products
WHERE NOT (UnitsInStock = 0);
```

Before moving on to the next section on SQL, I'd like share with you a paradigm shift. Believe it or not, most SQL programmers are the translators for their companies' information needs. To better understand this, think of SQL programmers as the intermediaries between business people and the unwieldy database. The business person comes in to your office and says: "I'm concerned about low inventories. Could you tell me what products we have in stock with unit quantities less than or equal to 5?" As the SQL programmer, you smile and say: "Sure, give me a minute." After digesting what your colleague said, you translate the inquiry into a question the database understands—in other words, a SQL query such as the following:

```
SELECT   *
  FROM Products
WHERE UnitsInStock <= 5;
```

Within seconds, your query executes and you print out the results for your amazed and thankful colleague. You're the superstar, the genius, the miracle worker. But most of all, you're the translator.

Computed Fields

Computed fields do not exist in the database as columns. Instead, computed fields are generated using calculations on columns that do exist in the database. Simple calculations such as addition, subtraction, multiplication, and division can be used to create computed fields.

When creating computed fields in SQL, the AS clause is used to assign a name to the computed field. The next SQL statement uses a computed field to calculate subtotals based on two columns (unit price and quantity) in the Order Details table. Output is seen in Figure 9.8.

```
SELECT OrderID, (UnitPrice * Quantity) AS SubTotals
  FROM [Order Details];
```

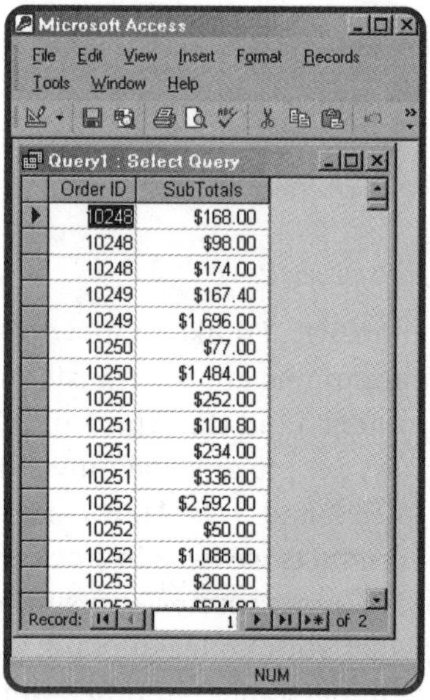

FIGURE 9.8

Using SQL to build computed fields

Note the presence of the SubTotals column name in Figure 9.8. The Sub-Totals field does not exist in the Order Details table. Rather, the SubTotals field is created in the SQL statement using the AS clause to assign a name to an expression. Though parentheses are not required, I use them in my computed field's expression to provide readability and order of operations if necessary.

Built-In Functions

Just as VBA incorporates many intrinsic functions such as Val, Str, UCase, and Len, SQL provides many built-in functions (also called aggregate functions) for determining information on your result sets. The SQL functions you will learn about in this section are:

- AVG
- COUNT

- FIRST, LAST
- MIN, MAX
- SUM
- DISTINCT

The **AVG** function takes an expression such as a column name for a parameter and returns the mean value in a column or other expression.

```
SELECT AVG(UnitPrice)
    FROM Products;
```

The preceding SQL statement returns a single value, which is the mean value of the UnitPrice column in the Products table. Output is seen in Figure 9.9.

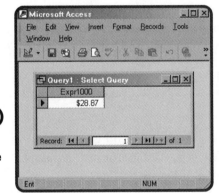

FIGURE 9.9

Using the AVG function to calculate the mean value of a column

Notice in Figure 9.9 that the column heading gives no clue as to the meaning of the SQL statement's return value. To correct this, simply use the AS clause:

```
SELECT AVG(UnitPrice) AS [Average Unit Price]
    FROM Products;
```

The **COUNT** function is a very useful function for determining how many records are returned by a query. For example, the following SQL query uses the COUNT function to determine how many customer records are in the Customers table:

```
SELECT COUNT(*) AS [Number of Customers]
    FROM Customers;
```

Figure 9.10 reveals the output from the COUNT function in the preceding SQL statement. Note that it's possible to supply a column name in the COUNT function, but the wildcard character (*) performs a faster calculation on the number of records found in a table.

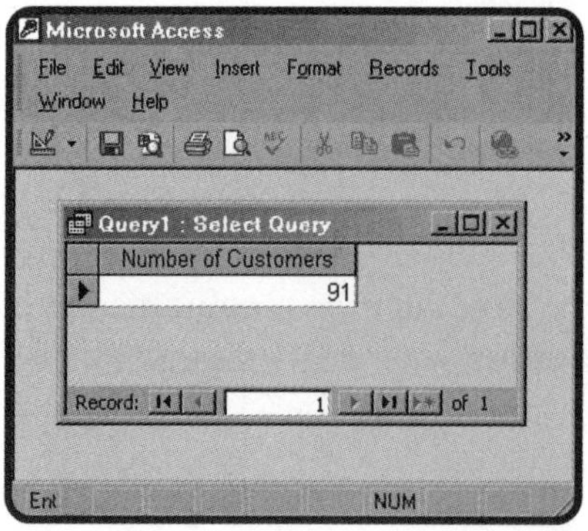

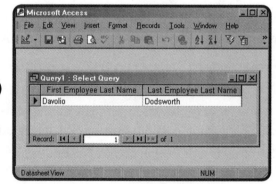

FIGURE 9.10

Displaying the result of a COUNT function

The **FIRST** and **LAST** functions return the first and last records in a result set, respectively. Because records are not necessarily stored in alphanumeric order, the FIRST and LAST functions may produce seemingly unexpected results. The results, however, are accurate, as these functions report the first and last expressions in a result set as stored in a database and returned by the SQL query.

```
SELECT FIRST(LastName) AS [First Employee Last Name],
            LAST(LastName) AS [Last Employee Last Name]
  FROM Employees;
```

The preceding SQL statement uses the **FIRST** and **LAST** functions to retrieve the first and last names (specifically the last name) of employee records in the **Employees** table. Output is seen in Figure 9.11.

FIGURE 9.11

Using the FIRST and LAST functions to retrieve the first and last values of a result set

To determine the minimum and maximum values of an expression in SQL, use the **MIN** and **MAX** functions, respectively. Like other SQL functions, the **MIN** and **MAX** functions take an expression and return a value. The next SQL statement uses these two functions to determine the minimum and maximum unit prices found in the **Products** table. Output is seen in Figure 9.12.

```
SELECT MIN(UnitPrice) AS [Minimum Unit Price],
             MAX(UnitPrice) AS [Maximum Unit Price]
   FROM Products;
```

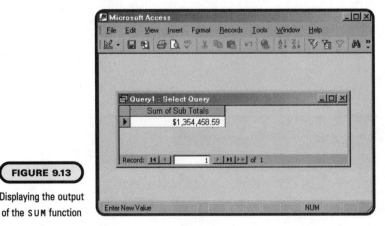

FIGURE 9.12

Retrieving the
minimum and
maximum values
from an expression
using the MIN and
MAX functions

The **SUM** function takes an expression as argument and returns the sum of values. The **SUM** function is used in the next SQL statement, which takes a computed field as an argument to derive the sum of subtotals in the Order Details table.

```
SELECT SUM(UnitPrice * Quantity) AS [Sum of Sub Totals]
   FROM [Order Details];
```

Output from the SQL statement using the **SUM** function is seen in Figure 9.13.

FIGURE 9.13

Displaying the output
of the SUM function

The last built-in function for this section is the **DISTINCT** function, which returns a distinct set of values for an expression. To demonstrate, if I wanted to know what countries the suppliers in the Northwind database were from, I'd need to sift through every record in the Suppliers table and count each distinct country name. Or, I could use the DISTINCT function to return a distinct value for each country in the Country column:

```
SELECT DISTINCT(Country)
    FROM Suppliers;
```

Sorting

You may recall from the discussions surrounding the FIRST and LAST functions that data stored in a database is not stored in any relevant order including alphanumeric. Most often, data is stored in the order in which it was entered into the database, but not always. If you need to retrieve data in a sorted manner, you'll want to learn how to work with the ORDER BY clause.

The ORDER BY clause is used at the end of a SQL statement to sort a result set (records returned by a SQL query) in alphanumeric order. Sort order for the ORDER BY clause can either be ascending (A to Z, 0 to 9) or descending (Z to A, 9 to 0) using the keywords ASC for ascending or DESC for descending.

Note that neither the ASC nor DESC keywords are required with the ORDER BY clause, and that the default sort order is ascending.

To properly use the ORDER BY clause, simply follow the clause with a sort key, which is a fancy way of saying a column name to sort on. The optional keywords ASC and DESC follow the sort key.

To exhibit SQL sorting techniques, study the next two SQL statements and their outputs, shown in Figures 9.14 and 9.15.

```
SELECT *
    FROM Products
ORDER BY ProductName ASC;
```

FIGURE 9.14

Using the ORDER BY clause and the ASC keyword to sort product records by product name in ascending order

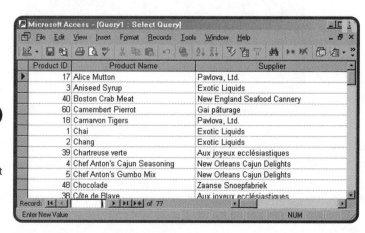

```
SELECT *
    FROM Products
ORDER BY ProductName DESC;
```

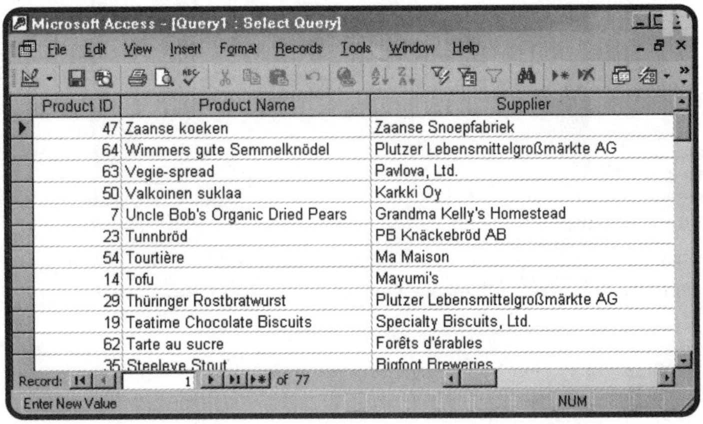

FIGURE 9.15

Using the ORDER BY clause and the DESC keyword to sort product records by product name in descending order

Grouping

Grouping in SQL provides developers with an opportunity to group like data together. Without the use of grouping, aggregate (built-in) functions, such as SUM and AVG, calculate every value in a column. To put like data into logical groups of information, SQL provides the GROUP BY clause.

In the next SQL statement, I use the GROUP BY clause to group a computed field by product id in the Products table:

```
SELECT ProductID, SUM(UnitPrice * Quantity) AS [Sub Total by Product]
    FROM [Order Details]
GROUP BY ProductID;
```

Notice the output from the preceding SQL statement in Figure 9.16. Even though I specified ProductID as the desired column, the outputted column and the data it contains show as a product name. This occurs because the Products table uses a SQL lookup to retrieve the product name by product id.

There will be times when you need conditions on your groups. In these events, you can *not* use the WHERE clause. Instead, SQL provides the HAVING clause for condition building when working with groups. To demonstrate, I'll modify the previous SQL statement to use a HAVING clause, which asks the database to retrieve only groups that have a subtotal by product greater than 15,000.00.

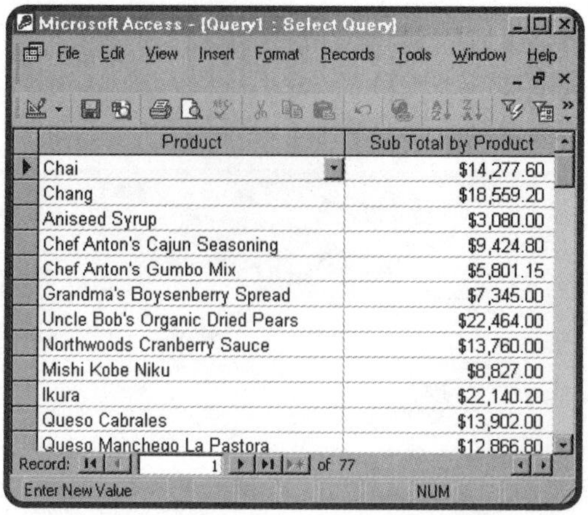

FIGURE 9.16

Using the GROUP
BY clause to group
like data together

```
SELECT ProductID, SUM(UnitPrice * Quantity) AS [Sub Total by Product]
    FROM [Order Details]
GROUP BY ProductID
    HAVING SUM(UnitPrice * Quantity) > 15000.00;
```

Joins

Joins are used when you need to retrieve data from more than one table. Specifically, a SQL join uses keys to combine records from two tables where a primary key from one table is matched up with a foreign key from another table. The result is a combination of result sets from both tables where a match is found. If a match is not found, information from either table is discarded in the result set returned.

SQL joins are created by selecting columns from more than one table in the SELECT clause, including both table names in the FROM clause, and matching like columns from both tables in the WHERE clause. An example join is shown below with output seen in Figure 9.17.

```
SELECT FirstName, LastName, OrderDate, ShipName
  FROM Employees, Orders
 WHERE Employees.EmployeeID = Orders.EmployeeID;
```

In Figure 9.17, I've retrieved columns from both the Employees and Orders table where the EmployeeID values from both tables match. Because the join keys from both tables (EmployeeID) are spelled the same, I must explicitly tell SQL what table name I'm referring to using dot notation, as seen again below:

```
WHERE Employees.EmployeeID = Orders.EmployeeID;
```

FIGURE 9.17

Joining the
Employees and
Orders table with
the WHERE clause

	First Name	Last Name	Order Date	Ship Name
▶	Andrew	Fuller	10-Apr-1998	Santé Gourmet
	Andrew	Fuller	03-Oct-1997	QUICK-Stop
	Andrew	Fuller	02-Feb-1998	QUICK-Stop
	Andrew	Fuller	29-May-1997	HILARIÓN-Abastos
	Andrew	Fuller	30-Jun-1997	Wartian Herkku
	Andrew	Fuller	09-Apr-1998	Reggiani Caseifici
	Andrew	Fuller	24-Nov-1997	North/South
	Andrew	Fuller	04-Nov-1996	QUICK-Stop
	Andrew	Fuller	16-Apr-1998	Königlich Essen
	Andrew	Fuller	19-Dec-1997	La maison d'Asie
	Andrew	Fuller	24-Apr-1997	Hungry Owl All-Night Grocers
	Andrew	Fuller	29-Nov-1996	Ernst Handel
	Andrew	Fuller	27-Feb-1998	Tortuga Restaurante
	Andrew	Fuller	17-Apr-1998	White Clover Markets
	Andrew	Fuller	09-Apr-1998	Romero y tomillo
	Andrew	Fuller	20-Apr-1998	Suprêmes délices
	Andrew	Fuller	08-Apr-1998	Godos Cocina Típica
	Andrew	Fuller	07-Apr-1998	Wilman Kala
	Andrew	Fuller	11-Dec-1996	Que Delícia
	Andrew	Fuller	06-Apr-1998	Folk och fä HB

Record: 14 ◄ | 1 | ► ►I ►* of 830

TRAP

If the expression in the WHERE clause is incorrect, a Cartesian join will result. A Cartesian result is when the query returns every possible number of combinations from each table involved.

INSERT INTO Statement

You can use SQL to insert rows into a table with the INSERT INTO statement. The INSERT INTO statement inserts new records into a table using the VALUES clause:

```
INSERT INTO Books
      VALUES ('1234abc456edf', 'Beginning SQL', 'Vine',

            'Michael', 'Technology Press');
```

Though not required, matching column names can be used in the INSERT INTO statement to clarify the fields you're working with.

```
INSERT INTO Books (ISBN, Title, LastName, FirstName, Publisher)
      VALUES ('1234abc456edf', 'Beginning SQL', 'Vine',

            'Michael', 'Technology Press');
```

Using matching column names is necessary, not just helpful, when you only need to insert data for a limited number of columns in a table. A case in point is when working with the `AutoNumber` field type, which Access automatically creates for you when inserting a record.

The concept of working with an `AutoNumber` and an `INSERT INTO` statement is shown in the following SQL statement and Figure 9.18.

```
INSERT INTO Shippers (CompanyName, Phone)
     VALUES ('Slow Boat Express', '123-456-9999');
```

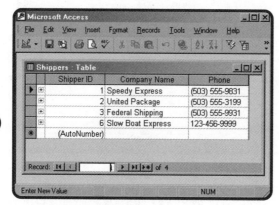

FIGURE 9.18

Inserting new records into a table with `INSERT INTO` statement

UPDATE Statement

Use the `UPDATE` statement to change field values in one or more tables. The `UPDATE` statement works in conjunction with the `SET` keyword:

```
UPDATE Products
     SET UnitsInStock = UnitsInStock + 5;
```

You supply the table name to the `UPDATE` statement, and use the `SET` keyword to update any number of fields that belong to the table in the `UPDATE` statement. In my example above, I'm updating every record's `UnitInStock` field by adding the number 5. Notice that I said every record. Because I didn't use a `WHERE` clause, the `UPDATE` statement updates every row in the table.

In the next `UPDATE` statement, I use a `WHERE` clause to put a condition on the number of rows that will receive updates.

```
UPDATE Products
    SET UnitsInStock = UnitsInStock + 5
  WHERE SupplierID = 1;
```

It is possible for SQL programmers to forget to place conditions on their UPDATE statements. Because there is no undo or rollback feature in Access, pay attention to the dialog box that appears before you commit to changes, as seen in Figure 9.19.

FIGURE 9.19

Information provided by Access when updating records

Always check the informational dialog presented by Access to ensure that the number of records updated aligns with the number of records you expect to update.

DELETE Statement

The DELETE statement is used to remove one or more rows from a table. It's possible to delete all rows from a table using the DELETE statement and a wildcard:

```
DELETE *
  FROM Products;
```

More often than not, conditions are placed on DELETE statements using the WHERE clause:

```
DELETE *
  FROM Products
WHERE UnitsInStock = 0;
```

Once again, pay close attention to Access's informational dialog boxes when performing any inserts, updates, or deletes on tables.

The DELETE statement can perform cascade deletes on tables with one-to-many relationships if the Cascade Delete Related Records option is chosen in the Edit Relationships window, as seen in Figure 9.20.

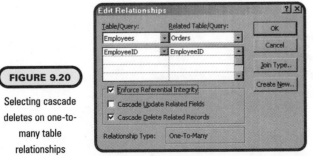

FIGURE 9.20

Selecting cascade deletes on one-to-many table relationships

With the Cascade Delete Related Records option chosen for the Employees and Orders tables, any employee records deleted would also initiate a corresponding deletion in the Orders table where a matching EmployeeID was found.

Data Definition Language

Data definition language, also known as DDL, is the database language that defines the attributes of a database. Most commonly, DDL is used to create, alter, and drop tables, indexes, constraints, views, users, and permissions.

In this section, you'll investigate a few of the more common uses for DDL in beginning database programming:

- Creating tables
- Altering tables
- DROP statements

Creating Tables

Creating tables in DDL involves using the CREATE TABLE statement. With the CREATE TABLE statement, you can define and create a table, its columns and column data types, and any constraints that might be needed on one or more columns. In its simplest form, the CREATE TABLE syntax and format is shown below:

```
CREATE TABLE TableName
            ( FieldName        FieldType,
              FieldName        FieldType,
              FieldName        FieldType);
```

The TableName attribute defines the table to be created. Each FieldName attribute defines the column to be created. Each FieldName has a corresponding FieldType attribute, which defines the column's data type.

The next CREATE TABLE statement creates a new table called Books that contains seven columns.

```
CREATE TABLE Books
            (ISBN Text,
             Title Text,
             AuthorLastName Text,
             AuthorFirstName Text,
```

```
Publisher Text,
Price Currency,
PublishDate Date);
```

The newly created table is shown in Figure 9.21.

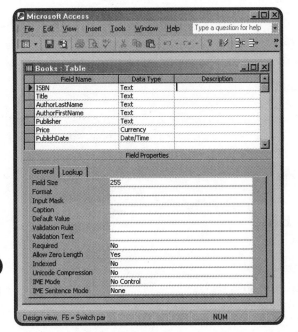

FIGURE 9.21

Creating new tables
with the CREATE
TABLE statement

The **CREATE TABLE** statement allows you to specify if one or more columns should not allow **NULL** values. By default, columns created in the **CREATE TABLE** statement are nullable—in other words, they allow **NULL** entries. To specify a not **NULL** column, use the **Not Null** keywords:

```
CREATE TABLE Books
                (ISBN Text Not Null,
                 Title Text,
                 AuthorLastName Text,
                 AuthorFirstName Text,
                 Publisher Text,
                 Price Currency,
                 PublishDate Date);
```

Using the **Not Null** keywords sets the column's **Required** attribute to **Yes**.

Altering Tables

You can use the ALTER TABLE statement to alter tables that have already been created. Three common uses of the ALTER TABLE statement are to add a column or columns to an existing table, to change the field type attributes of one or more columns, or to remove a column from a table.

The next ALTER TABLE statement adds a Salary column to the Employees table with the help of the ADD COLUMN keywords:

```
ALTER TABLE Employees
 ADD COLUMN Salary Currency;
```

Adding the Salary column with the ALTER TABLE statement, appends the new column to the end of the Employees table, as shown in Figure 9.22.

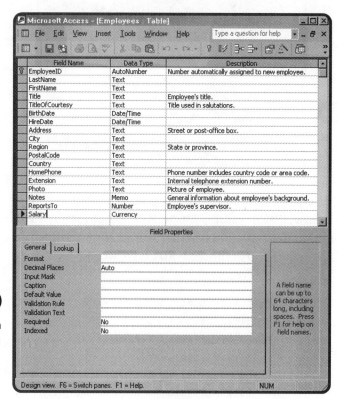

FIGURE 9.22

Adding columns with the ALTER TABLE statement appends new columns to the end of the table

To change the data type of a column, use the ALTER COLUMN keywords in conjunction with the ALTER TABLE statement.

```
ALTER TABLE Employees
ALTER COLUMN Extension Number;
```

In the preceding `ALTER TABLE` statement, I changed the data type of the `Extension` column from a `Text` data type to a `Number` data type.

To remove a column from a table in Access, use the `DROP COLUMN` keywords in conjunction with the `ALTER TABLE` statement:

```
ALTER TABLE Employees
DROP COLUMN Salary;
```

Note that Access does not always warn you of your impending database alterations. In the case of dropping (removing) a column, Access simply performs the operation without mention.

DROP Statement

The `DROP` statement can be used to remove (drop) many entities from a database such as tables, indexes, procedures, and views. In this section, you'll see how the `DROP` statement is used to remove a table from a database.

Removing a table from a database with the `DROP` statement is really quite easy. Simply supply the entity type to be dropped along with the entity name:

```
DROP TABLE Books;
```

In the preceding example, the entity typed to be dropped is a `TABLE` and the entity name is `Books`. Once again, beware: Access does not always warn you when it modifies the database. In the `DROP TABLE` example, Access simply executes the command without any confirmation.

Chapter Summary

This chapter covered many beginning database programming techniques for managing data and database entities without the help of Access wizards and graphical interfaces. In addition, you learned how to program in structured query language, also known as SQL, and data definition language, also known as DDL. You specifically learned the following key concepts:

- Most relational databases include languages such as SQL and DLL for retrieving data and manipulating entities, respectively.

- SQL statements are free form, meaning one SQL statement can be written on one or more lines. For readability, SQL programmers break SQL statements into one or more logical groups on multiple lines.

- Information is retrieved from a relational database using `SELECT` statements.

- Simple and compound conditions can be used in SQL statements using the WHERE clause.
- Computed fields do not exist as columns in a table; instead, they are derived data using calculations in SQL statements. Computed fields are given display names using the AS clause.
- SQL contains many aggregate or built-in functions such as COUNT, DISTINCT, MIN, MAX, and SUM.
- Database records returned by a SQL statement are not sorted by default. To sort SQL query results, use the ORDER BY clause.
- SQL query results can be grouped using the GROUP BY clause.
- SQL joins are made using key fields in two or more tables in the WHERE clause.
- Incorrect joins can produce an unwanted Cartesian product.
- Records can be manually inserted into a table using the INSERT INTO statement.
- The UPDATE statement can be used to update fields in a database table.
- Records in a table can be removed using the DELETE statement.
- Tables can be manually created using the CREATE TABLE statement.
- In its simplest form, the CREATE TABLE statement defines the table's name, its columns, and its column types.
- The ALTER TABLE statement can be used to add columns to an existing table, update a column's data type, and remove a column from a table.
- The DROP statement is used for removing tables, indexes, views, and procedures from a database.

CHALLENGES

Use the Microsoft Northwind database and a SQL View window for all challenges below.

1. Write and test a SQL query that retrieves all columns from the Categories table.

2. Write and test a SQL query that retrieves only the contact name and contact title from the Customers table.

3. Write and test a SQL query that uses a computed field to calculate the total cost of each record in the Order Details table.

4. Write and test the SQL query that returns the total number of records in the Employees table.

5. Use the Orders table to write and test the SQL query that returns the sum of freight shipments grouped by customer.

6. Using the INSERT INTO statement, write a SQL query that inserts a new record into the Employees table.

7. Update the unit price by $3.25 in the Products table for all products by the supplier Tokyo Traders.

8. Delete all records in the Products table where the product has been discontinued.

9. Using data definition language, create a new table called HomesForSale. The HomesForSale table should contain the following fields: StreetAddress, City, State, ZipCode, SalePrice, and ListDate. Ensure that the StreetAddress column is not nullable.

10. Using data definition language, add three new columns to the HomesForSale table called AgentLastName, AgentFirstName, and AgentPhoneNumber.

11. Using data definition language, remove the HomesForSale table from the database.

Database
Programming
with ADO

With a basic knowledge of VBA programming, you can leverage the power of Microsoft's ActiveX Data Objects (commonly referred to as ADO) to access and manage data sources such as Microsoft Access. In this chapter, I will show you the essentials for programming with ADO's application programming interface with the following key concepts:

- ADO overview

- Connecting to a database

- Working with recordsets

ADO Overview

For a number of years, Microsoft has implemented and supported quite a few database programming models such as RDO (Remote Data Objects), DAO (Data Access Objects), and most recently ADO (ActiveX Data Objects). ADO is an object-based programming model that allows programmers in many Microsoft programming languages such as Visual C++, Visual Basic, ASP (Active Server Pages), C#, and of course VBA to access and manage data sources. ADO has become Microsoft's most important and reliable method for data source connectivity, retrieval, and management through its suite of programming languages.

Data sources can be as simple as text files, or they can be more sophisticated relational data sources such as Microsoft Access, Microsoft SQL Server, or even non-Microsoft databases like Oracle's RDBMS. Specifically, ADO allows you to connect to data sources that support open database connectivity (ODBC). ADO also allows you to leverage the power of structured query language (SQL) for those data sources that support it.

Each ADO programming endeavor involves working with the ADO API, also called the ADO object model. An API (application programming interface) is a set of interfaces (classes) that allow you to access the low-level functionality of programming models such as ADO. The ADO API model consists of many objects, collections, events, methods, and properties.

Though most Microsoft programming languages support the ADO object model, there are some slight differences in how ADO is implemented and used within in each language. In this chapter, you will learn how ADO is implemented and used in Access VBA.

Before getting started, you may wish to familiarize yourself with some key ADO terminology and objects as outlined in Table 10.1.

Connecting to a Database

Before you and ADO can work with data in a data source, you must first establish a connection using the Connection object. To declare variables of ADO object type, use the ADODB library name followed by a period and a specific ADO object type such as Connection. An example of declaring an ADO object variable of Connection type is seen below.

TABLE 10.1   KEY ADO TERMINOLOGY

Item	Description
Connection	A connection is how you gain access to a data source. In ADO, connections are achieved through the `Connection` object.
Command	In ADO commands are defined as a set of instructions such as SQL statements or a stored procedure that typically inserts, deletes, or updates data. ADO commands are embodied in the `Command` object.
Field	ADO recordsets contain one or more fields. ADO fields are implemented with the `Field` object, which contain properties for field names, data types, and values.
Parameter	Parameters allow you to use variables to pass information to commands such as SQL statements. ADO uses the `Parameter` object to build parameterized queries and stored procedures.
Recordset	Rows returned by a command such as a SQL statement are stored in recordsets. ADO's `Recordset` object allows you to iterate through the returned rows and insert, update, and delete rows in the recordset.

```
Dim myConnection As ADODB.Connection
```

If you're using ADO to connect to your current Microsoft Access application, you can use the `CurrentProject` object's `AccessConnection` property to set an ADO connection object to your `Connection` object variable. An example of connecting to a local database is shown next.

```
Private Sub cmdConnectToLocalDB_Click()

    On Error GoTo ConnectionError

    'Declare connection object variable.
    Dim localConnection As ADODB.Connection

    'Set current Access connection to Connection object variable.
    Set localConnection = CurrentProject.AccessConnection

    MsgBox "Local connection successfully established."

    Exit Sub
```

```
ConnectionError:

    MsgBox "There was an error connecting to the database. " & Chr(13) _
            & Err.Number & ", " & Err.Description
```

```
End Sub
```

Using the Set statement, I'm able to assign the current Access ADO connection to my Connection object variable called localConnection. Note that whenever you open a connection, it's important to utilize error handling.

Many ADO programming occasions involve connecting to a remote database. Connecting to a remote database through ADO involves working with one or more Connection object properties and its Open method, as demonstrated below.

```
Private Sub cmdConnectToRemoteDB_Click()

    On Error GoTo ConnectionError

    'Declare connection object variable.
    Dim remoteConnection As New ADODB.Connection

    'Assign OLEDB provider to the Provider property.
    'Use the Open method to establish a connection to the database.
    With remoteConnection
        .Provider = "Microsoft.Jet.OLEDB.4.0"
        .Open "C:\work\tech\vba_access2002\chapter10\programs\chapter10.mdb"
    End With

    MsgBox "Remote connection successfully established."

    'Close the current database connection.
    remoteConnection.Close

    Exit Sub

ConnectionError:

    MsgBox "There was an error connecting to the database. " & Chr(13) _
            & Err.Number & ", " & Err.Description

End Sub
```

Remote database access using ADO can be one of two types: connecting to Access databases on your local machine, or connecting to databases across the network.

Depending on the type of database you're connecting to, you will use either ODBC or OLE DB as your connection provider. In the case of Microsoft Access databases, you assign an OLE DB provider name to the `Connection` object's `Provider` property. Microsoft's Jet 4.0 OLE DB provider uses the Microsoft Jet database engine to open a database in shared mode.

Once a provider has been set, use the `Open` method to establish a connection to your Access database. In the preceding example, I pass a connection string to the `Connection` object's `Open` method. This connection string tells ADO what my database name is and where it is located.

After working with the ADO object model for some time, you'll learn there are many programming methods for accomplishing the same task. Some ADO programmers like to use the `Connection` object's `Properties` collection to assign name/value pairs of connection attributes. As an example, the next procedure (http://msdn.microsoft.com) uses this technique for connecting to a remote Access database.

```
Private Sub cmdConnectToRemoteDB_Click()

    On Error GoTo ConnectionError

    'Declare connection object variable.
    Dim remoteConnection As New ADODB.Connection

    'Assign OLEDB providers.
    'Assign database name / location to Data Source.
    'Use the Open method to establish a connection to the database.
    With remoteConnection
        .Provider = "Microsoft.Access.OLEDB.10.0"
        .Properties("Data Provider").Value = "Microsoft.Jet.OLEDB.4.0"
        .Properties("Data Source").Value = _
"C:\work\tech\vba_access2002\chapter10\programs\chapter10.mdb"
        .Open
    End With

    MsgBox "Connection successfully established."
```

```
        remoteConnection.Close

    Exit Sub

ConnectionError:

    MsgBox "There was an error connecting to the database. " & Chr(13) _
            & Err.Number & ", " & Err.Description

End Sub
```

 TRAP **A common problem in beginning ADO programming is troubleshooting connection errors. One frequent error is to overlook the path and file name passed to the Data Source property or Open method. Make sure these values match correctly with the location and name of your database.**

Regardless of your connection choice, you should always close your database connections using the Connection object's Close method. The ADO Close method frees application resources, but does not remove the object from memory. To remove objects from memory, set the object to Nothing.

In general, connections should be opened once when the application is first loaded (e.g., Load event) and closed once when the application is closing (e.g., UnLoad event).

Working with Recordsets

In this section, I'll show you how to work with a key building block in the Microsoft ADO programming model called recordsets. The ADO programming model uses recordsets to work with rows in a database table. Using ADO recordsets, you can add, delete, and update information in database tables.

The Recordset object represents all rows in a table or all rows returned by a SQL query. The Recordset object, however, can refer to only a single row of data at time. Once a database connection has been established, Recordset objects can be opened in one of three ways :

- Using the Open method of the Recordset object.
- Using the Execute method of the Command object.
- Using the Execute method of the Connection object.

The most common way of opening recordsets is through the `Open` method of a `Recordset` object.

Recordset object variables are declared like any other variable using the ADODB library:

```
Dim rsEmployees As New ADODB.Recordset
```

Once a `Recordset` object variable has been declared, you can use its `Open` method to open a recordset and navigate through the result set. The `Open` method takes five arguments:

```
rsEmployees.Open Source, ActiveConnection, CursorType, LockType, Options
```

Before moving further into recordsets, you should investigate the concept of database locks and cursors and how Microsoft ADO uses them in conjunction with result sets and the `Recordset` object.

 A result set is the set of rows retrieved by a command or SQL query. In Microsoft ADO, recordsets are embodied in the `Recordset` object, which is used to manage result sets. In an abstract sense, however, the notion of a recordset is synonymous with a result set.

Introduction to Database Locks

Whether or not your `Recordset` objects can update, add, or delete rows depends on your database lock type. Most RDBMS implement various forms of table- and row-level locking. Database locking prevents multiple users (or processes) from updating the same row at the same time. For example, suppose both my friend and I attempt to update the same row of information at the same time. Left to its own devices, this type of simultaneous updating could cause memory problems or data loss. To solve this, very smart RDBMS developers designed sophisticated software locking techniques using a variety of algorithms.

Even though the locking dilemma has been solved and implemented for us, ADO developers still need to identity a valid locking mechanism such as read only, batch update, optimistic, or pessimistic. These types of locking mechanisms can be specified in the `LockType` property of the `Recordset` object. Table 10.2 describes available recordset lock types with a brief description.

Generally speaking, most VBA programmers need only decide whether their database locks should be read only or not. As a rule of thumb, use the read-only lock type (`adLockReadOnly`) when you simply need to scroll forward through a

TABLE 10.2 LOCKTYPE PROPERTY VALUES

Lock Type	Description
adLockBatchOptimistic	Used for batch updates.
adLockOptimistic	Records are locked only when the Recordset object's Update method is called. Other users can access and update the same row of data while you have it open.
adLockPessimistic	Records are locked as soon as record editing begins. Other users can't access or modify the row of data until you have called the Recordset's Update or CancelUpdate methods.
adLockReadOnly	Records are read only (default lock type).

result set without modifying its contents. If you need to perform any updates on the result set, an optimistic locking solution (adLockOptimistic) is sufficient.

Introduction to Cursors

Since Recordset objects represent a single of row of data, VBA programmers need a way to iterate through a list of rows. The ability to maneuver through a result set is implemented through database cursors.

In database terms, a cursor is a structure that names and manages a storage area in memory. Programmers use cursors to point to a row of data in a result set one row at a time. The concept of a cursor and a result set is depicted in Figure 10.1.

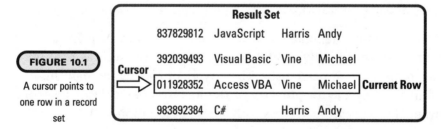

FIGURE 10.1

A cursor points to one row in a record set

Using a combination of other structures such as loops and objects, programmers navigate through a recordset with the cursor pointing to the current row. You can think of programming with cursors as similar to file processing (discussed in

Chapter 8) where you open a data file and read one record at a time. When programming with cursors, you establish a cursor and move the cursor's pointer to one row in a record set at a time.

When working with ADO's Recordset object, you can specify one of four cursor types in the CursorType property as outlined in Table 10.3.

TABLE 10.3 CursorType Property Values

Lock Type	Description
adOpenForwardOnly	Provides optimal performance through limited scrolling (forward only).
adOpenKeyset	Provides all types of movement in a Recordset object. Does not contain added or deleted rows.
adOpenDynamic	Provides all types of movement in a Recordset object. Includes added, deleted, and updated rows.
adOpenStatic	Provides all types of movement in a static Recordset object. Changes are not seen by users until the Recordset object is updated.

You should use forward only (adOpenForwardOnly) cursors when updating rows is *not* required and reading rows in a result set from start to finish is acceptable. If you require dynamic updates (adOpenDynamic) in your result set, a dynamic cursor type is recommended.

In addition to cursor types, ADO allows programmers to specify a cursor location for the Recordset and Connection object via the CursorLocation property. Depending on the location of your database and the size of your result set, cursor locations can have a considerable effect on your application's performance.

As outlined in Table 10.4, cursor locations can be either server-side or client-side.

When considering cursor locations, Microsoft recommends server-side cursors when working with Microsoft Access databases and client-side cursors when working with Microsoft SQL Server databases.

TABLE 10.4 CURSORLOCATION PROPERTY VALUES

Lock Type	Description
adUseClient	Records in the record set are stored in local memory.
adUseServer	Builds a set of keys locally for Access databases, and on the server for Microsoft SQL Server. The set of keys is used to retrieve and navigate through the result set.

Retrieving and Browsing Data

Once you have successfully established a connection to a database with ADO, retrieving and browsing data is quite easy. To retrieve data with ADO, you will work with the Recordset object. In addition to cursors and locks, the Recordset object has many features for managing record-based data.

In this section, I'll use Microsoft's sample database Northwind.mdb to demonstrate retrieving and browsing data with ADO. Figure 10.2 depicts a form I built, which remotely connects to the Northwind database and allows a user to browse through data found in the Categories table.

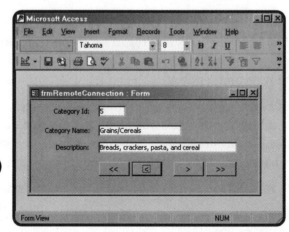

FIGURE 10.2

Using ADO to connect and browse record-based data

To build the application seen in Figure 10.2, simply create a similar form with similar controls. Next, add the connection-based program code to your application as seen next.

```
Option Compare Database

Dim remoteConnection As New ADODB.Connection
Dim rsCategories As New ADODB.Recordset


Private Sub Form_Load()

    Connect
    SetRecordset

End Sub

Public Sub Disconnect()

    On Error GoTo ConnectionError

    rsCategories.Close
    remoteConnection.Close

    Exit Sub

ConnectionError:
    MsgBox "There was an error closing the database." _
            & Err.Number & ", " & Err.Description

End Sub

Private Sub Connect()

    On Error GoTo ConnectionError

    With remoteConnection
        .Provider = "Microsoft.Jet.OLEDB.4.0"
        .Open "C:\Program Files\Microsoft" & _
            Office\Office10\Samples\Northwind.mdb"
    End With

    Exit Sub
```

```
ConnectionError:

    MsgBox "There was an error connecting to the database. " & Chr(13) _
            & Err.Number & ", " & Err.Description


End Sub
```

I created two procedures that handle connecting to the Northwind database and disconnecting. The Connect subprocedure is called during the form Load event.

 TRAP When applying code from this book in your own applications, remember to change the path of the Northwind.mdb database (or any other database for that matter) in the Open method of the Connection object.

Notice in the form's Load event that I call another subprocedure called SetRecordset. This procedure sets up my Recordset object by establishing a SQL query, opening the recordset, and applying the first row of data to the text boxes. The SetRecordset procedure is shown next.

```
Public Sub SetRecordset()

    Dim sql As String

    On Error GoTo DbError

    sql = "select * from Categories"

    rsCategories.CursorType = adOpenKeyset
    rsCategories.LockType = adLockReadOnly

    rsCategories.Open sql, remoteConnection, , , adCmdText

    If rsCategories.EOF = False Then
        Me.txtCategoryId = rsCategories!CategoryID
        Me.txtCategoryName = rsCategories!CategoryName
        Me.txtDescription = rsCategories!Description
    End If

    Exit Sub
```

```
DbError:

    MsgBox "There was an error retrieving information from the database." _
        & Err.Number & ", " & Err.Description

End Sub
```

Keep in mind that I declared my Recordset object variable (rsCategories) as a form-level variable. This allows me to access it throughout my Form Class module.

The following numbered list describes my process for opening a recordset.

1. Define a SQL query using a String variable, which will tell the Recordset object how to open.

2. Assign cursor and lock type values to corresponding Recordset object properties. Note that you can set these properties on separate lines (as I did) or in the Open method of the Recordset object.

3. Use the Open method and pass in three of five optional parameters. The first parameter (sql) tells the Recordset object how to open the record-set. In addition to SQL statements, you can use a table name surrounded by double quotes (e.g., "Categories"). The second parameter (remote-Connection) is the name of the active connection that points to my copy of the Northwind.mdb database. Note that this connection must have already been successfully opened. The last parameter I used is in the fifth parameter position. This is the options parameter, which tells the Recordset object how to use its first parameter. If the first parameter is a SQL string, use the constant adCmdText. If the first parameter is a table name (e.g., "Categories"), use the constant adCmdTable.

4. After the Recordset object has been successfully opened, I ensure that rows have been returned by using the EOF (end of file) property. If the EOF property is true, no records were returned and no further processing is done.

5. If the Recordset object contains one or more rows (EOF = False), I can access fields in a couple of ways. In my example, I use the Recordset object name (rsCategories) followed by an exclamation mark (!) and then the field name found in the database table. This is probably the most common way for ADO programmers to access recordset fields. Other ways of accessing fields involve using the Fields collection:

```
Me.txtCategoryName = rsCategories.Fields.Item("CategoryName")

Me.txtDescription = rsCategories.Fields.Item(2)
```

The first example passes a column name to the Item property of the Fields collection. The second example uses what's known as the ordinal position of the field returned. Ordinal positions start with 0.

Once data is successfully retrieved from a field, you can assign its value to variables or properties.

To browse through rows in a recordset, ADO's Recordset object provides the following four methods:

- MoveFirst. Moves the cursor to the first record in the result set.
- MoveLast. Moves the cursor to the last record in the result set.
- MoveNext. Moves the cursor to the next record in the result set.
- MovePrevious. Moves the cursor to the previous record in the result set.

When working with the MoveNext and MovePrevious methods, it's important to use cursors that allow forward and backward scrolling. Also, you will need to check that the cursor's position is not already at the beginning of the record-set before moving previous or at the end of the recordset before moving next. Use the Recordset object's AbsolutePosition and RecordCount properties for these conditions.

The AbsolutePosition property contains the ordinal position of the current record in the result set. The AbsolutePosition property contains a whole number beginning at 1. The RecordCount property contains the total number of rows contained in the recordset.

Using these properties and methods, you can build conditions for browsing through ADO records, which is demonstrated in the next four procedures.

```
Private Sub cmdMoveFirst_Click()

    On Error GoTo DbError

    'Move to the first record in the result set.
    rsCategories.MoveFirst
    Me.txtCategoryId = rsCategories!CategoryID
    Me.txtCategoryName = rsCategories!CategoryName
    Me.txtDescription = rsCategories!Description
```

```
        Exit Sub

DbError:

   MsgBox "There was an error retrieving information from the database." _
        & Err.Number & ", " & Err.Description

End Sub

Private Sub cmdMoveLast_Click()

    On Error GoTo DbError

    'Move to the last record in the result set.
    rsCategories.MoveLast
    Me.txtCategoryId = rsCategories!CategoryID
    Me.txtCategoryName = rsCategories!CategoryName
    Me.txtDescription = rsCategories!Description

        Exit Sub

DbError:

   MsgBox "There was an error retrieving information from the database." _
        & Err.Number & ", " & Err.Description

End Sub

Private Sub cmdMoveNext_Click()

    On Error GoTo DbError

    'Move to the next record in the result set if the cursor is not
    'already at the last record.
    If rsCategories.AbsolutePosition < rsCategories.RecordCount Then

        rsCategories.MoveNext
        Me.txtCategoryId = rsCategories!CategoryID
```

```vba
        Me.txtCategoryName = rsCategories!CategoryName
        Me.txtDescription = rsCategories!Description


    End If

    Exit Sub

DbError:

  MsgBox "There was an error retrieving information from the database." _
      & Err.Number & ", " & Err.Description


End Sub

Private Sub cmdMovePrevious_Click()

    On Error GoTo DbError

    'Move to the previous record in the result set, if the
    'current record is not the first record.
    If rsCategories.AbsolutePosition > 1 Then

        rsCategories.MovePrevious
        Me.txtCategoryId = rsCategories!CategoryID
        Me.txtCategoryName = rsCategories!CategoryName
        Me.txtDescription = rsCategories!Description


    End If

    Exit Sub

DbError:

  MsgBox "There was an error retrieving information from the database." _
      & Err.Number & ", " & Err.Description


End Sub
```

IN THE REAL WORLD

In ADO/database terms, the ordinal position refers to the relative position of a field or column in a collection such as the `Fields` collection. Believe it or not, using ordinal positions for accessing fields is not uncommon in ADO. Consider an example of accessing the return value of the SQL function `Count`. Since SQL does not return a column name, you must work with ordinal position in the `Fields` collection.

An example of using ordinal positions to retrieve the result of a SQL function is shown next.

```
Private Sub cmdCount_Click()

    Dim sql As String
    Dim rsCount As New ADODB.Recordset

    On Error GoTo DbError

    sql = "select count(*) from Categories"

    rsCount.Open sql, remoteConnection, adOpenForwardOnly, _
        adLockReadOnly, adCmdText

    If rsCategories.EOF = False Then
        MsgBox "There are " & rsCount.Fields.Item(0) & _
    " rows in the Categories table."
    End If

    Exit Sub

DbError:

    MsgBox "There was an error retrieving information " & _
           "from the database." & Err.Number & _
           ", " & Err.Description

End Sub
```

Updating Records

Updating records using ADO's `Recordset` object is relatively easy. Generally speaking, you will perform the following tasks:

1. First, declare a new `Recordset` object variable.

2. Define and create a SQL string that identifies the record you want to update.

3. Assign updatable cursor and lock types for updating a record.

4. Open the recordset, which should contain only one record, the record you wish to update.

5. Assign new data to the recordset fields.

6. Update the recordset using the `Recordset` object's `Update` method.

7. Close the recordset using the `Recordset` object's `Close` method.

8. Refresh other recordsets if applicable by closing the recordset and reopening it or calling the `Recordset` object's `Requery` method.

The tricky part in updating records is ensuring that your SQL queries are well defined. For example, to update a record in the `Categories` table of the Northwind database, I want to qualify my recordset using the table's primary key (in this case the `CategoryID` field):

```
sql = "select * from Categories where CategoryID = " & _
Val(Me.txtCategoryId.Value)
```

In the SQL string above, I assign value of the text box containing the category id. Since I'm using a `String` variable, I can build a dynamic SQL statement using control properties (input from the user). By using a condition in my SQL string and supplying it with the primary key of a record, I'm making sure that only the record with that primary key will be contained in the result set.

 TRICK **When concatenating string or text values to a dynamic SQL statement, you must use single quotes inside of double quotes to surround the expression.**

```
sql = "select * from Categories where CategoryName = '" & _
        Val(Me.txtCategoryName.Value) & "'"
```

You may be asking yourself, "How do I know what record to update?" The answer to this question is based on the record selected in the graphical interface. So long as my GUI allows a user to select only one record, I will be in good shape. For a demonstration of this concept, see Figure 10.3.

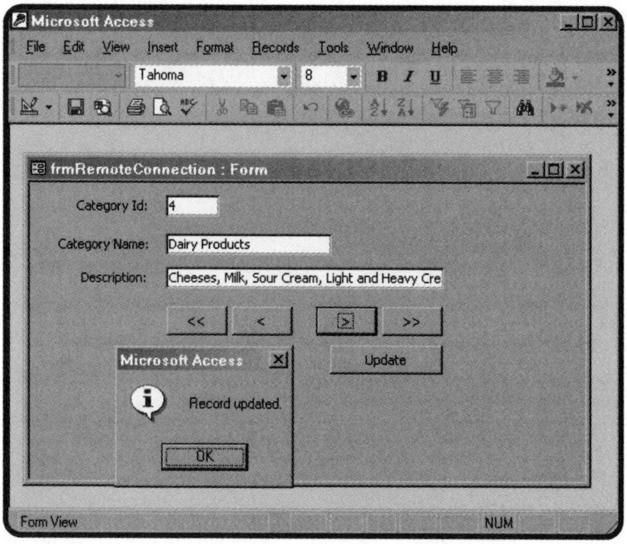

FIGURE 10.3

This graphical interface allows the user to select only one record at a time

In the `Click` event procedure below, I use concepts from the preceding numbered list to update the record selected on the form.

```
Private Sub cmdUpdate_Click()

    Dim sql As String
    Dim rsUpdate As New ADODB.Recordset

    On Error GoTo DbError

    'Build dynamic SQL statement based on record selected by the user.
    sql = "select * from Categories where CategoryID = " & _
        Val(Me.txtCategoryId.Value)

    'Assign updatable cursor and lock type properties.
    rsUpdate.CursorType = adOpenDynamic
    rsUpdate.LockType = adLockOptimistic

    'Open the Recordset object.
    rsUpdate.Open sql, remoteConnection, , , adCmdText

    'Don't try to update the record, if the recordset did not find a row.
    If rsUpdate.EOF = False Then

        'Update the record based on input from the user.
```

```
        With rsUpdate
            !CategoryName = Me.txtCategoryName
            !Description = Me.txtDescription
            .Update
            .Close
        End With

    End If

    MsgBox "Record updated.", vbInformation

    'Close the form-level Recordset object and refresh it to include
    'the newly updated row.
    rsCategories.Close
    SetRecordset

    Exit Sub

DbError:

    MsgBox "There was an error updating the database." _
        & Err.Number & ", " & Err.Description

End Sub
```

 TRICK The Recordset object's Update method is synonymous with saving.

Adding Records

Adding records with ADO does not necessarily require the use of SQL queries. In most scenarios, you simply need a record added to a table based on user input. As shown in Figure 10.4, I've added another command button to my form.

In the simplest form, records are added to tables using the following steps:

1. First, declare a new Recordset object variable.

2. Assign updatable cursor and lock types for adding a record.

3. Open the Recordset object using its Open method with a table name as the first parameter and the associated adCmdTable constant name for the options parameter.

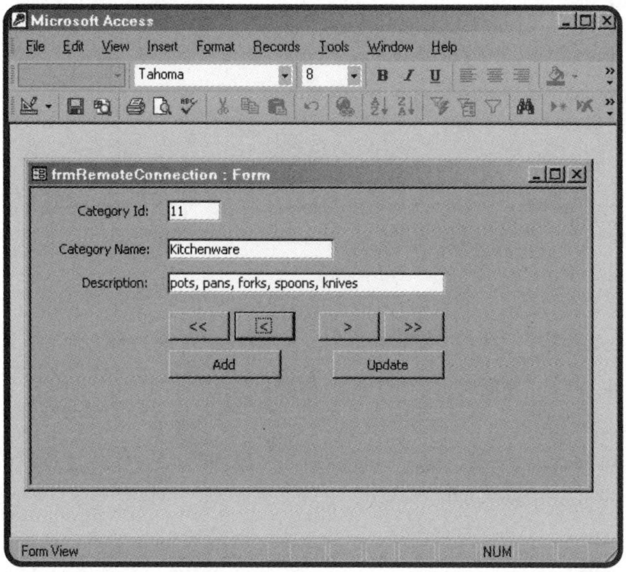

FIGURE 10.4

Using ADO and a graphical interface to add records

4. Call the `Recordset` object's `AddNew` method.

5. Assign new data to the recordset fields.

6. Save the new row of data using the `Recordset` object's `Update` method.

7. Close the recordset using the `Recordset` object's `Close` method.

8. Refresh other recordsets if applicable by closing the recordset and reopening it or calling the `Recordset` object's `Requery` method.

Using the preceding steps, I implemented the `Click` event procedure of the Add command button from Figure 10.4 with the following code.

```
Private Sub cmdAdd_Click()

    Dim sql As String
    Dim rsAdd As New ADODB.Recordset

    On Error GoTo DbError

    'Assign updatable cursor and lock type properties.
    rsAdd.CursorType = adOpenDynamic
    rsAdd.LockType = adLockOptimistic

    'Open the Recordset object.
    rsAdd.Open "Categories", remoteConnection, , , adCmdTable
```

```
'Add the record based on input from the user
'(except for the AutoNumber primary key field).
With rsAdd
    .AddNew
    !CategoryName = Me.txtCategoryName
    !Description = Me.txtDescription
    .Update
    .Close
End With

MsgBox "Record Added.", vbInformation

'Close the form-level Recordset object and refresh it to include
'the newly updated row.
rsCategories.Close
SetRecordset

Exit Sub

DbError:

MsgBox "There was an error adding the record." _
    & Err.Number & ", " & Err.Description

End Sub
```

Deleting Records

Deleting records using ADO is somewhat similar to updating records in that you need to use SQL queries to identify the record for updating or in this case deleting. The numbered steps below identify a typical ADO algorithm for deleting a record.

1. First, declare a new Recordset object variable.

2. Assign updatable cursor and lock types for deleting a record.

3. Construct a dynamic SQL string that uses a condition to retrieve the record selected by the user. The condition should use a field, which is a key (unique) value selected by the user.

4. Open the recordset, which should contain only one record, the record you wish to delete.

5. If the record was found, call the Recordset object's Delete method.

251

6. Save the record operation using the `Recordset` object's `Update` method.

7. Close the recordset using the `Recordset` object's `Close` method.

8. Refresh other recordsets if applicable by closing the recordset and reopening it or calling the `Recordset` object's `Requery` method.

Using these steps, I can implement ADO program code in the `Click` event procedure of the Delete command button shown in Figure 10.5.

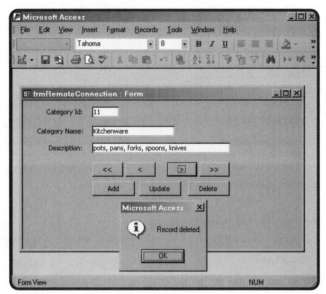

FIGURE 10.5

Using ADO and a graphical interface to delete records

All of the code required to delete a record in the `Categories` table is revealed next.

```
Private Sub cmdDelete_Click()

    Dim sql As String
    Dim rsDelete As New ADODB.Recordset

    On Error GoTo DbError

    'Build dynamic SQL statement based on record selected by the user.
    sql = "select * from Categories where CategoryID = " & _
        Val(Me.txtCategoryId.Value)

    'Assign updatable cursor and lock type properties.
```

```
        rsDelete.CursorType = adOpenDynamic
        rsDelete.LockType = adLockOptimistic

        'Open the Recordset object.
        rsDelete.Open sql, remoteConnection, , , adCmdText

        'Don't try to delete the record, if the recordset did not find a row.
        If rsDelete.EOF = False Then

            'Update the record based on input from the user.
            With rsDelete
                .Delete
                .Update
                .Close
            End With

        End If

        MsgBox "Record deleted.", vbInformation

        'Close the form-level Recordset object and refresh it to include
        'the newly updated row.
        rsCategories.Close
        SetRecordset

        Exit Sub

DbError:

        MsgBox "There was an error deleting the record." _
            & Err.Number & ", " & Err.Description

End Sub
```

Chapter Program: Choose My Adventure

Without a doubt, Choose My Adventure (Figure 10.6) is one of my favorites of the programs I've built for any of my Absolute Beginner books. Choose My Adventure uses ADO programming techniques to access tables that contain a short story. The

Using chapter-based
concepts to build the
Choose My
Adventure program

story presents questions on various pages and allows the reader to select an outcome. Depending on the selected outcome, the reader will get a different story and ending.

All of the code required to build the Choose My Adventure program is below.

```
Option Compare Database

    'Declare form-level Connection object variable.
    Dim localConnection As ADODB.Connection


Private Sub cmdAbout_Click()

    'Show the About form.
    DoCmd.OpenForm "frmAbout"


End Sub
```

```vba
Private Sub cmdChoose_Click()

    ' Use the assigned option button value to get the next page
    ' in the book.
    GetPage Me.fraQuestionAndOutcomes.Value

End Sub

Private Sub cmdQuit_Click()

    'Quit the application.
    End

End Sub

Private Sub cmdRead_Click()

    MsgBox "Welcome to The Night Before Halloween, " & _
            " a Choose My Adventure book by Michael Vine.", vbOKOnly, _
            "Chapter 10 - Datbase Programming with ADO"

    Me.cmdRead.Caption = "Start Over"
    ResetForm
    Me.txtPage.Value = ""
    Me.lblQuestion.Caption = ""
    Me.cmdChoose.Visible = False

    'Call the GetPage procedure to display the first page in the book.
    GetPage 1

End Sub

Private Sub Form_Load()

    'Perform some initial setup.
    ResetForm
    Me.txtPage.Value = ""
    Me.lblQuestion.Caption = ""
    Me.cmdChoose.Visible = False
    Me.cmdRead.Caption = "Read My Adventure"
```

```
    'Assign the current Access connection to my Connection object
    'variable.
    Set localConnection = CurrentProject.AccessConnection

End Sub

Private Sub Form_Unload(Cancel As Integer)

    On Error GoTo ErrorClosing

    'Close the connection.

    localConnection.Close

    Exit Sub

ErrorClosing:
    'Do nothing!

End Sub

Public Sub GetQuestion(pageID As Integer)

    Dim rsQuestion As New ADODB.Recordset
    Dim sql As String

    On Error GoTo BookError

    '   Using the incoming pageID, get and display the associated
    '   question (if one exists).
    '   This procedure calls the GetOutcome procedure.
    sql = "select * from Questions where PageID = " & pageID

    rsQuestion.Open sql, localConnection, adOpenForwardOnly, _
        adLockReadOnly, adCmdText

    If rsQuestion.EOF = False Then

        Me.lblQuestion.Caption = rsQuestion!Question
        GetOutcome rsQuestion!questionID
```

```
        Else

            ResetForm

        End If

        rsQuestion.Close

        Exit Sub

BookError:

        ErrorMessage

End Sub

Public Sub GetOutcome(questionID As Integer)

        Dim rsOutcomes As New ADODB.Recordset
        Dim x As Integer

        Dim sql As String

        On Error GoTo BookError

        'Using the incoming questionID, get all possible outcomes
        'for the associated question.
        sql = "select * from Outcomes where QuestionID = " & questionID

        rsOutcomes.Open sql, localConnection, adOpenForwardOnly, _
            adLockReadOnly, adCmdText

        ResetForm

        If rsOutcomes.EOF = False Then

            Me.lblOption1.Visible = True
            Me.optOption1.Visible = True
            Me.lblOption1.Caption = rsOutcomes!Outcome
```

```
            Me.optOption1.OptionValue = rsOutcomes!GoToPage
            rsOutcomes.MoveNext

        End If

        If rsOutcomes.EOF = False Then

            Me.lblOption2.Visible = True
            Me.optOption2.Visible = True
            Me.lblOption2.Caption = rsOutcomes!Outcome
            Me.optOption2.OptionValue = rsOutcomes!GoToPage
            rsOutcomes.MoveNext

        End If

        If rsOutcomes.EOF = False Then

            Me.lblOption3.Visible = True
            Me.optOption3.Visible = True
            Me.lblOption3.Caption = rsOutcomes!Outcome
            Me.optOption3.OptionValue = rsOutcomes!GoToPage

        End If

        rsOutcomes.Close

        Exit Sub

BookError:

        ErrorMessage

End Sub

Public Function AnyMoreQuestions(pageID As Integer) As Boolean

        Dim rsAnyMoreQuestions As New ADODB.Recordset
        Dim returnValue As Boolean
        Dim sql As String
```

```
    On Error GoTo BookError

    'This procedure is called by the GetPage procedure. It checks to see
    'if there are any more questions for the current page passed in.
    sql = "select * from Questions where PageID = " & pageID

    rsAnyMoreQuestions.Open sql, localConnection, _
        adOpenForwardOnly, adLockReadOnly, adCmdText

    If rsAnyMoreQuestions.EOF = False Then

        returnValue = True   'There are questions for this page.

    Else

        returnValue = False 'Ther are no questions for this page.

    End If

    rsAnyMoreQuestions.Close

    AnyMoreQuestions = returnValue

    Exit Function

BookError:

    ErrorMessage

End Function

Public Sub GetPage(pageID As Integer)

    Dim rsPage As New ADODB.Recordset
    Dim sql As String

    On Error GoTo BookError
```

```
'Gets and displays the requested page. Calls GetQuestion and
'AnyMoreQuestions procedures.
sql = "select * from Pages where PageID = " & pageID

rsPage.Open sql, localConnection, adOpenForwardOnly, _
    adLockReadOnly, adCmdText

If rsPage.EOF = False Then

    Me.txtPage.Visible = True
    Me.txtPage.Value = rsPage!Content

End If

GetQuestion rsPage!pageID

Me.txtPage.SetFocus
If AnyMoreQuestions(rsPage!pageID) = False Then

    Me.cmdChoose.Visible = False
    Me.lblQuestion.Caption = ""

Else

    Me.cmdChoose.Visible = True

End If

rsPage.Close

Exit Sub

BookError:

    ErrorMessage

End Sub

Public Sub ErrorMessage()
```

```
'A general error bin called by each error handler in the form class.
MsgBox "There was an error reading the book. " & Chr(13) _
    & Err.Number & ", " & Err.Description

End Sub


Public Sub ResetForm()

    Me.lblOption1.Visible = False
    Me.lblOption2.Visible = False
    Me.lblOption3.Visible = False
    Me.optOption1.Visible = False
    Me.optOption2.Visible = False
    Me.optOption3.Visible = False


End Sub
```

Chapter Summary

This chapter showed you essential ADO programming techniques such as connecting to a database and how VBA programmers use ADO to add, update, and delete records. This chapter specifically covered the following key concepts.

- ADO is Microsoft's most popular programming vehicle for managing data in databases such as Microsoft Access.

- ADO can be used to access and manage data in non-Microsoft databases such as Oracle's RDBMS.

- ADO's application programming interface (API) is made up of many objects such as the Connection and Recordset object and collections such as the Fields collection.

- It is considered good programming practice to use error handling whenever accessing a database through ADO.

- Connections to databases are established through ADO's Connection object.

- A result set is the set of rows retrieved by a command or SQL query.

- The Recordset object is used to work with rows in a database table.

- Database locking prevents multiple users (or processes) from updating the same row at the same time.

- A cursor is a structure that names and manages a storage area in memory. Programmers use cursors to point to a row of data in a result set one row at a time.

- The `Recordset` object methods `MoveFirst`, `MoveLast`, `MoveNext`, and `MovePrevious` are used to browse through records in a result set.

- Use the `Recordset` object properties `AbsolutePosition` and `RecordCount` to determine if the cursor position is at the end or beginning of a recordset.

- The `Recordset` object method `Update` is synonymous with saving a record.

- The `Recordset` object method `AddNew` is used to add a row to a table.

- The `Recordset` object method `Delete` is used to delete a row from a table.

CHALLENGES

1. Create a new Microsoft Access database application. Use the ADO `Connection` object to connect to a remote Northwind.mdb database. Display a successful confirmation in a message box. Use error handling to catch any connection errors.

2. Add controls to a form that mimic fields contained in Microsoft's Northwind `Products` table. Use ADO programming techniques to retrieve and fully browse the `Products` table. See Figure 10.2 for an example graphical user interface.

3. Update your application from Challenge 2 to allow a user to update records in the `Products` table.

4. Update your application from Challenge 2 to allow a user to add records to the `Products` table.

5. Update your application from Challenge 2 to allow a user to delete records from the `Products` table.

6. Build your own Choose My Adventure program with a unique story, questions, and outcomes.

Object-Oriented Programming with Access VBA

his chapter will show you how to leverage the power of object-oriented programming (also known as OOP) in Access VBA through Class Modules, custom objects, and collections. You will gain fundamental OOP concepts and best practices through clear explanations, examples, and challenges on the following key concepts:

- Introduction to object-oriented programming

- Creating custom objects

- Working with collections

Introduction to Object-Oriented Programming

Object-oriented programming is not a language unto itself, but rather a programming practice. OOP is seemingly easy at the surface, but can be quite challenging to master. In fact, many programmers coming from the procedural world of languages such as C or COBOL find they need to make a paradigm shift in how they think about programming. Even programmers who work with object-based languages such as VBA find the same paradigm shift inevitable. The paradigm shift I refer to is that of relating data, data structures, and business requirements to objects.

OOP contains five core concepts, which are **Objects**, **Classes**, **Encapsulation**, **Inheritance**, and **Polymorphism**:

- **Objects.** Objects represent a real-world thing such as person, place, or thing. Objects have behaviors and attributes.
- **Classes.** Classes are the blueprint for objects. They define how objects will behave and how they will expose attributes.
- **Encapsulation.** Encapsulation hides implementation details from a user.
- **Inheritance.** Inheritance allows one class to inherit the features of another class.
- **Polymorphism.** Polymorphism allows a class to implement the same operation in a number of different ways.

Unfortunately, VBA does not support inheritance or polymorphism in OOP's truest sense. Nevertheless, object-oriented programming in VBA allows the implementation of one of the most important benefits of OOP development known as *encapsulation*. In OOP terms, encapsulation allows programmers to reduce code complexity by hiding data and complex data structures in classes. You and other programmers simply instantiate these classes as objects and access the object's methods and properties. Encapsulating implementation details is a wonderful benefit of OOP. Not only are complex details hidden, but code reuse is promoted.

In VBA, OOP development is achieved through custom objects that are defined in Class Modules. Once built, custom objects don't necessarily add new functionality to your code. In fact, the same code you write in Class Modules could be written in event procedures, subprocedures, and function procedures. The purpose of using Class Modules is to provide encapsulation, code reuse, and self-documenting code. Programmers using your custom objects work with them just as they would with other built-in VBA objects such as the ones found in the ADO library.

Development with OOP generally requires more planning up front than in other programming paradigms. This design phase is crucial to OOP and your system's success. There are many books on OOP design, which use a number of techniques from CRC (Classes, Responsibilities, and Collaborators) cards to UML (Unified Modeling Language) and Use Cases to identify and graphically depict objects, their responsibilities, and their relationships.

At the very minimum, OOP design includes the following tasks:

- Identify and map objects to programming and business requirements.
- Identify the actions (methods) and attributes (properties) of each object. This action is commonly referred to as identifying the responsibilities of each object.
- Identify the relationships between objects.
- Determine the scope of objects and their methods and properties.

For more information on OOP design, try searching the web for UML and/or CRC cards. There are many free resources on the Internet for OOP design patterns.

Creating Custom Objects

You'll begin your investigation into object-oriented programming by creating custom objects that encapsulate implementation details. To create custom objects, VBA programmers use OOP techniques and Class Modules. You will specially learn how to build Class Modules that contain member variables and property and method procedures. After learning how to build custom objects with Class Modules, you'll see how to instantiate custom objects to access their methods and properties.

Working with Class Modules

Classes are the blueprints for an object. They contain the implementation details, which are hidden from users (programmers who use your custom objects). In object-oriented programming with VBA, classes are implemented as Class Modules.

Class Modules do not exist in memory. Rather, the instance of the class known as the object does. Multiple instances of a single class can be created. Each instance (object) created from a class shares the same access to the class's methods and properties. Even though multiple objects created from one class share the same characteristics, they are different in two ways. First, objects instantiated from the same class can have different property values. For example, an object called Bob instantiated from the Person class may have its hairColor property value set to brown, whereas an object called Sue also instantiated from the Person class could have its hairColor property value set to blond. Second, objects instantiated from the same class have unique memory addresses.

In OOP terms, an instance refers to the object that was created from a class. To instantiate means to create an object from a class.

To create a Class Module in Access VBA, simply open a Visual Basic window (VBE) and select the Class Module menu item from the Insert menu. Microsoft VBA automatically creates the Class Module for you as depicted in Figure 11.1. Looking at Figure 11.1, you will probably notice that the Class Module looks very similar to other code modules in VBA.

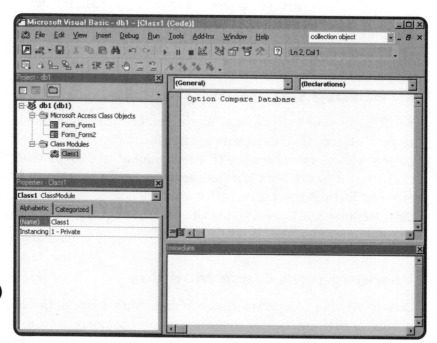

FIGURE 11.1

A newly created
Class Module

By default, VBA Class Modules contain two events called Initialize and Terminate. These events can be accessed by through the Code Window as seen in Figure 11.2.

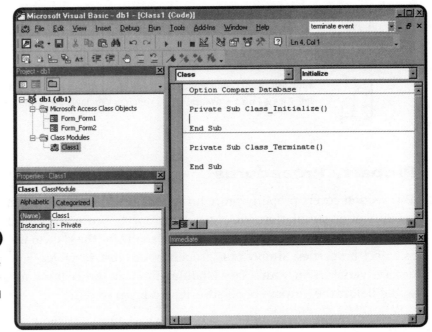

FIGURE 11.2

The Initialize and Terminate events are accessed through the VBE Code Window

The Initialize event for a Class Module is triggered each time the class is instantiated (created) using the New or Set keywords. The class module's Initialize event is similar to that of a constructor in OOP languages such as Java and C++. It is used to execute code when the object is first created. For example, you may wish to initialize certain member variables each time an instance of your class is created.

The Terminate event is triggered each time the instance is removed from memory. You can place code in this event procedure to free up other objects from memory or finalize any necessary transactions.

Another common use of the Initialize and Terminate events is in debugging your applications. If you'd like to know each time your application creates and destroys one of your custom objects, simply use the Initialize and Terminate events:

```
Private Sub Class_Initialize()


    Debug.Print "Object created."


End Sub


Private Sub Class_Terminate()
```

```
Debug.Print "Object destroyed."
```

```
End Sub
```

Note: Microsoft recommends *not* using message boxes in the `Initialize` and `Terminate` events, which requires Windows messages to be processed.

Property Procedures

This section covers property procedures, which will help you to understand the benefits of encapsulation. VBA provides property procedures for managing the attributes of a class, which are exposed internally for the class to use or externally as object properties. Simply put, properties are just variables. You could simply declare variables in your Class Modules for your procedures to use, but that would defeat the purpose of object-oriented programming.

To work with properties in VBA, you create variables of various scopes and use a combination of property procedures to manage them. VBA provides three types of property procedures:

- **Property Get.** Returns the value of a property.
- **Property Let.** Assigns a value to the property.
- **Property Set.** Sets the value of an object property.

Property Get procedures are often used in conjunction with both Property Let and Property Set procedures. When used together, a Property Let procedure and a Property Get procedure or a Property Set procedure and Property Get procedure must share the same name. Property Let and Property Set procedures, however, cannot be used together. They perform distinctly different roles in VBA object-oriented programming. Simply put, Property Let procedures are used for assigning data to scalar variables such as `String`, `Integer`, `Double`, or `Date` data types. Property Set procedures are used for assigning a reference to an object.

To add property procedures to your Class Module, access the Add Procedure dialog window from the Visual Basic Environment to add property procedures as demonstrated in Figure 11.3.

VBA automatically adds a matching set of Property Get and Property Let procedures for you as shown next.

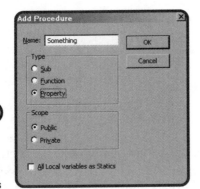

FIGURE 11.3

Use the Add
Procedure dialog
window to create
property procedures

```
Public Property Get Something() As Variant


End Property


Public Property Let Something(ByVal vNewValue As Variant)


End Property
```

The code required in each property procedure is short. You simply add a line to each respective procedure to assign a value and return a value. Before adding code to your property procedures, you must first have a property (sometimes referred to as a member variables) to manage. When working with property procedures, your properties are generally declared as `Private` in the general declarations area. By declaring the variable (property) in the general declarations area, you provide access to the property from any procedure in the Class Module. Declaring the variable (property) as `Private` provides encapsulation. Specifically, it forces users of your object to use the property procedures to access the member variable.

The concept of private properties and procedures is very important in OOP. Any procedure or property declared as private is only accessible to the Class Module (not instances of your Class Module). Examine this concept further by studying the next block of VBA code.

```
Option Compare Database


Private privateSomething As Variant


Public Property Get something() As Variant


    something = privateSomething
```

```
End Property

Public Property Let something(ByVal vNewValue As Variant)

    privateSomething = vNewValue

End Property
```

Notice that the Property Get procedure behaves much like a Function Procedure, in that a value is assigned to the procedure's name. This type of assignment statement returns the property's value to the calling procedure. The Property Let procedure takes a single argument as a parameter and assigns its value to the private property. This is how instantiated objects of this class access the `private-Something` property without knowing how it's declared or what its name is.

The previous code program statements typify a read/write property. In other words, instantiated objects of this class can read this property and write data to it. It's common, however, to require read-only properties in OOP. To do so, simply use a single Property Get procedure by removing the corresponding Property Let procedure:

```
Option Compare Database

Private readOnlySomething As Variant

Public Property Get something() As Variant

    something = readOnlySomething

End Property
```

With a private property and a single Property Get procedure, instantiated objects of this class can only read the property.

You can also use the Add Procedure dialog window to create matching Property Set and Property Get procedures. After VBA has created the matching property procedures, simply change the keyword `Let` to `Set`:

```
Option Compare Database

Private employee As Employee

Public Property Get NewEmployee() As Variant
```

```
    NewEmployee = employee

End Property

Public Property Set NewEmployee(ByVal vNewValue As Employee)

    employee = vNewValue

End Property
```

Instead of a `Variant` data type (or any other data type, for that matter), the Property Set procedure called `NewEmployee` takes in a parameter of `Employee` type. The Property Set procedure then assigns the object reference from the argument to the property of the same object type. A matching Property Get procedure is used to return an object reference of the property.

You've probably noticed by now that these procedures are very simple. That's because they should be! The primary purpose of property procedures is to manage access to member variables. It may seem like overkill for what appears to be variable access, but in sections to come and through practice you will see the power of property encapsulation through property procedures.

Method Procedures

Method procedures expose methods internally to the Class Module and/or externally to an instance of the class. They are the meat and potatoes of object-oriented programming—this is where encapsulation is truly evident.

Creating methods for custom objects is quite easy. Simply create and place sub- or function procedures in your Class Modules to represent methods. Remember from earlier in the book that function procedures return a value and subprocedures do not.

An example of each type of method is shown next.

```
Option Compare Database

Private result1 As Integer
Private result2 As Integer

Public Sub AddTwoNumbers(num1 As Integer, num2 As Integer)

    result1 = num1 + num2
```

```
End Sub


Public Function MultiplyTwoNumbers(num1 As Integer, num2 As Integer) As
Double

    MultiplyTwoNumbers = num1 * num2

End Function
```

The first method, AddTwoNumbers, takes two parameters and sets a property. If it's necessary for instances of this class to access this result, you should create a Property Get procedure that returns the value of the result1 member variable.

The second method, MultiplyTwoNumbers, is a function that also takes two arguments and performs a simple calculation. The big difference is that this method is a function, which returns a value to the calling procedure by assigning a value to the method's name.

To get a better understanding of object methods, consider the Connection object from the ADO library. The Connection object has a method called Open. You and I both know that this method establishes a connection to a database. But do we know how that method is implemented? No, we don't. And believe it or not, that's a good thing. Think about all the programming that must be involved to implement the Open method of the Connection object. It's a sure bet that it contains complicated data structures and algorithms. This is encapsulation at its finest. Because the implementation details are hidden, VBA programmers like us can simply call the method and pass it a few parameters to successfully open a database connection.

You can, of course, encapsulate the ADO library even further by writing your own classes to hide the dirty details of ADO programming. To demonstrate, imagine that a friend asks for your expertise in developing database connectivity. You agree to help by creating a class that performs all details of ADO programming for connecting to a database. You start your program design by thinking about what would be easiest for your colleague to use. During design, you decide to create a new class called DbConnection that will take care of all facets of connecting to a database and providing connection objects. Your DbConnection class will provide methods to connect and close the database connection and provide properties to access the ADO Connection object. After careful design, your class and its methods and properties look something like this:

```vba
Option Compare Database

Private cnn As New ADODB.connection

Public Sub OpenConnection(dbPath_ As String)

    On Error GoTo ConnectionError

    'Assign OLEDB provider to the Provider property.
    'Use the Open method to establish a connection to the database.
    With cnn
        .Provider = "Microsoft.Jet.OLEDB.4.0"
        .Open dbPath_
    End With

    Exit Sub

ConnectionError:

    MsgBox "There was an error connecting to the database. " & Chr(13) _
            & Err.Number & ", " & Err.Description

End Sub

Public Sub CloseConnection()

    On Error GoTo ConnectionError:

    'Close the database connection.
    cnn.Close

    Exit Sub

ConnectionError:

    MsgBox "There was an error connecting to the database. " & Chr(13) _
            & Err.Number & ", " & Err.Description

End Sub
```

```
Public Property Get ConnectionObject () As Variant

    'Return an object reference of the Connection object.
    Set dbconneciton = cnn

End Property
```

This simple class containing two methods (CloseConnection and Open-Connection) and one property (ConnectionObject) encapsulates the ADO programming required to manage a database connection. In the next section, you will see how easy it is for your friend to use your class for managing a database connection.

Creating and Working with New Instances

Once you've created a new Class Module, it becomes an available object type for you to use when declaring variables. Using the DbConnection class from the preceding section, I can declare an object variable in a Form Class module of DbConnection type:

```
Private Sub Form_Load()

    'Declare object variable as DbConnection type.
    Dim db As New DbConnection

    'Open the database connection.
    db.OpenConnection ("C:\temp\myDatabase.mdb")

End Sub
```

You can easily see how little code it takes to open a connection with the ADO programming encapsulated in the DbConnection class. Users of the DbConnection class need only know what methods and properties to use; they don't have to concern themselves with the specific ADO implementation details.

Working with object methods and properties is pretty straightforward. If you've been working with VBA even a little, you've already had exposure to objects and their properties and methods. When object methods or properties return an object reference, you will need to decide how the returned object reference is to be used. For example, the DbConnection class contains a Property Get procedure to return a reference of the current ADO Connection object:

```
Public Property Get DbConnection() As Variant

    'Return an object reference of the Connection object.
    Set dbconneciton = cnn

End Property
```

This property procedure appears as a property of the object when an instance of the class is created. Because this property returns an object reference, I will use a `Set` statement to retrieve and assign the object reference to another object:

```
Private Sub Form_Load()

    Dim db As New DbConnection
    Dim newConnection As New ADODB.connection

    db.OpenConnection ("C:\temp\myDatabase.mdb")

    Set newConnection = db.ConnectionObject 'Returns an object reference.

End Sub
```

Another example of using the `DbConnection` class's `ConnectionObject` property is to use it as an argument by passing it into methods for record-set processing. To demonstrate, I added a new method (function procedure) called `ReturnAThing` to my `DbConnection` class, which takes an ADO `Connection` object as an argument.

```
Public Function ReturnAThing(cnn_ As ADODB.connection) As Variant

    Dim rs As New ADODB.Recordset
    Dim thing As Variant
    Dim sql As String

    On Error GoTo DbError

    'Generate SQL string.
    sql = "select thing from AThing"

    'Open the read only / forward only recordset using SQL and the
    'Connection object passed in.
    rs.Open sql, cnn_, adOpenForwardOnly, adLockReadOnly, adCmdText
```

```
    If rs.EOF = False Then
        thing = rs!thing
    End If


    rs.Close


    'Return the thing back to the calling procedure.
    ReturnAThing = thing


    Exit Function

DbError:


    MsgBox "There was an error retrieving a thing from " & _
        " the database. " & Chr(13) _
        & Err.Number & ", " & Err.Description

End Function
```

I can now use this method and the `ConnectionObject` property in the Form Class module to return a thing:

```
Private Sub Form_Load()

    Dim db As New DbConnection
    Dim myThing As Variant
    Dim newConnection As New ADODB.connection

    db.OpenConnection ("C:\temp\myDatabase.mdb")

    myThing = db.ReturnAThing(db.ConnectionObject)

End Sub
```

Passing ADO `Connection` objects to methods allows me to be flexible in the type of connection (database) used in recordset processing. If users of my class are fluent in SQL or the database structure, I might add another parameter to the `ReturnAThing` method. This new parameter could be a SQL string or part of a SQL string, which would allow users to define what they want from the database or where they want it from.

An important part of working with object instances is freeing and reclaiming resources when your objects are no longer required. When objects are instantiated, VBA reserves memory and resources for processing. To free these resources, simply set the object to `Nothing`:

```
Private Sub Form_Load()

    Dim db As New DbConnection
    Dim myThing As Variant
    Dim newConnection As New ADODB.connection

    db.OpenConnection ("C:\temp\myDatabase.mdb")

    myThing = db.ReturnAThing(db.ConnectionObject)

    'Reclaim object resources
    Set db = Nothing

End Sub
```

It's good programming practice to reclaim resources not only from custom objects but from built-in objects such as the ones found in the ADO library. If you neglect to free object resources, VBA does not remove them from memory until the application is terminated. If your application uses a lot of objects, this can certainly lead to performance problems.

Working with Collections

Collections are a data structure similar to arrays in that they allow you to refer to a grouping of items as one entity. Collections, however, provide an ordered means for grouping not just items such as strings and numbers, but objects as well. As demonstrated next, the `Collection` object is used to create a collection data structure.

```
Dim myCollection As New Collection
```

Collections are popular data structures in object-oriented programming because they allow the grouping of objects using an ordered name/value pair. In fact, collections are objects themselves!

Items in a collection are referred to as members. All collection objects have one property and three methods for managing members as described in Table 11.1.

TABLE 11.1 COLLECTION OBJECT PROPERTIES AND METHODS

Type	Name	Description
Property	Count	Returns the number of members in the collection (beginning with 1).
Method	Add	Adds a member to the collection.
Method	Remove	Removes a member from the collection.
Method	Item	Returns a specific member in the collection.

Adding Members to a Collection

Use the Add method of the Collection object to add members to a collection. The Add method takes four parameters:

```
object.Add item, key, before, after
```

- **item.** A required expression that identifies the member to be added.
- **key.** An optional expression (string-based) that uniquely identifies the member.
- **before.** An optional expression that adds before the member position identified.
- **after.** An optional expression that adds the member after the member position identified.

 HINT

When adding a member to a collection, only the *before* or *after* parameter can be used, not both.

The following VBA code creates a new collection and adds three string-based members:

```
Dim myColors As New Collection

myColors.Add "red"
myColors.Add "white"
myColors.Add "blue"
```

As mentioned, collections are useful for grouping objects. The next VBA code creates three ADO Recordset objects and adds them to a Collection object:

```
Dim books As New ADODB.Recordset
Dim authors As New ADODB.Recordset
Dim publishers As New ADODB.Recordset
Dim myRecordsets As New Collection

myRecordsets.Add books
myRecordsets.Add authors
myRecordsets.Add publishers
```

By grouping objects in a collection, I can simplify code by accessing all objects through one Collection object.

Removing Members from a Collection

Members are removed from a collection using the Collection object's Remove method. The Remove method takes a single parameter that identifies the index or key value of the member.

Removing a collection member using both the index value and key value is demonstrated below.

```
Dim myColors As New Collection

myColors.Add "red", "r"
myColors.Add "white", "w"
myColors.Add "blue", "b"

myColors.Remove 1
myColors.Remove "w"
```

Accessing a Member in a Collection

To access a member in a collection, use the Item method, which takes a single parameter that matches the index or key value of a member.

```
Dim myColors As New Collection

myColors.Add "red", "r"
myColors.Add "white", "w"
myColors.Add "blue", "b"

MsgBox myColors.Item(1)
MsgBox myColors.Item("b")
MsgBox myColors.Item(4)    'Generates an error.
```

If the index or key value of the member is not found in the collection, an error is generated as shown in Figure 11.4.

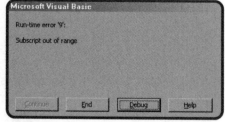

FIGURE 11.4

An error is generated when trying to access a member's key value or index that does not exist

For Each Loops

VBA provides a looping structure specifically designed for iterating through members in a collection. Specifically, the `For Each` loop executes one or more statements for each object in a collection:

```
Dim myColors As New Collection


myColors.Add "red", "r"
myColors.Add "white", "w"
myColors.Add "blue", "b"


For Each clr In myColors


    MsgBox clr


Next
```

Notice the syntax of the `For Each` statement. The statement basically says "for every object in the collection," where the object is simply an undeclared variable (in this case I called my object variable `clr`, short for "color").

Chapter Program: Monster Dating Service

The Monster Dating Service program seen in Figure 11.5 uses chapter-based concepts to build a simple and funny application. Essentially, the application allows a user to find an available monster by selecting character criteria.

The Monster Dating Service application uses object-oriented programming techniques and is split into two modules. The Class Module defines a Monster object,

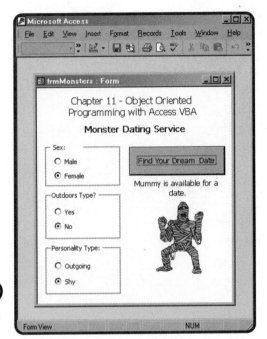

FIGURE 11.5

The Monster Dating
Service application

which encapsulates all the functionality required to connect to the current database and retrieve monster details based on user input.

All of the code for the Monster class is shown next.

```
Option Compare Database


Private name As String
Private picture As String
Private id As Integer


Public Sub FindMonster(sql_ As String)

    Dim rs As New ADODB.Recordset
    Dim sql As String

    'This method finds and sets all necessary monster details.
    'If does not return a value. Users of this method must use
    'the read-only property procedures to access the monster
    'attributes.
    On Error GoTo MonsterError
```

```
'Open the recordset based on the SQL string passed in as an argument.
rs.Open sql_, CurrentProject.AccessConnection, adOpenForwardOnly, _
    adLockReadOnly, adCmdText

If rs.EOF = False Then

    'Retrieve the monster's id, which will be used later.
    id = rs!monsterId

Else

    'No monster found with those attributes. Raise a custom error.
    Err.Raise vbObjectError + 512, , "No monster found."

End If

rs.Close

'Generate a new SQL string to retrieve the monster's name and picture
sql = "select * from Monsters where MonsterId = " & id

rs.Open sql, CurrentProject.AccessConnection, adOpenForwardOnly, _
    adLockReadOnly, adCmdText

If rs.EOF = False Then

    'Assign monster name and picture to properties.
    name = rs!MonsterName
    picture = rs!picture

End If

rs.Close

Exit Sub

MonsterError:

MsgBox "Sorry, there was a problem finding the monster. " & Chr(13) _
    & Err.Number & ", " & Err.Description
```

```
End Sub

Public Property Get MonsterName() As Variant

    'This property procedure returns the monster's name.
    MonsterName = name

End Property

Public Property Get MonsterPicture() As String

    'This property procedure returns the path and file name of
    'the monster's picture.
    MonsterPicture = picture

End Property
```

The next module is the Form Class module, which builds a SQL query based on
user input and passes it to the instantiated Monster object. After successfully
finding a monster, the Form Class module uses Monster object properties to display monster attributes. All of the code required to build the Form Class module
is revealed below.

```
Option Compare Database

Private Sub cmdFindMonster_Click()

    Dim aMonster As New monster
    Dim sex As String
    Dim personality As String
    Dim outdoors As Boolean
    Dim sql As String

    'Generate a SQL string based on user selection criteria.
    If Me.fraSex.Value = 1 Then
        sex = "Male"
    Else
        sex = "Female"
    End If
```

```
        If Me.fraOutdoors.Value = 1 Then
            outdoors = True
        Else
            outdoors = False
        End If


        If Me.fraPersonality = 1 Then
            personality = "Outgoing"
        Else
            personality = "Shy"
        End If


        sql = "select * from MonsterAttributes where Outdoors = " & _
            outdoors & " and Sex = '" & sex & "'" & _
            " and Personality = '" & personality & "'"


        'Try to find a monster based on the search criteria.
        aMonster.FindMonster sql


        'If a monster was found, display their name and picture.
        If aMonster.MonsterName = "" Then

            Me.lblMonsterName.Caption = "Sorry, no one is available with " &_
                "that search criteria."

            Me.imgPicture.picture = _
            "C:\work\tech\vba_access2002\chapter11\programs\logo.gif"

        Else

            Me.lblMonsterName.Caption = aMonster.MonsterName & _
            " is available for a date."

            Me.imgPicture.picture = aMonster.MonsterPicture

        End If

    End Sub
```

Chapter Summary

This chapter covered the basics of Object-Oriented Programming as it applies to Microsoft Access VBA. You learned how to incorporate OOP into your VBA applications through Class Modules and how OOP leverages encapsulation through object methods and properties.

The following key concepts were covered in this chapter.

- OOP maps data, data structures, and business requirements to objects.
- Encapsulation allows programmers to reduce code complexity by hiding data and complex data structures in classes.
- Class Modules contain member variables and property and method procedures.
- Class Modules do not exist in memory.
- Multiple instances of a single class can be created.
- By default, VBA Class Modules contain two events called `Initialize` and `Terminate`.
- The `Initialize` event for a Class Module is triggered each time the class is instantiated (created) using the `New` or `Set` keywords.
- The `Terminate` event is triggered each time the class's instance is removed from memory.
- VBA provides property procedures for managing the attributes of a class.
- VBA provides three types of property procedures, Property Get, Property Let, and Property Set.
- Property Get procedures return the value of a property.
- Property Let procedures assign a value to a property.
- Property Set procedures set the value of an object property.
- Use a single Property Get Procedure to create a read-only property.
- Method procedures are created in Class Modules with `Sub` and `Function` procedures.
- Setting objects to `Nothing` frees system resources.
- Collections are objects that contain an ordered list of items.
- Items in a collection are called members.
- Members in a collection can be referenced with an index or key value.
- VBA provides the `For Each` loop to iterate through members in a collection.

CHALLENGES

1. Create a new database called `BookStore` with one table called `Books`. Add the columns `ISBN`, `Title`, `PublishDate`, and `Price` to the `Books` table. Create a new connection class called `CustomConnection` that will connect to your `BookStore` database. The new class should have two methods, one method for opening an ADO `Connection` object and a second method for closing the ADO `Connection` object. The method that opens a database connection should take a single string argument, which represents the path and file name of the database.

2. In the same database application from Challenge 1, create a new class called `Books`. This class should have a read-only property for each column in the `Books` table.

   Create a method in the `Books` class called `FindBook`. The `FindBook` method should take in an ISBN. Build a SQL string based on the ISBN and use ADO programming techniques to open a recordset and assign the recordset field values to the class's matching properties. You should use the `CustomConnection` class to create and retrieve any `Connection` objects.

3. Create a user interface in the database application from Challenge 1. Add form elements that allow a user to find a book by entering an ISBN. Use your `Books` class from Challenge 2 to find and retrieve book details.

4. Enhance the user interface from Challenge 3 to allow a user to add and remove books. To accomplish this, you will need to modify the `Books` class from Challenge 2 by adding two methods called `AddBook` and `RemoveBook`.

5. In a new Access application, create a `Collection` object called `friends`. Construct a user interface that allows a user to add and remove names of friends in the `friends` collection.

   Add an additional command button to the user interface that displays each friend in a message box. Hint: Use the `For Each` loop to iterate through members in the collection.

Microsoft Office Objects

By providing access to internal Microsoft Office functionality and utilities, Microsoft Office Objects are an excellent example of what makes VBA such a powerful object-based language. In this chapter I'll show you how to leverage the power of Microsoft Office Objects through various VBA programming techniques. You'll specifically learn how to work with the following Microsoft Office Objects:

- `Assistant` object

- `CommandBar` object

- `FileDialog` object

Introduction to Microsoft Office Objects

VBA is an object-based programming language, which means VBA exposes many objects for you to work with. In addition to objects such as `DoCmd`, `Err`, and `Debug` and objects found in the ADODB library, VBA provides the Microsoft Office Objects for use in the suite of applications found in Microsoft Office. Microsoft Office Objects provide functionality for file searching, file management, interfaces to the Office Assistant, and custom menus and toolbars.

Most of the Microsoft Office Objects can be used in any Microsoft Office application such as Microsoft Word, Microsoft Excel, and Microsoft Access. Note, however, that some of these objects are application specific.

By default, Microsoft Office Object references are not set. To work with many of the examples in this chapter, you will need to let VBA set the references for you or simply set them yourself. You will know if a reference is *not* set as soon as you try to access a property, constant, or method of an object, which requires a reference. At which time, VBA will notify you with the message in Figure 12.1.

FIGURE 12.1

Accessing Object
items for which no
reference has
been set

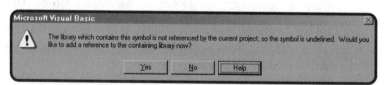

If you select *Yes* in the dialog seen in Figure 12.1, VBA automatically adds a reference to the Microsoft Office Objects library for you. You can select *No* and add the reference yourself through the References window seen in Figure 12.2.

To set the reference manually, access the References dialog window through the Tools menu in the VBE. From the Reference window, select the Microsoft Office Object Library as seen in Figure 12.2.

In VBA, the concept of setting a reference involves creating a link to another application's objects for use in your code.

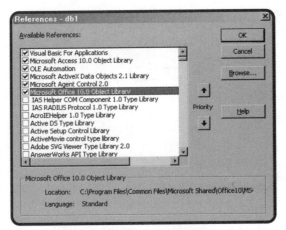

FIGURE 12.2

Using the References
dialog window to set
object library
references

Assistant Object

Because of its professional graphics and animation, the `Assistant` object is a
popular Microsoft Office Object to work and learn with. More than likely, you
have already seen the `Assistant` object with Microsoft applications such as
Microsoft Word, Microsoft Excel, and Microsoft Access.

In a nutshell, the `Assistant` object exposes the animated Microsoft Assistant.
There are eight different Office Assistant characters you can install with
Microsoft Office. Through VBA, you can choose which Assistant character is displayed to the user, or you can let a user choose the character themselves through
the Choose Assistant menu option. Figures 12.3 through 12.10 show each Assistant character provided by Microsoft Office.

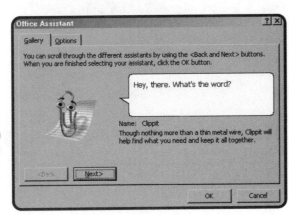

FIGURE 12.3

The *Clippit* Office
Assistant Character.
File name:
CLIPPIT.ACS

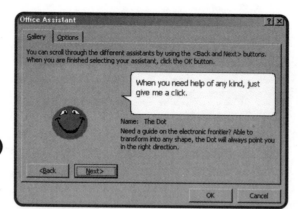

FIGURE 12.4

The *Dot* Office
Assistant Character.
File name: DOT.ACS

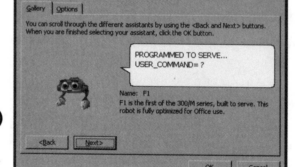

FIGURE 12.5

The *F1* Office
Assistant Character.
File name: F1.ACS

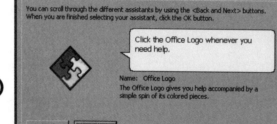

FIGURE 12.6

The *Office Logo*
Office Assistant
Character. File name:
LOGO.ACS

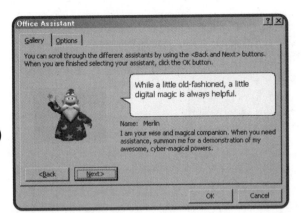

FIGURE 12.7

The *Merlin* Office
Assistant Character.
File name:
MERLIN.ACS

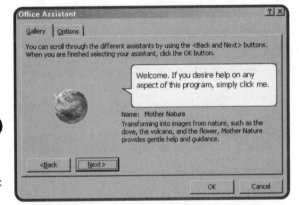

FIGURE 12.8

The *Mother Nature*
Office Assistant
Character. File name:
MNATURE.ACS

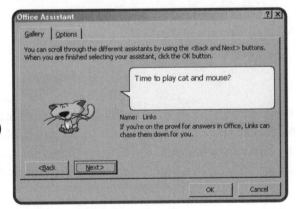

FIGURE 12.9

The *Links* Office
Assistant Character.
File name:
OFFCAT.ACS

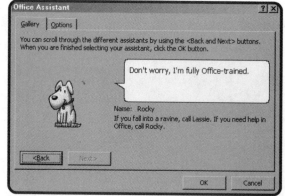

To display the Office Assistant, you'll need to work with the `Application` object's `Assistant` property. The `Assistant` property returns an object of `Assistant` type. Once the `Assistant` object is returned, you can use its properties and methods as shown in the code example below.

```
Private Sub cmdShowAssistant_Click()

    With Application.Assistant

        .On = True
        .FileName = "F1.ACS"
        .Animation = msoAnimationBeginSpeaking
        .Visible = True

    End With

End Sub
```

In the preceding code example, I've used a minimal number of `Assistant` object properties to display the character. The `On` property enables and disables the Assistant. The `FileName` property takes a string that identifies the Assistant character to be displayed. There are more than thirty different animations that can be assigned to the `Animation` property:

- `msoAnimationAppear`
- `msoAnimationBeginSpeaking`
- `msoAnimationCharacterSuccessMajor`
- `msoAnimationDisappear`
- `msoAnimationEmptyTrash`

- msoAnimationGestureDown
- msoAnimationGestureLeft
- msoAnimationGestureRight
- msoAnimationGestureUp
- msoAnimationGetArtsy
- msoAnimationGetAttentionMajor
- msoAnimationGetAttentionMinor
- msoAnimationGetTechy
- msoAnimationGetWizardy
- msoAnimationGoodbye
- msoAnimationGreeting
- msoAnimationIdle
- msoAnimationListensToComputer
- msoAnimationLookDown
- msoAnimationLookDownLeft
- msoAnimationLookDownRight
- msoAnimationLookLeft
- msoAnimationLookRight
- msoAnimationLookUp
- msoAnimationLookUpLeft
- msoAnimationLookUpRight
- msoAnimationPrinting
- msoAnimationRestPose
- msoAnimationSaving
- msoAnimationSearching
- msoAnimationSendingMail
- msoAnimationThinking
- msoAnimationWorkingAtSomething
- msoAnimationWritingNotingSomething

Each animation constant above repeats until the animation type is changed or the Assistant character is hidden. The Visible property hides or shows the Assistant character.

The next program code demonstrates how you can show, hide, and animate Office Assistants using VBA. Output is seen in Figure 12.11.

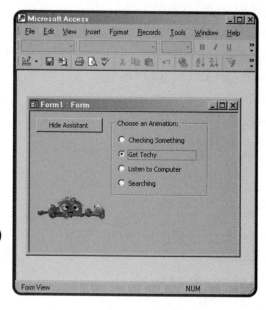

FIGURE 12.11

Using VBA to manage the Office Assistant

```
Private Sub cmdShowAssistant_Click()

If cmdShowAssistant.Caption = "Show Assistant" Then

    With Application.Assistant

        .FileName = "F1.ACS"
        .Animation = msoAnimationBeginSpeaking
        .Visible = True

    End With

    cmdShowAssistant.Caption = "Hide Assistant"

Else

    With Application.Assistant

        .Visible = False
```

```
        End With

        cmdShowAssistant.Caption = "Show Assistant"

    End If

End Sub

Private Sub optCheckingSomething_GotFocus()

    With Application.Assistant

        .Animation = msoAnimationCheckingSomething

    End With

End Sub

Private Sub optGetTechy_GotFocus()

    With Application.Assistant

        .Animation = msoAnimationGetTechy

    End With

End Sub

Private Sub optListenToComputer_GotFocus()

    With Application.Assistant

        .Animation = msoAnimationListensToComputer

    End With

End Sub

Private Sub optSearching_GotFocus()
```

```
With Application.Assistant

    .Animation = msoAnimationSearching

End With

End Sub
```

Once the `Assistant` object is displayed in an Office application (e.g., Access), the user can left-click it to use the Assistant's help and search features. The user can also right-click the Assistant character to display character options.

Balloon Object

With the help of the `Assistant` object, you can even create your own specialized balloons. Balloons are the graphical text area that the Office Assistant uses to display information. To create your own custom balloons, simply access the `NewBalloon` property from the `Assistant` object.

```
Application.Assistant.NewBalloon
```

The `NewBalloon` property returns a new `Balloon` object that contains its own methods and properties for managing custom balloons. You can customize your balloons to include labels, check boxes, icons, and various button and balloon types. In the program below, I create a new balloon that provides information as a tip of the day. Sample output is seen in Figure 12.12.

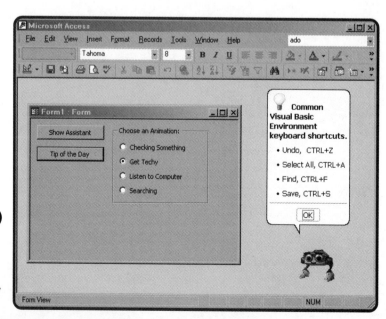

FIGURE 12.12

Using the
Assistant and
Balloon objects
to create and display
custom balloons

```
Private Sub cmdTip_Click()

    With Application.Assistant.NewBalloon
        .BalloonType = msoBalloonTypeBullets
        .Icon = msoIconTip
        .Button = msoButtonSetOK
        .Heading = "Common Visual Basic Environment keyboard shortcuts."
        .Labels(1).Text = "Undo,   CTRL+Z"
        .Labels(2).Text = "Select All, CTRL+A"
        .Labels(3).Text = "Find, CTRL+F"
        .Labels(4).Text = "Save, CTRL+S"
        .Show
    End With


End Sub
```

NewBalloon property uses are described next.

- Use built-in Office Object constants in the BalloonType, Icon, and Button properties to change the appearance of your custom balloon.

- The Heading property is used to display information in the balloon's heading.

- The Labels property contains a collection of BalloonLabels. The Labels property can be used in conjunction with the BalloonType property to display labels with different types of bulleted lists.

- The Show method displays the balloon and returns a constant that contains the value of the button or label clicked by the user.

To determine what label or button the user has clicked in a balloon, assign a Variant variable to the result of the Show method. The next program demonstrates this using a more informative balloon with different Label types (clickable). Output is seen in Figure 12.13.

```
Private Sub cmdTip_Click()

    Dim choice
    Dim heading As String
    Dim txt As String
```

```
With Application.Assistant.NewBalloon
    .heading = "Common Visual Basic Environment keyboard shortcuts."
    .Labels(1).Text = "Undo,  CTRL+Z"
    .Labels(2).Text = "Select All, CTRL+A"
    .Labels(3).Text = "Find, CTRL+F"
    .Labels(4).Text = "Save, CTRL+S"
    choice = .Show
End With

Select Case choice

    Case 1

        heading = "Undo, CTRL+Z"
        txt = "Undoes the most recent change."

    Case 2

        heading = "Select All, CTRL+A"
        txt = "Selects all text in the current window."

    Case 3

        heading = "Undo, CTRL+F"
        txt = "Opens the Find and Replace window to search for text."

    Case 4

        heading = "Undo, CTRL+S"
        txt = "Saves current work."

End Select

If choice <> -1 Then

    With Application.Assistant.NewBalloon
        .BalloonType = msoBalloonTypeBullets
        .Icon = msoIconTip
        .heading = heading
        .Labels(1).Text = txt
```

```
        .Show
    End With


    End If


End Sub
```

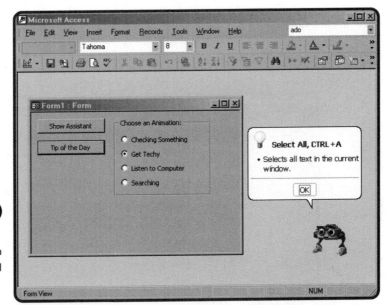

FIGURE 12.13

Using the result of
the Show method to
determine what label
or button has been
clicked in a balloon

By assigning the result of the Show method to the choice variable, I can easily
determine what the user clicked. Based on the user's selection, I customize variables that will be used later. If the value of the choice variable is −1, I know the
user has clicked the OK button and that it's unnecessary to show any other balloons. If the value of the choice variable is anything other than −1, I show a
new balloon with a custom header and label.

Command Bars

In VBA, command bars represent a number of user interface entities such as toolbars, menu bars, and shortcut menus (via right-click). You can declare variables in
VBA as a CommandBar object type. To demonstrate, the next program code declares
a CommandBar object variable and uses a For Each loop to iterate through each
CommandBar object found in the CommandBars collection. Each command bar's
name is printed to the Immediate Window. Output is seen in Figure 12.14.

```
Private Sub cmdFindCommandBars_Click()

    Dim myCommandBar As CommandBar

    For Each myCommandBar In CommandBars

        Debug.Print myCommandBar.Name

    Next myCommandBar

End Sub
```

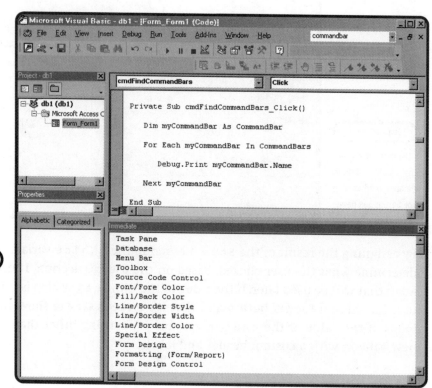

FIGURE 12.14

Using the
CommandBar
object to iterate
through each
command bar in a
CommandBars
collection

The CommandBars collection contains all command bar objects in the current
application.

TRAP

**VBA will generate an error when working with Microsoft Office Objects if a refer-
ence to the Microsoft Office Object library has not been set.**

CommandBarControl Object

The `CommandBarControl` object represents controls found in menus and tool-bars. Command bar controls can be buttons, boxes, and pop-up controls. Using the `CommandBars` collection, you can identify each command bar control found in a command bar. This concept is revealed in the next program code, which outputs the `Caption` property for each control found in the `Database` command bar. Output is seen in Figure 12.15.

```
Private Sub cmdFindCommandBarControls_Click()

    Dim myControl As CommandBarControl

    For Each myControl In CommandBars("Database").Controls
        Debug.Print myControl.Caption
    Next myControl


End Sub
```

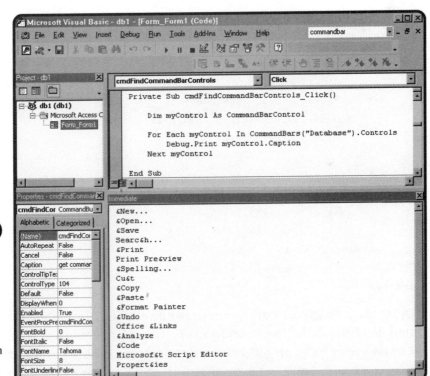

FIGURE 12.15

Using the
CommandBar–
Control object
and Command–
Bars collection to
identify captions of
each control found in
the Database
command bar

The `CommandBarControl` is a general object for working with built-in command bar controls. Its properties and methods are common among more specialized command bar control objects such as the `CommandBarButton`, `CommandBarComboBox`, and `CommandBarPopUp` objects.

CommandBarButton Object

The `CommandBarButton` object is a specialized command bar control that represents a button on a toolbar or menu that the user can click. You can use the `CommandBarButton` object in conjunction with the `CommandBar` object to build your own custom toolbars as demonstrated in the next procedure.

```
Private Sub cmdAddCustomCommandBar_Click()

    Dim customBar As CommandBar
    Dim newButton As CommandBarButton

    Set customBar = CommandBars.Add("Sheila")

    Set newButton = customBar.Controls _
        .Add(msoControlButton, CommandBars("Insert") _
        .Controls("Table").ID)

    Set newButton = customBar.Controls _
        .Add(msoControlButton, CommandBars("Insert") _
        .Controls("Query").ID)

    Set newButton = customBar.Controls _
        .Add(msoControlButton, CommandBars("Insert") _
        .Controls("Form").ID)

    customBar.Visible = True

End Sub
```

Using the `Add` method of the `CommandBar` object, I can create a new custom command bar called `MyCommandBar`. Then, I can use `Add` methods of new `CommandBarButton` objects to create buttons on my custom command bar. Note that the `Controls` property of the `CommandBar` object returns a `CommandBarsControls` collection. I use this collection's `Add` method to add a new button to the command bar. The `Add` method takes five optional parameters. In my example, the first parameter determines the type of control to be added. The options for this parameter are `MsoControlType` constants `msoControlButton`, `msoControlEdit`, `msoControlDropdown`, `mso-ControlComboBox`, or `msoControlPopup`. The next parameter in the `Add` method requires an `Integer` value, which represents a built-in control. In my example, I use the `ID` property of the `Controls` collection to return an `Integer` value representing a known control.

 TRICK You can pass a `String` into the `Controls` collection, which identifies a specific control name. The control name, however, must match a control name found in the `CommandBars` collection. Note that control and command bar names are found in Access command bars, not in VBE command bars.

After executing the preceding procedure, a new custom command bar is created as seen in Figure 12.16.

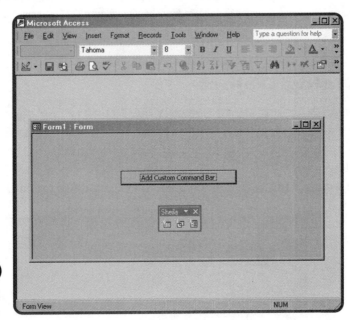

FIGURE 12.16

A custom command bar called Sheila

Once a custom command bar has been created, it is added to your current application. To manage your newly added custom command bar, simply right-click a toolbar and select Customize or select Customize from the View/Toolbars menu group. Shown in Figure 12.17 is my newly added custom toolbar called Sheila.

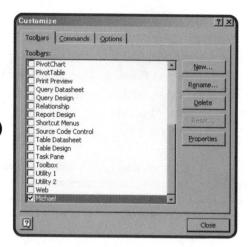

FIGURE 12.17

Managing custom
and built-in
command bars
through the
Customize dialog
window

Once you've added a custom command bar, it is available to your application. Use the Customize dialog window shown in Figure 12.17 to remove a custom command bar.

FileDialog Object

A very useful Microsoft Office Object is the `FileDialog` object. Believe it or not, you've already seen the `FileDialog` object in action. Almost all Microsoft Windows applications uses some variation of it. In a nutshell, the `FileDialog` object allows you to display and manage standard Open and Save file dialog boxes. An example of the Windows Open dialog window is seen in Figure 12.18.

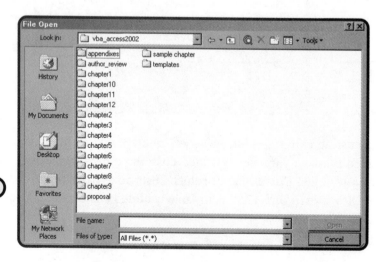

FIGURE 12.18

A Microsoft
Windows Open
dialog box

To work with the FileDialog object, you will also need to work with the Application object. More specifically, you will access the Application object's FileDialog property, which takes a single dialog type parameter. Valid FileDialog property parameters are one of four MsoFileDialog-Type types:

- **msoFileDialogFilePicker**. Allows users to select one or more files. Selected files are saved in the FileDialogSelectedItems collection.

- **msoFileDialogFolderPicker**. Allows the user to select a path. Selected items are saved in the FileDialogSelectedItems collection.

- **msoFileDialogOpen**. Allows the user to select one or more files to open. Files are opened in the application using the Execute method.

- **msoFileDialogSaveAs**. Allows the user to select only one file for saving using the Execute method.

The return value of the Application object's FileDialog property should be assigned to your FileDialog object variable:

```
Set myFileDialog = Application.FileDialog(msoFileDialogOpen)
```

After doing this, you can use the FileDialog object's Show method to display the specified dialog window. Use a For Each loop and the FileDialog object's SelectedItems property to iterate through each of the users selection. An example program that uses the FileDialog object is shown next. Output is seen in Figure 12.19.

```
Private Sub cmdAddFiles_Click()

    'Declare a FileDialog object variable.
    Dim myFileDialog As FileDialog

    'Declare a variant to hold each file selected.
    Dim vFileSelected As Variant

    'Create a FileDialog object as an Open dialog window.
    Set myFileDialog = Application.FileDialog(msoFileDialogOpen)

    'If the user didn't press Cancel, process each selection.
    If myFileDialog.Show = -1 Then

        For Each vFileSelected In myFileDialog.SelectedItems
```

```
                    lstFiles.AddItem vFileSelected

            Next vFileSelected

        Else

            'The user pressed Cancel.
            MsgBox "No files selected."

        End If

        'Set the myFileDialog object variable to Nothing.
        Set myFileDialog = Nothing


    End Sub
```

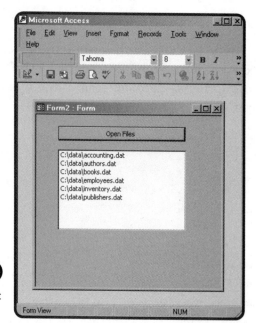

FIGURE 12.19

Items added to a list
box using the
FileDialog object

After clicking the command button seen in Figure 12.19, I use the `FileDialog` object to show an Open dialog window from which the user can select one or more files. Files selected by the user are added to the list box. If the user elects to press Cancel, a message is displayed instead. After finishing with the `File-Dialog` object variable, I set it to `Nothing`, freeing memory.

Chapter Program: Animated Math

Seen in Figure 12.20, the Animated Math game uses chapter based concepts to make simple math problems fun. Specifically, I used the `Assistant` object to present and guide users through simple addition problems.

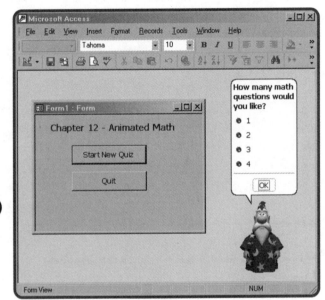

FIGURE 12.20

The Animated Math
program uses the
Assistant
object to make
math fun

All of the VBA code required to build the Animated Math program is seen next.

```
Option Compare Database


Private Sub cmdStartNewQuiz_Click()


    Dim choice
    Dim question As String
    Dim txt As String
    Dim loopNumber As Integer
    Dim iNumber1 As Integer
```

```vba
Dim iNumber2 As Integer
Dim randomAnswerOrder As Integer


'Display the Assistant and prompt the user for number of
'questions to ask.
Application.Assistant.On = True
Application.Assistant.Visible = True
With Application.Assistant.NewBalloon
    .Animation = msoAnimationGreeting
    .Icon = msoIconNone
    .heading = "How many math questions would you like?"
    .Labels(1).Text = "1"
    .Labels(2).Text = "2"
    .Labels(3).Text = "3"
    .Labels(4).Text = "4"
    choice = .Show
End With


'Prompt the user with math questions, based on their
'initial response.
If choice <> -1 Then

    For loopNumber = 1 To choice

        'Generate random numbers for math problems.
        iNumber1 = Int((100 * Rnd) + 1)
        iNumber2 = Int((100 * Rnd) + 1)

        'Generate a random number that will be used for placing
        'the correct answer in a random order for each question.
        randomAnswerOrder = Int((4 * Rnd) + 1)

        With Application.Assistant.NewBalloon

            Animation = msoAnimationThinking
            Icon = msoIconNone
            heading = "What is " & iNumber1 & "+ " & iNumber2 & " ?"
```

```
'Based on the random location of the answer, populate four
'labels with possible answers.
    Select Case randomAnswerOrder
        Case 1
            .Labels(1).Text = iNumber1 + iNumber2 'correct
            .Labels(2).Text = iNumber1 + iNumber1 'wrong
            .Labels(3).Text = (iNumber1 + iNumber2) - 1 'wrong
            .Labels(4).Text = (iNumber1 + iNumber2) + 1 'wrong
        Case 2
            .Labels(1).Text = iNumber1 + iNumber1 'wrong
            .Labels(2).Text = iNumber1 + iNumber2 'correct
            .Labels(3).Text = (iNumber1 + iNumber2) - 1 'wrong
            .Labels(4).Text = (iNumber1 + iNumber2) + 1 'wrong
        Case 3
            .Labels(1).Text = (iNumber1 + iNumber2) - 1 'wrong
            .Labels(2).Text = iNumber1 + iNumber1 'wrong
            .Labels(3).Text = iNumber1 + iNumber2 'correct
            .Labels(4).Text = (iNumber1 + iNumber2) + 1 'wrong
        Case 4
            .Labels(1).Text = (iNumber1 + iNumber2) + 1 'wrong
            .Labels(2).Text = iNumber1 + iNumber1 'wrong
            .Labels(3).Text = (iNumber1 + iNumber2) - 1 'wrong
            .Labels(4).Text = iNumber1 + iNumber2 'correct
    End Select


    choice = .Show

End With

If choice = -1 Then
    'user canceled
    Exit For
End If

If choice = randomAnswerOrder Then
    MsgBox "That's right!"
Else
    MsgBox "Sorry, incorrect answer."
End If
```

```
        Next LoopNumber

    End If

End Sub


Private Sub Form_Load()
    Randomize
End Sub


Private Sub cmdQuit_Click()
    End
End Sub
```

Chapter Summary

This chapter showed you how to leverage the power of Microsoft Office Objects such as the `Assistant` object, the `Balloon` object, the `CommandBarControl` object, the `CommandBarButton` object, and the `FileDialog` object. More specifically, this chapter covered the following key concepts:

- Most Microsoft Office Objects are available to the suite of Microsoft Office applications. Some Microsoft Office Objects, however, are available only to specific applications in the suite.

- Sometimes Microsoft Office Object references are not set automatically. To set object references in VBA, use the References window.

- Setting an object reference sets a link to another application's objects for use in your code.

- The `Assistant` object exposes an animated Microsoft assistant character.

- Customized balloons can be created to work with the assistant character using the `Balloon` object.

- Command bars represent a number of user interface entities such as toolbars, menu bars, and shortcut menus.

- The `CommandBars` collection contains all command bar objects in the current application.

- The `CommandBarControl` object represents controls found in menus and toolbars.

- Command bar controls can be buttons, boxes, and pop-up controls.

- The `CommandBarButton` object is a specialized command bar control that represents a button on a toolbar or menu that the user can click.

- Use the Customize dialog window seen in Figure 12.17 to remove a custom command bar.

- The `FileDialog` object allows you to display and manage standard Open and Save file dialog boxes.

CHALLENGES

1. Using the `Assistant` object, build a custom balloon that displays three useful Access VBA tips you've learned about in this book.

2. Build a custom command bar named after you. Your custom command bar should have four controls. Use existing controls found in the Access File menu (CommandBar).

3. Use the `FileDialog` object to show a file picker dialog window. Output each file selected by the user to a message box.

Common Character Codes

The items in this table represent the most common characters and associated character codes used in conjunction with the Chr and Asc functions.

Code	Character	Code	Character
8	Backspace	44	,
9	Tab	45	-
10	Linefeed	46	.
11	Carriage return	47	/
32	Space bar	48	0
33	!	49	1
34	"	50	2
35	#	51	3
36	$	52	4
37	%	53	5
38	&	54	6
39	'	55	7
40	(	56	8
41	)	57	9
42	*	58	:
43	+	59	;

Code	Character	Code	Character
60	<	92	\
61	=	93	]
62	>	94	^
63	?	95	_
64	@	96	`
65	A	97	a
66	B	98	b
67	C	99	c
68	D	100	d
69	E	101	e
70	F	102	f
71	G	103	g
72	H	104	h
73	I	105	i
74	J	106	j
75	K	107	k
76	L	108	l
77	M	109	m
78	N	110	n
79	O	111	o
80	P	112	p
81	Q	113	q
82	R	114	r
83	S	115	s
84	T	116	t
85	U	117	u
86	V	118	v
87	W	119	w
88	X	120	x
89	Y	121	y
90	Z	122	z
91	[	123	{

Code	Character
124	|
125	}
126	~
127	Del (Delete key)

Keyboard Shortcuts for the Code Window

The items in the following table represent common keyboard shortcuts that can be used in the Visual Basic Environment's Code Window.

Task	Shortcut	Task	Shortcut
Beginning of module	Ctrl+Home	Move to end of line	End
Clear all breakpoints	Ctrl+Shift+F9	Next procedure	Ctrl+Down Arrow
Delete current line	Ctrl+Y	Outdent	Shift+Tab
Delete to end of word	Ctrl+Delete	Previous procedure	Ctrl+Up Arrow
End of module	Ctrl+End	Replace	Ctrl+H
Find	Ctrl+F	Shift one screen down	Ctrl+Page Down
Find next	F3	Shift one screen up	Ctrl+Page Up
Find previous	Shift+F3	Undo	Ctrl+Z
Go to last position	Ctrl+Shift+F2	View Code window	F7
Indent	Tab	View definition	Shift+F2
Move one word to left	Ctrl+Left Arrow	View Object Browser	F2
Move one word to right	Ctrl+Right Arrow	View Shortcut menu	Shift+F10
Move to beginning of line	Home		

Index

Index

GAME DEVELOPMENT.

IT'S SERIOUS BUSINESS.

"Game programming is without a doubt the most intellectually challenging field of Computer Science in the world. However, we would be fooling ourselves if we said that we are 'serious' people! Writing (and reading) a game programming book should be an exciting adventure for both the author and the reader."

—André LaMothe,
Series Editor

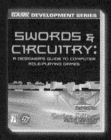

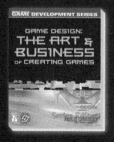